Grok 1.0 Web Development

Create flexible, agile web applications by using the power of Grok—a Python web framework

Carlos de la Guardia

BIRMINGHAM - MUMBAI

Grok 1.0 Web Development

First published: February 2010

Production Reference: 1040210

Published by Packt Publishing Ltd.
32 Lincoln Road
Olton
Birmingham, B27 6PA, UK.

ISBN 978-1-847197-48-1

www.packtpub.com

Cover Image by Parag Kadam (paragvkadam@gmail.com)

Credits

Author
Carlos de la Guardia

Reviewers
Carola Brand
Iasson Grabowski
Marcel Klapschus
Jan-Wijbrand Kolman
Lennart Regebro

Acquisition Editor
Rashmi Phadnis

Development Editor
Amey Kanse

Technical Editor
Namita Sahni

Indexer
Monica Ajmera Mehta

Editorial Team Leader
Akshara Aware

Project Team Leader
Priya Mukherji

Project Coordinator
Leena Purkait

Proofreader
Dirk Manuel

Graphics
Nilesh R. Mohite

Production Coordinator
Adline Swetha Jesuthas

Cover Work
Adline Swetha Jesuthas

Foreword

A little less than a year ago, Zope 4 was released. As the successor of the complex, verbose, and certainly not agile Zope 3 (now called BlueBream), it was instantly welcomed with much cheer. Naturally, I chimed in and announced without much hesitation that the forthcoming 4th edition of my book would already be based on the lean and mean Zope 4.

Sadly, these were all just April fool's jokes.

Sadly? No, I should say luckily! Because something much better came out of Zope land just a few months after we jokingly invented a new Zope version. Grok 1.0 was released. And thanks to Carlos' tremendous effort, there's now a book to accompany and celebrate this achievement, too.

There is much to say about this book, but I'm sure you're eager to get started with your web application. So let me just tell you what I like best about it.

Carlos has managed to capture the Grok spirit in this book. It is concise, not too heavy and doesn't beat about the bush. Yet it manages to hit all the bases of web development, with a spikey club, of course. It is as smashing as the framework itself and I hope you'll enjoy both as much as I have.

Have fun!

Philipp von Weitershausen
Author of Web Component Development with Zope 3

About the Author

Carlos de la Guardia has been doing web consulting and development since 1994, when selling any kind of project required two meetings just to explain what the Internet was, in the first place. He was the co-founder of Aldea Systems—a web consulting company—where he spent ten years working on all kinds of web projects, using a diverse range of languages and tools. In 2005, he became an independent developer and consultant, specializing in Zope and Plone projects. He frequently blogs about Plone and other Zope-related subjects.

Acknowledgement

This book would not have been possible without the understanding and constant encouragement from my wife, Liz. You are the love of my life, thanks for constantly pushing me to try more things and be what I can be.

My three little kids, Rodrigo, Santiago, and Valeria, had to put up with daddy being working on a book instead of playing with them. I can't imagine my life without them.

Thanks to my parents for their constant support and love. I am very fortunate for being part of our family.

Thanks to Martijn Faassen for being so kind and open with advice, even though I got him at a very busy time in his life. I was fortunate as well to have a great team of reviewers. Lennart Regebro and Jan-Wijbrand Kolman are Zope and Grok veterans who provided experimented advice. Carola Brand, Iasson Grabowski, and Marcel Klapschus helped me understand how a person unfamiliar with Zope technologies might look at the book. Thanks to all of them, my book is a better product. Thanks also to the Grok community, which keeps improving and evolving Grok, making it a great web development framework.

Thanks to Rashmi Phadnis for helping me through the initial stages of the book, and Amey Kanse for doing the heavy editing after that. Special thanks to Leena Purkait for her patience when managing this project.

About the Reviewers

Carola Brand lives in Lübeck, Germany. After studying bioinformatics for a year, she discovered her liking for programming. In 2007, she started an apprenticeship as an IT specialist in a small company that develops web applications based on Zope. She reviewed this book while working on a project with Grok for the first time.

Iasson Grabowski started his apprenticeship in 2007, after he obtained his general qualification for university entrance. He made his apprenticeship in a small company in Lübeck, where he had his first experiences in programming with Python and web development with Zope. While reading this book, he started his first project with Grok. In addition to programming, Iasson is very interested in sports, and likes to use his free time for sportive activities, watching movies, or just meeting with friends.

Marcel Klapschus lives in a small town near Lübeck, Northern Germany. He started his apprenticeship as an IT specialist, with a main focus on web development with Zope and Grok, in 2008. As a beginner, he knows the "stumbling blocks" of first-time programmers very well, which led to the motivation to write this review. When Marcel is not programming or reviewing, he is engaged in writing fantasy novels, on rainy evenings, while listening to some great music.

Jan-Wijbrand Kolman has been involved in the development of Grok since its early beginnings. He joined the original Grok founders when they held the second Grok "sprint", where the foundation was laid for what Grok currently is.

With a background in User Interface design, Jan-Wijbrand became more and more involved in software development when working at the V2_ institute for art, media, and technology, from 1998 on. In 2001, he became acquainted with Grok's "father", Martijn Faassen, and worked with him at Infrae. There, he worked on the Silva Content Management System, and other projects based on Zope 2, the predecessor of Zope 3.

Since the second Grok "sprint", Jan-Wijbrand has collaborated with the Grok community members on the advancement of Grok. Currently, he works for The Health Agency, where he develops highly personalized web applications with Grok.

I'd like to thank Sandra, Sverre, and Rune. I'd also like to thank my past and current employers for facilitating the work with and on Zope and Grok.

Lennart Regebro is an independent Python contractor who has done little but worked with computers since a friend showed him how to program in Basic in 1982. He has been using Zope since the fall of 1999, and wrote his first Python program during Christmas of the same year. Lennart became a full-time Zope developer in 2001, and has been an occasional core contributor to Zope since 2002. Lennart has been an enthusiastic fan of Grok since the beginning.

Although born in Sweden, Lennart has lived both in Norway and Iceland, and in 2003 he moved to Paris.

Table of Contents

Chapter 9: Grok and the ZODB — **159**

Chapter 10: Grok and Relational Databases — **179**

Preface

There are many options these days for web development frameworks. Grok is one of the many that are written in the Python programming language, but it may be one of the least known. This book is a step towards getting the word out that Grok can be a very good fit for many kinds of web development projects.

For one thing, Grok is based on a body of software known as the Zope Toolkit (ZTK), which is a huge set of libraries that are used for web development in Python. The ZTK is itself the result of more than ten years of work that started with the Zope web framework, which was one of the very first Python web frameworks.

Grok is also a modern web framework, which means, it has also learned from the innovations of popular web frameworks such as Django or Ruby on Rails. All in all, as we go through the book, you will find Grok as a framework that is agile enough for small applications, yet powerful enough for really complex projects.

What this book covers

Chapter 1, *Getting to Know Grok*, goes into what makes Grok an attractive option for Python web development. You'll learn how Grok makes use of the Zope Toolkit and why this makes Grok powerful and flexible. Then some of Grok's most important concepts will be introduced. Finally, you'll briefly see how Grok compares to other web development frameworks.

Chapter 2, *Getting Started with Grok*, shows you how to install Python on different platforms, in case you are new to it. You'll learn what the Python Package Index (PyPI) is and how to work with EasyInstall to quickly install packages from it over the network. Next, you'll create and run your first project using a tool called grokproject.

Chapter 3, *Views*, explains what views are and where in the Grok application code should they be defined. For templating, Grok uses the ZPT templating language, so you'll learn how to use it and see examples of the most common statements in action. To test this knowledge, we'll see how to write a full Grok application using only views. Other topics covered include how to get form parameters from a web request, how to add static resources to a Grok application, and how to create and work with additional views.

Chapter 4, *Models*, introduces the concept of models and what relationship they have with views. Among other key topics, you'll learn how to persist model data on the ZODB and how to structure your code to maintain the separation of display logic from application logic. Next, we'll see what a container is and how to use one. Finally, we'll explain how to use multiple models and associate specific views to each.

Chapter 5, *Forms*, will start with a quick demonstration of automatic forms. We'll briefly touch the concepts of interface and schema and show how they are used to generate forms automatically. Among other things, you'll learn how to filter fields and prevent them from appearing in a form, and how to change form templates and presentation.

Chapter 6, *The Catalog: An Object-Oriented Search Engine*, will discuss how to search for specific objects in the database using a tool called the catalog. We'll cover what a catalog is and how it works, what indexes are and how they work, and how to store data in the catalog. Next, we'll learn how to perform simple queries on the catalog and how to use that knowledge to create a search interface for our application.

Chapter 7, *Security*, will cover authentication and authorization. Grok security is based on the concepts of principals (users), permissions, and roles. It has a default security policy, which you'll learn to modify. Grok has a pluggable authentication system, which allows us to set up custom security policies. We'll create one and learn how to manage users as well.

Chapter 8, *Application Presentation and Page Layout*, deals with Grok's layout and presentation machinery that is based on the concept of viewlets. We'll learn what viewlet managers and viewlets are and how to define a layout using them. Then we'll cover the concepts of layers and skins, which allow Grok applications to be delivered with alternative presentations and styles. Finally, we'll define an alternative skin for the application.

Chapter 9, *Grok and the ZODB*, tells us more about the ZODB, including how to take advantage of its other features, such as blob handling. We'll also learn a bit about ZODB maintenance and the need to pack the database frequently. Finally, we'll try our hand at using the ZODB as a regular Python library, outside Grok.

Chapter 10, *Grok and Relational Databases*, will help us find out what facilities Grok has for relational database access. Here are some specific things that we will cover — why is it important that Grok allows developers to use relational databases easily, what an Object Relational Mapper is, how to use SQLAlchemy with Grok, and how to change our authentication mechanism to use a relational database instead of the ZODB.

Chapter 11, *Key Concepts Behind Grok*, goes into a little more depth with the main concepts behind the Zope Component Architecture, a pillar of Grok. We'll start by explaining the main ZCA concepts, such as interfaces, adapters, and utilities, using the code from the last ten chapters for illustration. We'll learn about one of the main benefits of the ZCA, by using some of its patterns to extend our application. Most importantly, we'll cover how to extend a package without touching its code.

Chapter 12, *Grokkers, Martian, and Agile Configuration*, will introduce grokkers. A grokker is a piece of code that allows developers to use framework functionality by making declarations in the code instead of using configuration files. Grok uses a library called Martian to create its own grokkers and we'll see how to create our own as well.

Chapter 13, *Testing and Debugging*, comments briefly on the importance of testing and then explains how to do testing in Grok. We'll start with extending the functional test suite provided by grokproject and then go on to other kinds of testing. Finally, we'll cover some debugging tools, including live web debuggers.

Chapter 14, *Deployment*, discusses how to deploy our application by using the standard paster server. Then, we'll find out how to run the application behind Apache, first by using a simple proxy configuration, and then under mod_wsgi. Finally, we'll explore how ZEO provides horizontal scalability for our application, and will briefly discuss how to make a site support high traffic loads by adding caching and load balancing into the mix.

What you need for this book

All you will need for getting the sample Grok application on this book working is a computer with a net connection running the Python programming language, version 2.4 or 2.5. In Unix environments, you'll also need a C compiler.

Who this book is for

This book is intended for Python developers who want to create web applications but have little or no experience in web development. If you have used other web frameworks but are looking for one that enables you to create more complex applications without losing agility, you will also benefit from this book. The reader is expected to have a general idea of how a web application works.

Conventions

In this book, you will find a number of styles of text that distinguish between different kinds of information. Here are some examples of these styles, and an explanation of their meaning.

Code words in text are shown as follows: "Now that we have a `title` attribute, we can modify the `index.pt` template to show that instead of the old text".

A block of code is set as follows:

```
class SetTitle(grok.View):
    def update(self,new_title):
        self.context.title = new_title

    def render(self):
        return self.context.title
```

When we wish to draw your attention to a particular part of a code block, the relevant lines or items are set in bold:

```
# Comment this line to disable developer mode. This should be done in
# production
# devmode on
```

Any command-line input or output is written as follows:

```
$ bin/paster serve --stop-daemon parts/etc/deploy.ini
```

New terms and **important words** are shown in bold. Words that you see on the screen, in menus or dialog boxes for example, appear in the text like this: "Under the **Base classes** section there is an **Interfaces provided** section.".

Warnings or important notes appear in a box like this.

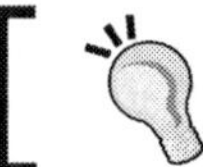

Reader feedback

Feedback from our readers is always welcome. Let us know what you think about this book—what you liked or may have disliked. Reader feedback is important for us to develop titles that you really get the most out of.

To send us general feedback, simply send an e-mail to `feedback@packtpub.com`, and mention the book title via the subject of your message.

If there is a book that you need and would like to see us publish, please send us a note in the **SUGGEST A TITLE** form on `www.packtpub.com` or e-mail `suggest@packtpub.com`.

If there is a topic that you have expertise in and you are interested in either writing or contributing to a book on, see our author guide on `www.packtpub.com/authors`.

Customer support

Now that you are the proud owner of a Packt book, we have a number of things to help you to get the most from your purchase.

Downloading the example code for the book
Visit `http://www.packtpub.com/files/code/7481_Code.zip` to directly download the example code.

Errata

Although we have taken every care to ensure the accuracy of our content, mistakes do happen. If you find a mistake in one of our books—maybe a mistake in the text or the code—we would be grateful if you would report this to us. By doing so, you can save other readers from frustration and help us improve subsequent versions of this book. If you find any errata, please report them by visiting `http://www.packtpub.com/support`, selecting your book, clicking on the **let us know** link, and entering the details of your errata. Once your errata are verified, your submission will be accepted and the errata will be uploaded on our website, or added to any list of existing errata, under the Errata section of that title. Any existing errata can be viewed by selecting your title from `http://www.packtpub.com/support`.

Piracy

Piracy of copyright material on the Internet is an ongoing problem across all media. At Packt, we take the protection of our copyright and licenses very seriously. If you come across any illegal copies of our works, in any form, on the Internet, please provide us with the location address or website name immediately so that we can pursue a remedy.

Please contact us at `copyright@packtpub.com` with a link to the suspected pirated material.

We appreciate your help in protecting our authors, and our ability to bring you valuable content.

Questions

You can contact us at `questions@packtpub.com` if you are having a problem with any aspect of the book, and we will do our best to address it.

Getting to Know Grok

Grok is a web application framework written in the Python programming language. Currently, there are lots of fine options available for web development frameworks for Python, and Grok might be one of the least well known. This book presents Grok in detail, through the development of a complete web application. In the process, this book will let us know why Grok is a very good option for building web applications, no matter if they are small and simple, or large and complex. In this chapter, we'll start with:

- What makes Grok an attractive option for Python web development
- How Grok makes use of the Zope Toolkit and why this makes Grok powerful and flexible
- Which are Grok's most important concepts and why they are useful
- How Grok compares to other web development frameworks

Why Grok?

Grok is a modern web framework, which means:

- It offers an agile development process, with an emphasis on producing working code quickly, but always with an eye on clarity and testability. It doesn't require extensive configuration.
- It provides a set of conventions for developing applications, including a file system layout and code structure. Grok's design encourages developers to share standards and provides them with a good practice to follow, when organizing their code. This allows less experienced developers to be productive from the start.

Grok supports strong integration with relational databases, including the use of many object relational mappers, and also offers a transparent way to store Python objects, by using its own object-oriented database. Grok offers a solid foundation for developing powerful, extensible, and secure web applications without too much complexity. This is in part because it uses, at its core, the **Zope Toolkit**, which is a set of libraries intended for reuse by projects in order to develop web applications or frameworks. This collection of libraries uses a common component development model, known as the **Zope Component Architecture (ZCA)**.

The ZCA is developed in the Zope community, which has been developing web applications by using Python for more than a decade. Grok builds on that experience and offers a strong combination of experience and agility. When using Grok, you will get:

- A core framework that has been evolving for more than ten years, always learning new lessons and looking for improvements, based on extensive experience on projects deployed in all kinds of production environments.
- A flexible, forward-looking architecture that allows developers to create applications that can be evolved and extended over long periods of time, even by other developers and, sometimes, without having to touch the original code at all.
- A practical, knowledgeable development community, which has been around for a long time, and is willing to offer advice on how best to learn and take advantage of the framework.
- A wide range of integrated features, such as internationalization, form generation and validation, security, cataloguing, and templating.
- An impressive number of ready-to-use components that can be used as building blocks for your own applications. As with Zope 3 itself, these are usually thoroughly tested, solid components with good API documentation.

Grok gives web developers a range of useful features for our applications which can easily be integrated as dependencies into our code.

Distinguishing Grok concepts

Grok has many things in common with other modern web development frameworks, but it also offers some very unique features, which make it stand apart from the crowd. We'll briefly mention three of them here:

- The component architecture
- The object database
- The concept of object publishing and traversal

The Zope Component Architecture

One distinguishing feature of Grok is its use of a component architecture that is intended to enable developers to create independent components that can be freely reused and exchanged.

Components are simply objects that perform a specified functionality. In the ZCA, this functionality is declared formally by using Interfaces, which are classes that describe the various methods and attributes of an object. A component that implements the same interface as some other component can easily be exchanged for it, giving the developer the option of combining components in different ways and substituting any specific component with newer or better implementations.

The ZCA includes two kinds of components — adapters and utilities. An **adapter** is a component that extends another component with additional data, functionality, or presentation capabilities. A **utility** is a standalone component that provides some kind of service, such as database connectivity, encryption, or mail delivery. In Grok, the term **content component** is used to define the code with which these adapters and utilities interact.

For example, a common paradigm used to describe modern web frameworks is called **Model/View/Controller**, or **MVC** for short. The *model* is the content itself, which is usually stored in a relational database, along with the business rules that define how to modify it; the *view* is the HTML page that the user sees and with which he interacts; the *controller* is the code that gathers dynamic data from the view and pushes it to the model for processing and assembling a new HTML page with the results.

In MVC terms, the model is a component that provides data and is called a content component in Grok. The view and the controller are both adapters that act on this component, the former providing presentation capabilities to it, and the latter giving it additional functionality.

Using the ZCA gives Grok developers several advantages — we get a standard way to extend other objects, which can even be used to add functionality to them from outside, without even touching their code. Also, we are able to both create reusable components, and use existing components that were developed elsewhere. In addition to this, we get a global registry that we can use to easily create our own component registries, thus avoiding code duplication.

This may sound somewhat abstract, so imagine an actual web application where we have several types of objects that represent items in a store catalog. Suppose that this application was developed by a third party, but we need to add a web page that shows specific information for each item, depending on where in the world the user browsing the catalog is located. In Grok, we can easily do that by creating the new view in an independent package and using the ZCA to hook it up with the original object with one single line of code. There is no need to touch the third-party application at all.

Object database

Most Python web frameworks use relational databases to store their object data, which, for complex data structures, can mean that the data is spread over different tables and then joined together by using complex queries. As Python is an object-oriented language, it makes a lot more sense to store the objects directly, which Zope 3 accomplishes by using its own object database, known as the ZODB.

The **ZODB** is a transactional object store with load-balancing capabilities, and is one of the defining concepts of Zope since the very beginning. It allows developers to work with their objects and persist them almost transparently (it's enough to inherit from a persistent class). There is no need to worry about putting together the objects at read time and taking them to pieces when writing.

The ZODB is one of the pieces of Grok that can be used independently in any Python environment.

Object publishing and traversal

In other web frameworks, URLs are usually mapped into code, which calls the correct template or returns the requested result. In Grok, URLs are mapped to objects, which means that any object can have a corresponding view.

If you think of the ZODB storage as a tree, you can visualize how Grok resolves URLs as going from the root node of the tree to the branches, and then sub-branches, until it reaches an object instance to display. This process of "walking the tree" is known as **traversal**.

The traversal mechanism "just works", which means that in practice, you can have nested hierarchies of any length and never have to worry about it as long as you provide default views for all of your object classes (these are called index views in Grok).

In contrast, many Python web frameworks use the concept of "URL routing", which requires the assignment of known paths to database objects by using some sort of regular expression syntax that involves object attributes on the database, such as ID, and a number of possible actions. Modifying these routes from outside the application is not easy.

In addition to the default traversal mechanism, Grok also allows the use of custom traversal methods, which can return arbitrary object instances and views. This can be used to traverse results from a relational mapper query, for example.

Other Grok features

There are lots of other goodies that Grok offers for web application development. Here's a look at just a handful.

Integrated security model

Grok has a very granular security model, based on permissions and roles. It allows the developer to assign specific permissions to a given view and then map those permissions to different roles. It uses the ZCA to permit pluggable components to be used for authentication and authorization.

Easy use of existing Python libraries and modules

Of course, Python web frameworks are very powerful because they allow easy access to the multitude of Python libraries and modules available, starting with Python's own standard library. Grok allows developers to take advantage of this body of software, of course, but that's not the best part. Using the ZCA, it is possible to add views and functionality to objects instantiated from any of these modules without modifying their code, thus allowing us to reuse them more easily.

Static resources

Grok has a special directory name reserved for all of the static files, such as images, CSS stylesheets, or JavaScript files. You can work with these resources like you would in any other web development environment.

Relational database access

Grok includes the powerful ZODB for transparent object persistence, but, of course, there are times when a relational database is better suited for storing some kinds of data. Grok also features easy access to relational databases by using object relational mappers such as SQLAlchemy, so we can get the best of both worlds.

Python Web Server Gateway Interface compatibility

Grok can be configured as a WSGI application and plugged into a pipeline together with other Python applications. This allows the developer to combine different web frameworks and applications into a single site, enabling him to use the best of breed applications wherever possible.

How Grok compares to other web frameworks

Developers who have used, or are familiar with, other web frameworks may like to know a bit about how Grok compares to them. Although a full comparison is out of scope of this book, a few sentences about popular frameworks may be helpful.

PHP

PHP allows a quick development pace, but does not encourage structured and secure web development practices. Grok offers an agile but a much more structured experience, which encourages good practices from the start. Grok also has a clean separation of concerns. Its templating language, ZPT, focuses on presentation, and avoids too much application logic, unlike PHP, which by its own nature combines everything into one template.

Java frameworks

Like Java frameworks, Grok is designed with an eye on developing large and complex applications. Developers coming from Java web frameworks will find that Grok's conventions will drastically reduce configuration file usage. Grok uses a dynamic language, and the lack of a compile cycle greatly speeds up the development cycle. The Python language makes it easier to even test out things from the command line.

Ruby on Rails

Grok is heavily inspired by Ruby on Rails. Rails was one of the earliest frameworks to articulate agile philosophies into two general principles: *Don't Repeat Yourself* (*DRY*) and *Convention over configuration*. DRY means to avoid repeating the same code or information in different places—something that Rails strongly enforces in its development practices. Convention over configuration means that instead of depending on explicit configuration to work, many framework aspects and code constructs have sensible default values. Grok takes these concepts to heart and combines them with the Zope Toolkit and the Zope Component Architecture, to offer a powerful and unique development platform.

Django

Django is one of the most popular Python web development frameworks. One of its key selling points is the automatic generation of administrative interfaces for its applications, which Grok doesn't do. Django is similar to Grok in the use of the *Convention over configuration* and *Don't Repeat Yourself* principles. It also offers the full power of the Python programming language and wants to be a full stack solution for web development problems. Unlike Grok, its architecture is focused on building relational database backed applications and integrating third-party pieces into its stack, while still keeping features such as the administration interfaces working, which is not easy.

Pylons

Pylons is more of a minimal web framework, whereas Grok is trying to offer a full stack of components. Developers using Pylons may find a more powerful framework in Grok, at the expense of some of the flexibility that a minimal framework enables.

Summary

In this chapter, we have introduced Grok and shown why it is a great option for modern web application development. In the next chapter, we'll see how to put Grok into action, and will get our first, simple application up and running.

Getting Started with Grok

Now that we know something about Grok and its history, let's get started with it. The first thing to do, of course, is to install the programs on which Grok is dependent. Luckily, most of this work will be performed automatically for us, but there are three key programs that you may need to install manually: Python, a C compiler (not necessary on Windows systems), and EasyInstall. Also, please be aware that Grok installs itself over the network, so an internet connection is required.

In this chapter, we will cover:

- How to install Python on different platforms
- What the Python Package Index (PyPI) is
- How to work with EasyInstall to quickly install packages from the PyPI over the network
- How `virtualenv` allows us to set up clean Python environments for our development work
- How to create a project using `grokproject`
- How to run an application using paster
- What the Grok admin UI is, and how to use it

Because Python runs on many different platforms, Grok can be installed almost anywhere. In this chapter, we will provide instructions for installing it on three specific platforms: Unix/Linux, Mac OS X, and Windows.

Getting a C compiler

If you use Linux or Mac OS X, your first step is to obtain a compiler. Grok depends on the Zope Toolkit, which includes some C extensions in its source code, and thus we need a compiler to build these extensions, on most platforms.

Windows users need not worry about this because the Grok installation process uses precompiled packages, but the other systems do require a compiler to be installed, in order for Grok to be built.

Many Linux distributions include a compiler in the default setup, so no action is needed for these distributions, but Ubuntu in particular needs a special package containing the compiler and other development tools to be installed. The package name in this case is `build-essential` and you install it by using the following command:

```
# sudo apt-get install build-essential
```

On Mac OS X systems, there's a compiler included in the Developer Tools package on the system DVD. See `http://developer.apple.com/tools/xcode/` for more information.

Installing Python

One of Grok's greatest strengths is that it is written in Python. Grok requires Python version 2.4 or 2.5 to run (at the time of writing, 2.6 support is around the corner), but be aware that it won't run on the recently released 3.0 version, because this version breaks compatibility with older versions of Python and thus is still not supported by most libraries and frameworks.

Installing Python on Unix/Linux

Unix/Linux distributions generally come with Python already installed, so the chances are that your system already has a suitable version of Python installed. To see which version you have, type the command `python -v` at the shell prompt; you'll get a result similar to this:

```
# python -V
```

```
Python 2.5.2
```

If you get an error, then this means that Python is not installed on your machine, and so you will have to install it yourself. This should not happen in any mainstream Linux distribution, but it could conceivably happen with some Unix variants. This is highly unlikely though, so you should get a version number similar to the previous example.

If your version number is 2.4 or 2.5, you may use your system's Python installation for developing with Grok. However, depending on your Linux distribution, you may need additional packages. Some distributions bundle the development libraries and headers for Python in separate packages, so it could be necessary to install these on your system.

If you use Ubuntu or Debian, for example, you will need to install the `python-dev` package as well. You can easily do this by using the command line.

```
# sudo apt-get update
# sudo apt-get install python-dev
```

Other distributions may require different packages to be installed. Consult your system's documentation for instructions.

If you don't have Python installed, you should be able to install it easily using your system's package manager, similar to the way we set up additional packages:

```
# sudo apt-get install python
```

If you have Python, but it's not version 2.4 or 2.5, it's very likely that your Linux distribution includes the package for version 2.5. In Ubuntu or Debian, you can use the following command:

```
# sudo apt-get install python2.5
```

You don't necessarily have to use the system's version of Python. Some developers prefer to manually compile their own Python from the source. This can give you more flexibility and also avoid package conflicts, which can occur when different Python frameworks or tools are installed on the same system (note that similar goals may be accomplished without compiling your own version, by using the `virtualenv` tool, as described elsewhere in this chapter).

To install from the source you need to download the desired version from `http://www.python.org/download/` and go through the usual **configure-build-install** cycle required for Unix/Linux packages. Remember to use Python 2.4 or 2.5.

Installing Python on Mac OS X

Mac OS X always comes with Python pre-installed, but due to the Mac release cycle, the version installed on your computer can be one or even two years old. Therefore, in many cases, Python-Mac community members recommend that you install your own version.

If your OS X version is 10.5, you should be fine with the installed version of Python. For older versions, you might want to check `http://www.python.org/download/mac/` for available installers and suggestions.

Grok has a known dependency clash with **Twisted,** a networking package included in recent versions of Mac OS X, so it's best to use a separate Python environment for Grok. You could, of course, build your own version, as described at the end of the *Installing Python on Unix/Linux* section of this chapter. If, for some reason, you are not comfortable with building your own Python from the source, the recommended approach is to use a virtual environment. This will be covered later in this chapter.

Installing Python on Windows

In addition to the source download, Python releases come with a very good Windows installer. All you have to do to install Python on Windows (we suggest you use at least XP or Vista) is to select a Python version from `http://www.python.org/download/` and choose to download the corresponding `.msi` installer from the available options.

After downloading the installer, double-click the installer file, select an appropriate directory to install Python (the default should be fine), and you can begin to use Python. Since you need to work from the command line to use Grok, you might want to add the Python installation path to your system path so that you can easily access the Python interpreter from any directory.

To do this, go to the Windows **Control Panel**, click on the **System** icon, and select the **Advanced** tab. From there, click on the **Environment Variables** button and select **Path** from the **System Variables** windows (the one at the bottom). Click on **Edit**, and a window with a text box will be displayed, in which you can edit the current value. Be sure to leave the current value exactly as it is, and add the path to your Python installation at the end. The path is the one you selected when running the installer, and is usually in the form `C:\PythonXX`, where XX represents the Python version without a dot (for example, **C:\Python25**, as shown in the following screenshot). Separate this path from the previous paths already present in the system path by using a semicolon. You might also want to add `C:\PythonXX\Scripts` after this, so that the Python scripts that we are going to install in this chapter can also be invoked from anywhere.

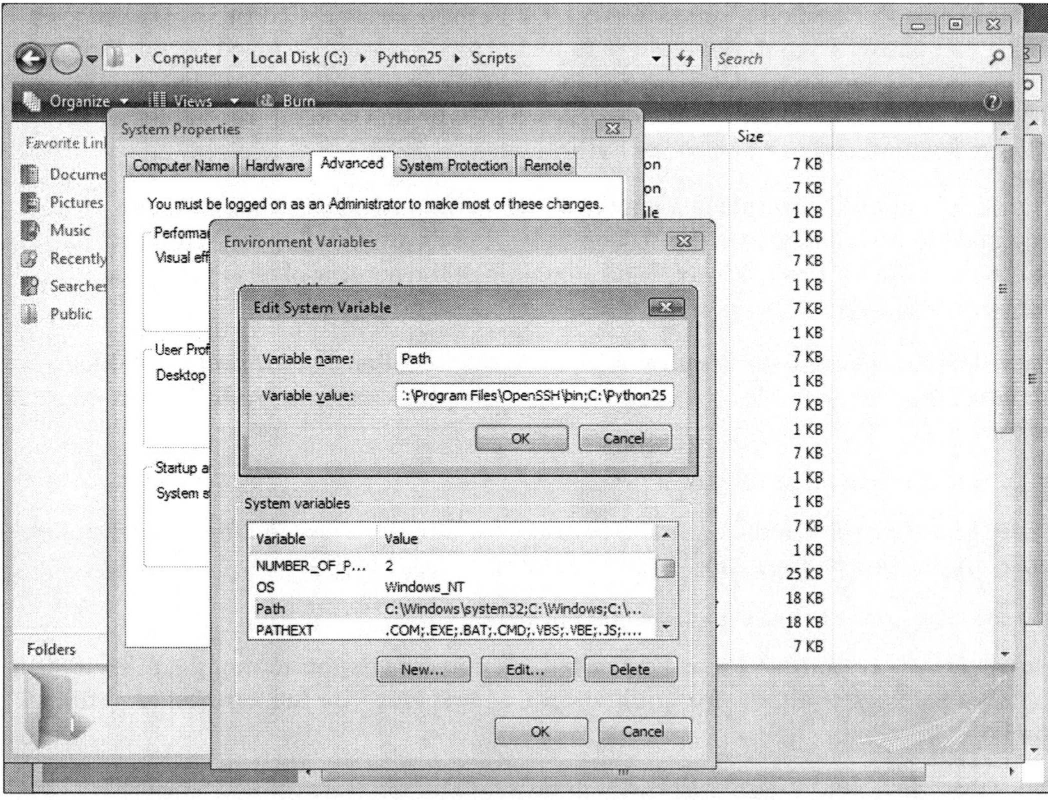

To use Grok, you will also need to install the `win32all` package, which includes the Win32 API, COM support, and Pythonwin. This package also comes with an installer, so it should be easy to set up. Just go to `http://sourceforge.net/projects/pywin32/files` and download the corresponding `win32all` version for your already installed version of Python. Simply run the installer after downloading it, and everything will be ready.

EasyInstall and the Python Package Index (PyPI)

The **Python Package Index (PyPI)** is a repository of software for Python, where thousands of packages are available for download. You can find many kinds of libraries and applications there, and Zope and Grok are well represented, with hundreds of packages at your disposal.

What makes PyPI much more powerful is a Python script called `easy_install`—a script that allows Python developers to install any package indexed on the PyPI over the network, keeping track of dependencies and versions. Packages that can be easy installed are packaged either as compressed files or in a special format, using the `.egg` extension, and are known as **Python eggs**.

The `easy_install` module is a part of a package known as `setuptools`, so you need to install that in order to obtain it. There's an installer for Windows and a `.egg` file for Unix/Linux/Mac available at the setuptools PyPI page on `http://pypi.python.org/pypi/setuptools`.

To install `setuptools` on Windows, just run the installer. For Unix/Linux/Mac systems, run the `.egg` file as a shell script, like in this example (your version may vary):

```
# sh setuptools-0.6c11-py2.4.egg
```

Many Linux distributions include a package for `setuptools`. In Ubuntu or Debian, for example, you can use `apt-get` to install it:

```
# sudo apt-get install python-setuptools
```

However, we recommend that you install the newest version manually, even if there's a package available for your system, as this way you are assured of getting the latest version.

After this, the `easy_install` script will be available on the system Python's path, and from then onwards any package from PyPI can be installed on your system using:

```
# sudo easy_install <package name>
```

It could be possible that you already have `setuptools` installed, but some package that you want to easy install might need a more recent version. In this case, you will receive an error informing you of this fact. To quickly update your `setuptools` version, use the following command:

```
# sudo easy_install -U setuptools
```

The `-U` switch tells `easy_install` to get the latest version of a package and update the previous version in place. The `easy_install` commands are identical on Windows systems. Just leave out the word `sudo` at the beginning.

As mentioned before, Grok and dozens of packages that you can use with both Grok and plain Zope, are available on PyPI, so we will use `easy_install` to install the packages required by Grok. But first, we'll learn how to set up a clean environment for our Grok development work.

Grok and the Python environment

Grok uses a fairly large number of packages. If other large Python packages, or even a number of smaller Python packages, are installed under the same installation of Python dependency problems or version conflicts can sometimes arise. This is because, the code for Python packages installed by `easy_install` or other Python installation methods are usually stored inside the `site-packages` directory of the Python library.

Grok isolates its packages by placing them inside the `.buildout/eggs` directory, but the Python interpreter still looks into `site-packages` for finding a required package, which means that if another Python tool installs a different version of a library used by Grok, a conflict could occur.

This probably will not be a problem for you unless you use another Zope-based technology, such as **Plone**. If you are starting with Grok, the easiest course is probably to just go ahead and install it, but if you run into any version conflicts there's a tool that can help you out of the mess; it's called `virtualenv`.

Virtualenv

`virtualenv` is a Python package that allows the creation of isolated Python environments. This is a way to avoid conflicting packages inside the `site-packages` directory from interfering with your Grok application.

`virtualenv` can be installed by using `easy_install`:

```
# sudo easy_install virtualenv
```

Once it's installed, you can work with it by creating environments for any new projects. For example, to create a test environment for Grok, go to a directory of your choice under your home directory, and type:

```
# virtualenv --no-site-packages-no-site-packages-no-site-packages
testgrok
```

This command will create a directory named `testgrok`, with subdirectories `bin` and `lib` (`Scripts` and `Lib` under Windows). Inside the `bin` directory you will find the `python` and `easy_install` commands, which will run under the context of the virtual environment that you just created. This means, `python` will run the Python interpreter by using the `lib` directory under `testgrok`, and `easy_install` will add new packages under the `site-packages` directory there.

The `--no-site-packages` option tells `virtualenv` that none of the existing packages under the system's Python `site-packages` should be available in the new `virtualenv`. It is recommended that you use this option when building environments for Grok. However, if you have many different environments for applications that tend to use the same general libraries, it is possible to install those libraries under the main Python environment and just add the required packages for each application under the virtual environment. In this case, the `--no-site-packages` option should not be used, but you will need to plan your setup very carefully.

When working inside a `virtualenv`, you must remember to use the full path to the `python` and `easy_install` commands, or you may inadvertently install a package in the main Python environment, or run your application with a different set of packages than you intended. To prevent this problem, a batch script named `activate` is included in the `bin` directory of the `virtualenv` (`Scripts` directory under Windows). Once you run it, all further invocations of the `python` and `easy_install` commands will use their `virtualenv` versions until you end the session by using the corresponding `deactivate` script.

Use the following command to activate the `virtualenv` under Unix/Linux/Mac for our `testgrok` environment:

```
# source testgrok/bin/activate
```

And in Windows:

```
> testgrok\scripts\activate
```

As `buildout` itself takes care of this, the `activate` and `deactivate` scripts are not needed for Grok; they are only mentioned here for completeness.

Installing Grok using grokproject

We are finally ready to install Grok. To make it easy to create a project along with a basic directory structure, Grok uses the `grokproject` package, which can be installed using `easy_install`. Go to a directory where you want to create your application (if you are using `virtualenv`, go inside the `testgrok virtualenv` we created in the previous section). Now type the following command:

```
# easy_install grokproject
```

You have now installed it, but keep in mind the `-U` switch for `easy_install` that allows you to update a package in place, because `grokproject` is under continuous development, and updating it frequently is a good idea. Now we can create our first Grok project.

Creating our first project

As mentioned earlier, the `grokproject` package we just installed is a tool for creating projects. A Grok project is a directory that constitutes a working environment in which Grok applications can be developed. It's a template that includes a simple executable application that can be used as a base for development and as a guide for where things usually go in Grok.

Creating a project is very easy. Let's create the traditional hello world example using Grok:

```
# grokproject helloworld
```

`grokproject` takes as an argument, the name of directory where the project will be created. After you run the command, you will immediately be asked for an administrator username and password. Take note of this because you will need it later, to run the application for the first time.

Once it has the required information, `grokproject` downloads and installs the Zope Toolkit packages that Grok requires, as well as Grok itself. This can take a few minutes, depending on the speed of your network connection, because Grok consists of many packages. Once the download is finished, `grokproject` configures Grok, and sets up the Grok application template, leaving it ready for use.

Running the default application

To run the default application that is created along with the project workspace, we need to start up Grok. Let's change the current directory to that of our hello world example, and do that.

```
# cd helloworld
```

```
# bin/paster serve parts/etc/deploy.ini
```

Note that the command needs to be run directly from the project's directory. Please do not change to the `bin` directory and try to run `paster` there. In general, all project scripts and commands are meant to be run from the main project directory.

This command will start Grok on port 8080, which is its default port. Now you can see Grok in action at last by opening a web browser and pointing it to `http://localhost:8080`.

If, for some reason, you have to use a different port on your system, you will need to edit the `deploy.ini` file inside the `parts/etc/` directory. This file holds Grok's deployment configuration. You will find the line where the port is set (very near to the bottom of the file). Simply change it to whatever number you want, and run `paster` again. Here is an example of how the relevant part of the file should look:

```
[server:main]
use = egg:Paste#http
host = 127.0.0.1
port = 8888
```

When you go to that URL, you will see a login prompt. Here you have to use the login and password that you selected when you created the project in the previous section. After that, you will be inside the Grok administration interface (refer the following screenshot).

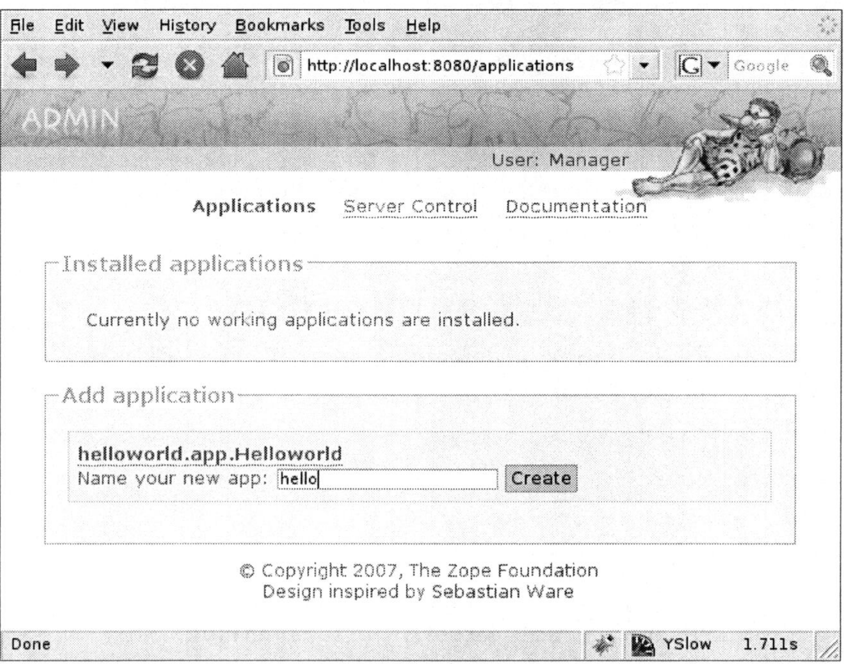

All you need to do to create a copy of the default application is to type a name for it in the text box with the label **Name your new app** label and click the **Create** button. Call it **hello**, for example. After that, you will see a new section on the page where installed applications are shown, and **hello** should be the only one in the list, as shown in the next screenshot. You can either click the name from there, or point your browser to `http://localhost:8080/hello`, to see the application running.

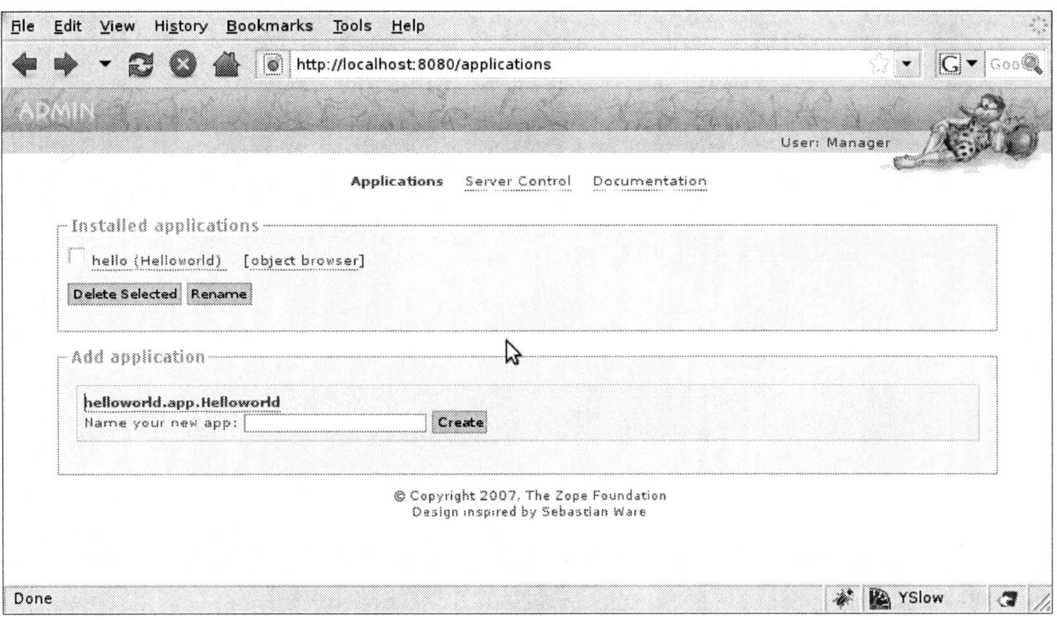

At this point, your browser should display a very simple HTML page with a message telling you that Grok is up and running, as seen in the following screenshot:

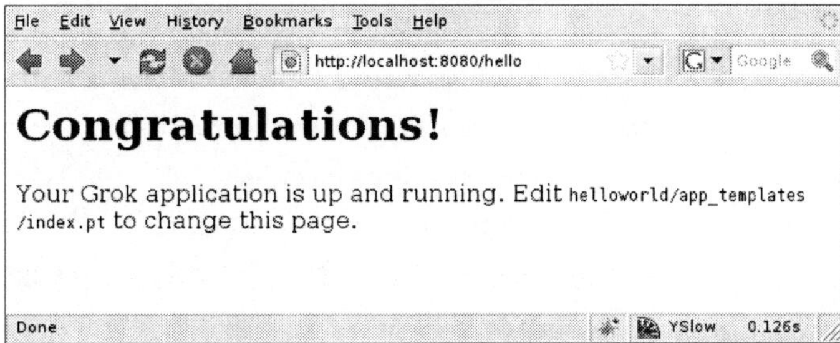

To stop the server, you need to press *Ctrl + C*, which will let you regain control of the shell. To restart it again, just rerun the `paster serve` command.

What's inside a Grok project?

As we mentioned earlier, the `grokproject` command that we used to create a project in the last section uses (behind the scenes) a tool called `zc.buildout`—a system for managing repeatable development and production environments. `buildout` took care of downloading all of Grok's dependencies, building and installing them under the project directory. It also installed all of the scripts required to run Grok, like the `paster` command that we used before.

We'll take a closer look at `buildout` and its directory structure later in this book. For now, just note that the files in the main project directory are a part of the `buildout`. The actual Grok application will be stored under the `src` directory.

Let's take a look at the directories and files specifically associated with the hello world Grok application that we created.

Overview of the application structure

The hello world application code is stored inside the `src` subdirectory under the `helloworld` directory that `grokproject` created for us, earlier in this chapter. Let's take a look at the files stored there:

File	Description
`app.py`	Contains the models and views for the application
`app_templates`	Directory where application templates are stored
`app.txt`	Functional tests for the application
`configure.zcml`	Zope 3 XML configuration file
`ftesting.zcml`	XML configuration for functional tests
`__init__.py`	This file exists to make the directory a package
`startup.py`	WSGI application factory
`static`	Directory for static resources, such as images and CSS
`tests.py`	Contains application testing code

We'll have more to say about all of these files in further chapters, but for now the most important points to take home are:

- The file `app.py` contains the actual application code, which in this case is minimal.

- The message that was displayed in the browser window when we executed the application comes from the `index.pt` template stored inside the `app_templates` directory.

- An XML configuration file, which is used mainly to load Grok's configuration.

Creating our first template

In the last section, we presented a template that comprises the only visible part of the hello world application. This template can be found inside the `src/app_templates` directory of our Grok project. To get our feet wet with Grok, let's change that template and add a message of our own.

From the `helloworld` directory, open the file `src/app_templates/index.pt` using your favorite text editor. The file has the following contents:

```
<html>
<head>
</head>
<body>
  <h1>Congratulations!</h1>
  <p>Your Grok application is up and running.
  Edit <code>testdrive/app_templates/index.pt</code> to change
  this page.</p>
</body>
</html>
```

Change the file to look like this:

```
<html>
<head>
</head>
<body>
  <h1>Hello World!</h1>
  <p>Grok the caveman says hi.</p>
</body>
</html>
```

Actually, you can change the message to say whatever you like; just be aware that Grok templates require XHTML.

Finally, save the template and run the server instance using `paster` again:

```
# bin/paster serve parts/etc/deploy.ini
```

If you left the server running before, there's no need to restart it for this change, as modifications to page templates, images, and CSS can be viewed immediately.

Open the URL `http://localhost:8080/hello` in your browser. You should see something similar to the following screenshot:

Grok says hi. Now rejoice, you have finished your first Grok application.

The Grok admin UI

You briefly interacted with the Grok admin application manager before, when you named and launched the hello world application. Let's take a look in more detail at the three tabs in this admin UI.

Applications

In this tab, you can manage all your application instances. For any application that you define, you will see its dotted class path, such as `helloworld.app.Helloworld` in our example, and a text box and button for creating and naming an instance.

Once you create an instance of an application, you will see it listed at the top of the page, along with any other application that you might have created before. From there you can launch an application by clicking on its name, or can delete it, or rename it by using the checkbox on its left and the corresponding button.

You can also use the **object browser** link next to the application's name to inspect the instance and take a look at its base classes, attributes, properties, and methods. For example, it's possible to explore the documentation included in the docstrings of a class or module. You can take a look at the second screenshot under the *Running the default application* section to see the link to the object browser in the Grok admin UI.

Server control

The **Server Control** tab allows you to take a look at the server process information, such as uptime, platform, and software versions. It also allows you to start, stop, or restart the server process, provided you are running it as a daemon and not from the command line. See the next screenshot for an example of the information found in this tab.

Because the **ZODB** that Grok uses for persistence is transactional and supports undo, it tends to grow a lot in size as more and more objects are added to it and modified constantly. To keep your project's database neat and tidy, it is recommended to "pack" it regularly. The packing process deletes older revisions of your objects and keeps only the latest information, thus reducing file size.

You can pack the ZODB from Grok from the server control panel. Just pick the number of days for which you would like to preserve object information and click on the **Pack** button. A value of **0** clears all previous object revisions leaving only the latest versions of all objects. The packing process runs on the background, so your application can still serve requests while it takes place.

One last feature you can use from this tab is administrative message, which allows you to type in a message that will be seen by all administrators on every page of the Grok admin UI until someone resets the text.

Documentation

The **Documentation** tab presents links to the DocGrok package and object browsers, which allow you to look at all the information provided by most of the things living under the running Grok process. This includes, but is not limited to objects, classes, modules, functions, and text files.

Summary

In this chapter, we installed Grok and its dependencies and created our first Grok project and application.

Now that we can create our own Grok projects, it's time to learn how to define and create different kinds of views and develop our first working application using that knowledge.

3

Views

In the previous chapter we created our first Grok project and learned how to start a simple hello world application. Now we are going to learn about views and templates, which comprise the presentation layer of our web applications. To do this, we will create a simple application to manage to-do lists. The objective is to produce, by the end of this chapter, a working application that allows the user to create and manage any number of lists, add items to them, and mark them off as completed.

In order to reach our objective, we'll go through the following topics in this chapter:

- What are views and where in the Grok application code should they be defined
- How to use the ZPT templating engine, and examples of the most common statements in action
- How to write a full Grok application using only views
- How to get form parameters from a web request
- How to add static resources to a Grok application
- How to create and work with additional views
- How to use views that do not require an associated template

Grok views

A **web application** is just a series of web pages that help the user to carry out one or more tasks by allowing him to enter some data, working with it in various ways, and presenting some result or confirmation back to him. In a web application framework, the web pages that allow the user to see what is going on and the web forms that permit him to capture information are known as **views**.

A view is typically implemented by using some sort of page templates, but in Grok we can also have separate Python code to handle more complex logic more easily. In fact, we could even have the view rendered using only Python code without templates. This gives the developer more power (the full power of Python, indeed) and allows a clean separation of view presentation and view logic, resulting in a more readable code both in the template and the Python sides.

We already worked with the template part of a view at the end of Chapter 2, when we modified the file `index.pt` in the `helloworld` project. Besides this page template, if you look at the `app.py` file inside the `src/helloworld` directory of this project, you will see the Python part of the view. Here's the full source code for the `helloworld` application:

```python
import grok

class Helloworld(grok.Application, grok.Container):
    pass


class Index(grok.View):
    pass # see app_templates/index.pt
```

In this case, the Python code for the view consists only of a single class declaration, which we inherit from `grok.View`, which is the basic Grok view. Since we are just going to show the template, we don't need any more code, but we can see one of Grok's conventions at work here if we look at the name of the class: `Index`. As the comment after the class definition says, the template for this class will be found under `app_templates/index.pt` in the `application` directory. Grok doesn't need to be told this either in code or configuration because by convention, the template name will be the same as the class name, with the template name in lowercase and the extension `.pt` appended to it.

To add a new view to the application, all we need to do is to define a class that inherits from `grok.View` and create the corresponding template inside the `app_templates` folder. Then we can refer to this view in a URL by using the template name. Note that the name `index.pt` is a special case and represents another convention, because a view with that name will be considered the default view of the application, which means that it's not necessary to specify its name in the URL.

Zope Page Templates (ZPT)

For the HTML generation, Grok uses **Zope Page Templates** (ZPT). They fit Grok's philosophy nicely because one of the driving principles behind their design is the strict separation of logic from presentation. Wherever possible, a view template should contain only presentation and structural logic, along with name and method calls from the view class.

Another important design principle of ZPT is to work well with editing tools, thus allowing designers to take template code back from developers and still be able to see and work with a complete HTML representation of the page without losing any logic. This is achieved by using valid HTML/XHTML for the page template.

The Template Attribute Language (TAL)

To accomplish its objective of working well with editing tools, ZPT uses the **Template Attribute Language** (TAL). Statements from this language use HTML attributes with an XML namespace, which basically means that they are prefixed with the letters "tal" and a colon, as in `tal:content` or `tal:replace`. Editing tools usually ignore statements which are not a part of regular HTML, and so they leave the TAL statements alone.

Let's take a quick overview of the most important TAL statements and constructs. We'll cover the basics here, but the complete reference can be found at `http://docs.zope.org/zope2/zope2book/AppendixC.html`.

Let's begin our introduction to TAL by showing a simple example:

```
<h1 tal:content="python:5*5">Me Grok can multiply</h1>
```

`content` is a TAL statement that leaves the tag alone, but replaces its contents with the result of the expression in quotes. In this case, when the page is rendered, we'll get the following:

```
<h1>25</h1>
```

Note that the tag remains an `<h1>` tag, but the contents of the tag change to the result of the expression, which will be dynamically calculated each time the page renders. A designer using a WYSIWYG tool will see the words "A simple multiplication" instead, but will be able to correctly see the intended structure of the page.

By design, ZPT is not a general programming language, so complex code will be better off inside Python code in the view class. However, it is still possible to repeat tags, omit, or display them according to some conditions, or even include parts of other page templates. This will generally be enough for most page structures and even if it's not, part of the HTML can be generated in Python code and inserted inside a template as well.

ZPT is not the only templating engine that can be used with Grok, as it was carefully designed to allow pluggable engines. At the time of writing, there are packages available for two such engines: `megrok.genshi` and `megrok.chameleon`. A developer can choose which templating engine fits his style better and use that instead of ZPT.

Expression types

In the previous example, we used the expression `python:5*5` to get the result of a multiplication. These are known as Python expressions and can include any valid Python expression after the colon. Of course, as one of the principles of Grok is the clear separation of presentation and logic, we want to avoid very large expressions. But Python expressions are sometimes very useful, especially when we are dealing with conditions or Python objects such as lists or dictionaries.

There are several reasons why keeping most of the logic out of the templates is a good idea. Debugging and testing code is much easier if we can use Python development tools, for one thing. Also, by using this strategy, we can potentially alter the presentation of an application (the templates) without touching the main code.

There are other kinds of expressions, though. The default type of expression in ZPT is called **path expression**. Here is an example:

```
<p tal:content="request/URL">Me Grok want current URL</p>
```

The reason it's called a path expression is because it starts with a variable name and uses a slash to separate calls to subobjects of that variable, returning the result of calling the last object in the path, or the object itself if it is not callable. In the preceding example, we get the current URL from the special name `request`, by using a path from `request` to `URL`.

If a component of the path is not found, an error occurs, but it's possible to fall back to other objects or values in this case. To do that, we use the | symbol to separate possible expression values. For example, to get some parameter from the request:

```
<span tal:content="request/param1|request/param2|nothing">Me Grok will
settle for any value here</span>
```

In this path expression, we look for the request parameter `param1`; if it's not defined, we use the value of `param2`, and if none of the two are defined, the special value `nothing` is used. This value is equivalent to Python's `None` value, so nothing will be inside the span tag if this happens, but no error will occur.

In addition to path and Python expressions, there is a third type, known as **String expressions**. These are useful when you need to combine arbitrary strings with the result of path expressions. Here is an example:

```
<p tal:content="string:Me Grok web page is at this URL: ${request/
URL}"></p>
```

Everything after the colon is treated as the string to display, except that the string is searched for path expressions marked with the $ sign and the results of those expressions are substituted in. When the path expression consists of more than one part (when we have to use the / separator) or when it's not separated by spaces from other characters in the string, it is necessary to enclose the expression in { } braces, as in the preceding example. To insert a $ sign, a double $ is used, like this:

```
<p tal:content="string: Me Grok is richer by $$ $amount"></p>
```

If the variable `amount` has the value 45, the previous expression will output the following HTML:

```
<p>Me Grok is richer by $ 45</p>
```

Inserting text

We already saw that the `content` statement replaces all of the content of a tag, including any nested tags inside. There is another statement, `replace`, which gets rid of the tag altogether, and inserts the desired text in its place.

```
<span tal:replace="string:Me Grok need no tag here">text</span>
```

In this case, the `<span>` tag is only a placeholder tag because it will not be output when the template is rendered.

In addition to inserting text, the `replace` statement can be used for including dummy content on a page, which can be helpful for some designers who want to work with a more detailed mock web page for illustrative purposes, without this content appearing on the final rendered page. To do that, we simply replace the HTML with the special name `nothing`:

```
<p tal:replace="nothing">Me Grok will not use this content</p>
```

Repeating tags

When working with HTML tables and lists, we will often need to add a table row or a list item for every item in a Python sequence, such as a list or a tuple. For example, we could have a list of weapons for 'Grok the caveman' that we need to display as an HTML unordered list. The repeat statement causes a tag, and all of its contents, to be repeated once for every element in a sequence. To see how it works, suppose that we have a list of weapons that is passed to the template as an attribute of the view, with the name weapon:

```
<h1>Grok's Arsenal</h1>
<ul>
<li tal:repeat="weapon python:view.weapons"
    tal:content="weapon">Weapon</li>
</ul>
```

If weapon contains the list ['Rock','Club','Spear'], the template will be rendered like this:

```
<h1>Grok's Arsenal</h1>
<ul>
<li>Rock</li>
<li>Club</li>
<li>Spear</li>
</ul>
```

The repeat statement takes two parameters. The first is the name of the loop variable, which will be assigned the value of each element in the list in order. The second is an expression that returns the sequence where the elements are stored. Notice how we use our chosen name weapon, together with the content statement, to insert the name of the current weapon inside the <li> tag.

It is possible to nest multiple repeat statements, which is why we need to assign a name to the loop variable. This name can also be useful for determining where on the list are we by using it together with the special repeat variable. For example, the expression repeat/weapon/number will return 1 for the first element, 2 for the second, and so on. The expression repeat/weapon/index does the same, but starts at 0.

Conditional elements

The condition statement is used when we want to decide, at render time, if a tag and its contents should be displayed on the page or not. It evaluates the expression passed to it and removes the tag if the result is false. When the expression is true, the tag is shown as normal.

To help 'Grok the caveman' keep better track of his arsenal, we could turn the list into a table to also show the number of each weapon that he has. A helpful reminder can be added to each row when the number of items is considered too low. The `view` variable would contain a list of dictionaries in this case, such as this one: [{'name':'Rock','quantity':10},{'name':'Club','quantity':1},{'name':'Spear','quantity':3}]. To show the table, we could use this markup:

```
<table>
<tr>
<th>Weapon</th>
<th>Quantity</th>
<th>Notes</th>
</tr>
<tr tal:repeat="weapon view/weapons">
<td tal:content="weapon/name">Weapon</td>
<td tal:content="weapon/quantity">Quantity</td>
<td tal:condition="python:weapon['quantity']>=3">OK</td>
<td tal:condition="python:weapon['quantity']<3">Need to get
  more!</td>
</tr>
</table>
```

This will produce the following HTML:

```
<table>
<tr>
<th>Weapon</th>
<th>Quantity</th>
<th>Notes</th>
</tr>
<tr>
<td>Rock</td>
<td>10</td>
<td>
OK
</td>
</tr>
<tr>
<td>Club</td>
<td>1</td>
<td>
Need to get more!
</td>
</tr>
```

```
<tr>
<td>Spear</td>
<td>3</td>
<td>
OK
</td>
</tr>
</table>
```

There are a few things to note about this code. First, notice how we used path expressions to refer to the dictionary keys in the `name` and `quantity` columns. Path expressions work the same way for dictionary keys, object attributes, and methods. By contrast, in the Python expressions for the `condition` statements we had to use the dictionary syntax. The other thing to note is that we essentially need to repeat the same `<span>` tag twice with different conditions. The rendered template only shows those tags which are true. In this case, we have mutually exclusive conditions, but in other cases we could have multiple conditions, with independent true or false values.

Variables

Sometimes we have expressions that we need to reuse throughout a page template. We could just repeat the expression in multiple places, but that would cause it to be evaluated multiple times, which is inefficient. For these situations, ZPT provides a `define` statement that allows us to assign the result of an expression to a variable. Here is an example of a template fragment where a variable definition would be helpful:

```
<ul>
<li tal:repeat="weapon view/weapons">
<span tal:replace="weapon">weapon</span> is weapon
<span tal:replace="repeat/weapon/number">number</span> of
<span tal:replace="python:len(view.weapons)">total number of weapons
</span>
</li>
</ul>
```

In this example, the expression `view/weapons` is calculated once at the `repeat` statement and then once more for every item in the list. The length of the list is also calculated once for every item in the `weapons` list. If we use the `define` statement, this can be avoided:

```
<ul tal:define="weapons view/weapons;total_weapons
   python:len(weapons)">
<li tal:repeat="weapon weapons">
<span tal:replace="weapon">weapon</span> is weapon
<span tal:replace="repeat/weapon/number">number</span> of
```

```
<span tal:replace="total_weapons">total number of weapons</span>
</li>
</ul>
```

The `define` statement takes the name of the variable and a expression for its value, with a space in between. Note that we can have multiple definitions in a single statement, separated by semicolons. Now, let's say that we need to add a header at the top of the list where the total number of weapons must be displayed again:

```
<h1>Grok's Arsenal (<span tal:replace="python:len(view.weapons)">
    number</span> total weapons)
</h1>
```

We can't define the length only in the `<h1>` tag because the scope of the `define` statement is limited to the tag where it is used and its contents. Nevertheless, we would like to have just one definition that we can reuse throughout the template. The `global` keyword can be used in this case:

```
<h1 tal:define="global weapons view/weapons;total_weapons
    python:len(weapons)">Grok's Arsenal (<span tal:replace="python:
    total_weapons">number</span> total weapons)
</h1>
```

Once a variable is defined using the `global` keyword, it can be reused anywhere in the template, independent of the tag structure of the page.

One important thing to keep in mind regarding definitions is that path expressions always return the result of calling the last element of the path. Thus, when we are working with callable objects, we could end up assigning the wrong thing to a variable and messing up the page. This can sometimes be hard to debug, so it's not a bad idea to use Python expressions wherever possible, because they are more explicit.

This doesn't mean that we can't use path expressions (after all, they are the default type), but we have to make sure that we are getting the value that we want. When we need to get an object and not the result of calling that object, we can use the special `nocall` path expression to get it:

```
<p tal:define="object nocall:view/object">Me Grok need object</p>
```

Special variables

Grok also makes some special variables available to every page template, so that template authors can refer to the different application's objects and views.

- `view`: Using this special name, all of the methods and attributes of the view class associated with the template can be accessed.
- `context`: The context name refers to the model that is being viewed, and also allows access to its methods and attributes.
- `request`: The request object contains data from the current web request.
- `static`: This special name allows the creation of URLs referring to static resources.

Modifying HTML tag attributes

In addition to inserting text in a page, it's very common to require the attributes of an HTML tag to be defined dynamically at rendering time. The `attributes` statement allows us to do precisely this. For example, let's add links to a description page for every weapon in Grok the caveman's arsenal:

```
<h1>Grok's Arsenal</h1>
<ul>
<li tal:repeat="weapon view/weapons">
<a tal:content="weapon" href=""
   tal:attributes="href string:${request/URL}/${weapon}">Weapon</a>
</li>
</ul>
```

In this example, we modify the link's `href` attribute to use the current page's URL and append to it the name of the weapon, assuming that a weapon description page with that name exists for every weapon in the list.

As with the `define` statement, `attributes` statements allow multiple attribute definitions separated by semicolons.

Inserting structure

For security reasons, strings inserted by using the `content` and `replace` tags are quoted, in order to escape any HTML tags, so the < bracket becomes `<` and the > bracket becomes `>`. This results in HTML tags being displayed in the rendered page, instead of being interpreted as HTML. This is useful for preventing some cross-site scripting attacks, but does get in the way of generating HTML from Python code. The `structure` keyword is used before an expression to tell ZPT that the returned text should be interpreted as HTML and rendered like the rest of the tags on the page.

For instance, if we suppose that the variable text contains the following HTML:

```
<p>This is the text</p>
```

This tag will escape the HTML:

```
<div tal:content="text">The text</div>
```

The resulting HTML will look like this:

```
<div>&lt;p&gt;This is the text&lt;/p&gt;</div>
```

Let's use the `structure` keyword:

```
<div tal:content="structure text">The text</div>
```

Now we get this result:

```
<div><p>This is the text</p></div>
```

Multiple statements in one tag

In some of the earlier examples, we have used more than one TAL statement inside a single tag. As XML doesn't allow repeating attributes inside a tag, we can use only one of each type of TAL statement inside a given tag, and we can combine them as we see fit, with the exception of the `content` and `replace` statements, which are mutually exclusive and can't be used in the same tag at all.

The most important thing to know when using multiple statements in one tag is that the order in which they are executed is fixed. It doesn't matter how we place them in the tag, they will be executed in the following order:

1. `define`
2. `condition`
3. `repeat`
4. `content/replace`
5. `attributes`

For this reason, if we need one statement that is lower in this list to be executed before a statement that is higher, we have to add `<div>` or `<span>` tags as required to get around the fixed order. For example, suppose we want to define some variable for every element in a `repeat` statement. We can't add the `define` statement in the same tag as the `repeat` statement itself, because `define` is executed before `repeat`, so we would get an error due to the loop variable being undefined at that point.

A possible solution would be to use a `<span>` tag to define the variable after the `repeat` statement, as shown in the following example:

```
<h1>Grok's Arsenal</h1>
<ul>
<li tal:repeat="weapon view/weapons">
<span tal:define="weapon_uppercase python:weapon.upper()"
      tal:content="weapon_uppercase">
Me Grok want uppercase letters
</span>
</li>
</ul>
```

A slightly better solution is to use a tag with the XML namespace `tal`, which will serve as a structural marker but not appear in the final page rendering:

```
<h1>Grok's Arsenal</h1>
<ul>
<li tal:repeat="weapon view/weapons">
<tal:weapon define="weapon_uppercase python:weapon.upper()"
            content="weapon_uppercase">
Me Grok want uppercase letters
</tal:weapon>
</li>
</ul>
```

Instead of the `<span>` tag, we use `<tal:weapon>`. It's not that ZPT has a `weapon` tag; the trick is in the `tal` part of the name. We could use anything else in place of `weapon` here. Note that as the tag itself explicitly uses the `tal` namespace, when using ZPT, the `define` and `content` statements in the same tag do not need to be prefixed by it.

Macros and slots

Many websites use standard elements on every page, such as headers, footers, sidebars, and more. One nice feature of ZPT is that it allows us to reuse elements like these without having to repeat them everywhere. The mechanisms used for doing this are called macros and slots.

A **macro** is a page or part of a page that is declared as one and given a name. Once this declaration is done, the markup so named can be reused in different pages. This way, we can have a single-page macro defining the look and feel of our site and have every other page look like it and, most importantly, automatically change whenever the macro changes.

A macro is defined using HTML attributes, just like TAL statements are. The macro definition language is known as **Macro Expansion Template Attribute Language**, or just **METAL** for short. Here's an example:

```
<div metal:define-macro="about">
<h1>About Grok</h1>
<p>Grok is a friendly caveman who likes smashing websites</p>
</div>
```

The `define-macro` statement creates a macro with the name given in quotes, which is `about` in this case. This name is added to the list of macros defined on the page, which is appropriately named macros. We can define any number of macros inside a page template, as long as we use different names for each. To use a macro, we access the `macros` attribute of the page in which it was created, by using the desired name. Supposing the `about` macro is defined inside a page template named `main.pt`, we can then use the macro from any other page, like this:

```
<p metal:use-macro="context/main.pt/macros/about">
About
</p>
```

When this other template is rendered, the entire `<p>` tag is substituted by the `<div>` tag that encloses the macro. It's just as if the HTML from the macro was copied and pasted in place of the tag containing the `use-macro` statement.

By using macros, you can easily reuse big or small pieces of HTML in multiple pages, but what makes this much more useful is the concept of slots. Think of slots as placeholders for custom HTML inside an existing macro. Although the general structure of the HTML remains the same, a template using macros can fill in these placeholders at rendering time, thus allowing much more flexibility than simple macros alone can provide.

The best use for slots is to define sections within a full-page macro that can be filled in by different templates using the macro. We can then define the structure of our web pages in one single place, and have the whole site take advantage of it.

Let's define a page macro to show these concepts in action:

```
<html metal:define-macro="page">
<head>
<title tal:content="context/title">title</title>
</head>
<body>
<div metal:define-slot="header">
<h1 tal:content="context/title">Grok's Cave</h1>
</div>
```

```
<div metal:define-slot="body">
<p>Welcome to Grok's cave.</p>
</div>
<div metal:define-slot="footer">
<p>Brought to you by Grok the caveman.</p>
</div>
</body>
</html>
```

Notice how we define the macro right inside the very first tag, so that the entire page is a single big macro. Then, using the `define-slot` statement, we define three slots, one each for the header, footer, and body. Other templates can reuse the macro and fill in one or more of these slots to customize the final page rendering. Here's how to do that:

```
<html metal:use-macro="context/main.pt/page">
<div fill-slot="body">
Me Grok likes macros!
</div>
</html>
```

The `fill-slot` statement takes the name of a slot and replaces its content with the section beginning with the tag where it is used. Everything else in the `main.pt` template is used exactly as it appears there. This is what the rendered HTML looks like:

```
<html>
<head>
<title>example</title>
</head>
<body>
<div>
<h1>example</h1>
</div>
<div>
<p>Me Grok likes macros!</p>
</div>
<div>
<p>Brought to you by Grok the caveman.</p>
</div>
</body>
</html>
```

Going beyond ZPT basics

This has been a short introduction to ZPT, although we did cover a handful of concepts, including inserting text into templates, repeating tags, conditions, variables, attributes, and macros. For more information, a good resource is the Zope book, which is available online at `http://docs.zope.org/zope2/zope2book/`.

The to-do list application

Now that we have learned about ZPT, let's begin with the code for our to-do list application. The idea is that the user will have a web page where he can manage his tasks by using lists. Instead of using a single list, he will be able to create several lists for high-level tasks, each with a number of smaller tasks to carry out. The application will allow the user to create a list with a description, add tasks to it, and check them off as completed when he is done. He can add as many lists as he needs, and remove any of them at any time.

This is all very simple, so for now the list manager will use a single view with an associated template. We will add additional functionality as we advance through the chapter.

The first step of course is to create a new Grok project:

```
# grokproject todo
```

For now, we'll hold our to-do lists in a Python list. Each one will be a dictionary containing keys of title, description, and items. Our next step will be to create a template to show all of the lists and their items. We'll replace the content of the `index.pt` template inside `app_templates` with this code:

```
<html>
<head>
  <title>To-Do list manager</title>
</head>
<body>
  <h1>To-Do list manager</h1>
  <p>Here you can add new lists and check off all the items that
    you complete.
  </p>
  <tal:block repeat="todolist context/todolists">
    <h2 tal:content="todolist/title">List title</h2>
    <p tal:content="todolist/description">List description</p>
    <ul>
        <li tal:repeat="item todolist/items"
            tal:content="item">item 1</li>
```

```
            <li tal:replace="nothing">item 2</li>
            <li tal:replace="nothing">item 3</li>
        </ul>
    </tal:block>
  </body>
</html>
```

Examine the code. Make sure that you understand all of the ZPT statements that we are using. Go look at the ZPT section again, if necessary. We are assuming that the special name `context` will include the lists in an attribute named `todolists` and that it iterates over all of the lists by using the `repeat` statement. We also have a nested `repeat` statement inside that, to list all of the items in each to-do list.

Before doing anything else, open the `index.pt` file by using the open file option in your web browser. Notice how we get a nice preview of how the page will look once it has real data (see the following screenshot). That's one of the benefits of working with ZPT. We expressly took advantage of this feature by including two dummy list items in the list, by using the `replace="nothing"` trick.

Now let's see its working in Grok. Remember that the template assumes that there will be a list named `todolists` available in the `context`. This would in fact refer to the application model, but for now let's just hardcode some value there to see how the template is rendered. We'll use a real model later. Open the `app.py` file in the `src` directory and change it to look like this:

```python
import grok


class Todo(grok.Application, grok.Container):
    todolists = [{
        'title' : 'Daily tasks for Grok',
```

```
        'description' : 'A list of tasks that Grok does everyday',
        'items' : ['Clean cave',
                   'Hunt breakfast',
                   'Sharpen ax']
    }]

class Index(grok.View):
    pass
```

Now start the application:

```
# bin/paster serve etc/deploy.ini
```

Create an application by using the admin control panel and click on its link. A screen similar to the following screenshot will be displayed. Notice the similarity to the preview template that we opened before.

Handling form data

We can now display to-do lists and their items correctly, but we need a way to add new lists and items, and we also need to be able to check them off somehow. We need forms to handle these actions, so let's modify the template to look like this:

```
<html>
<head>
  <title>To-Do list manager</title>
</head>
```

```
<body>
  <h1>To-Do list manager</h1>
  <p>Here you can add new lists and check off all the items that
     you complete.
  </p>
  <tal:lists repeat="todolist context/todolists">
     <form method="post" tal:attributes="action view/url">
       <fieldset>
           <legend tal:content="todolist/title">
             title</legend>
           <p tal:content="todolist/description">
               description</p>
           <div tal:repeat="item todolist/items">
               <span tal:content="item/description">
                 </span>
           </div>
       </fieldset>
     </form>
  </tal:lists>
</body>
</html>
```

We now use a form for each list, and every form has the same action, defined at
rendering time by using the `attributes` statement. A Grok view always has a
`url` method that returns the view URL, so what we are doing here is submitting
the form to itself. We'll deal with form submissions a bit later, when we add the
view's Python code.

To separate the lists visually, each one is inside a `fieldset`, with its title and
description. To list individual items, we drop the `<ul>` from our first template and
use a `<div>`, because we now need to have a checkbox to mark the items completed.
Let's add the checkbox, and also provide a way to delete items from the list while we
are at it:

```
<div tal:repeat="item todolist/items">
   <input type="checkbox"
      tal:attributes="name string:item_{repeat/item/index};
                      checked item/checked"/>
   <span tal:content="item/description"></span>
   <input type="submit"
      tal:attributes="name string:delete_${repeat/item/index}"
      value="Delete"/>
</div>
<br/>
<input type="hidden" name="list_index"
   tal:attributes="value repeat/todolist/index"/>
<input type="submit" name="update_list" value="Update list"/>
<br />
```

Note the use of the `repeat/item/index` variable to name each item according to its place in the list, so that we can refer to them individually in the view. We'll also need to know to which list the item belongs, which is why every list form has a hidden input field with its index, using `repeat/todolist/index` to get that value. Finally, we have an update list button which is used to check and uncheck multiple list items in one go.

All that's needed now is a way to add new items to a list. We'll just append to the preceding code a text area for the item description, and a submit button for adding it. Nothing really special here:

```
<label for="item_description">Description:</label><br/>
<textarea name="item_description"></textarea>
<input type="submit" name="new_item" value="Add item"/>
```

After all of the lists are displayed, we want another form to be able to add new lists. This one also submits to itself. Place this code after the closing `</tal:lists>` tag above.

```
<form method="post" tal:attributes="action view/url">
  <fieldset>
    <legend>Create new list</legend>
    <label for="list_title">Title:</label>
    <input type="text" name="list_title"/><br/>
    <label for="list_description">Description:</label>
    <br/>
    <textarea name="list_description"></textarea><br/>
    <input type="submit" name="new_list" value="Create"/>
  </fieldset>
</form>
```

The view template is ready. Now let's create the view class. Remember that in Grok, a view usually consists of a template for the UI, and a class for passing calculated data to the template and handling any form input. As we now have various submit buttons that will send form data to the view, we need a way to handle that data. The easiest way to do that is to define an `update` method, which Grok knows to call just before rendering the page template for the view.

To get at the form data, we will use the `request` variable that is available in every view class. This variable contains all of the data for the current HTTP request, including form fields. Using `request.form` we'll get a dictionary with all of the available form fields, with the `name` attribute of the field used as the key. Each submit button has its own name, so we can test for it's presence to see which action we need to carry out.

Change `app.py` to look like the following code:

```python
import grok

class Todo(grok.Application, grok.Container):
    todolists = []

class Index(grok.View):
    def update(self):
        form = self.request.form
        if 'new_list' in form:
            title = form['list_title']
            description = form['list_description']
            self.context.todolists.append({'title':title,
            'description':description, 'items':[]})
            return
        if 'list_index' in form:
            index = int(form['list_index'])
            items = self.context.todolists[index]['items']
            if 'new_item' in form:
                description = form['item_description']
                items.append({'description':description,
                'checked':False})
                return
            elif 'update_list' in form:
                for item in range(len(items)):
                    if 'item_%s' % item in form:
                        items[item]['checked'] = True
                    else:
                        items[item]['checked'] = False
                return
            else:
                for item in range(len(items)):
                    if 'delete_%s' % item in form:
                        items.remove(items[item])
```

First of all, in the application definition, we remove the test data that we added before, leaving the `todolists` attribute defined as an empty list, so that we have a clean slate when we start the application.

In the `update` method, we assign the form data to the `form` variable by using `self.request.form`, as discussed earlier. We then have three possible cases.

- **Case one**: The add list form was submitted, in which case the name `new_list` will be in the form.

- **Case two**: One of the buttons for adding an item, removing an item, or updating a particular list was pressed, so the `list_index` hidden field will be in the form.

- **Case three**: No form submission occurred, such as when the view is accessed for the first time, so no action should be taken.

In the case of a new list, we get the values of the title and description fields and then simply append a new dictionary with an empty item list to the `todolists` variable of the application.

If one of the specific list buttons was pressed, then we get the list index from the form and use it to get the list items of the affected list. If the `new_item` button was pressed, we get the item description and append a dictionary with this description and a checked key to keep track of its on/off state. If `update_list` was pressed, we go through each of the list items and set its state to `True`, if it is present on the form and `False` otherwise. The last possible case is when the delete button of a list item was pressed, so we go through the items and remove any of them whose name is present in the form.

Run the application and play with it a little. It doesn't look pretty, but it has the complete functionality that we sketched at the start of the chapter. The following screenshot shows how a test run looks:

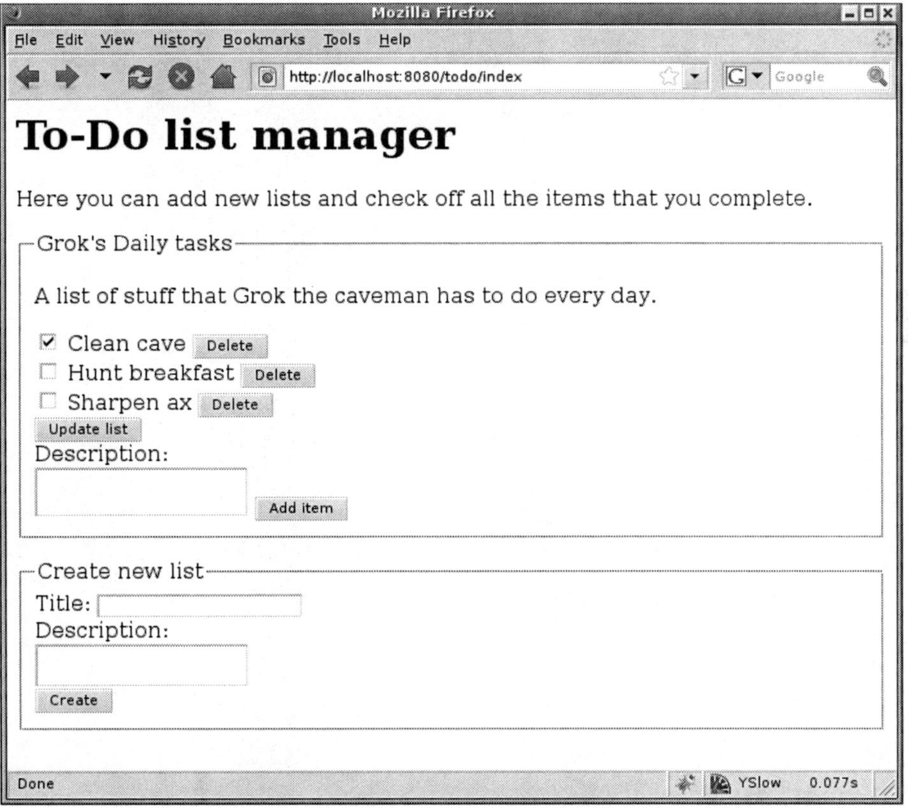

Adding static resources

We now have a working application, so the next step will be to make it look better. We obviously need to add some styles using CSS. In addition, the **Delete** button to the right of the list items is too distracting, so let's use a small trash can icon instead.

In this case, we will be working with static resources, such as images and stylesheets, and not with dynamic templates and classes. To handle these type of resources, Grok uses, by convention, a directory named `static`, which you will find in the same directory as the project source. We can simply place our static files in this directory, and Grok will be able to find them and generate links to them.

The icon that we will use here is available in the book's code, under the `static` directory of the project. You'll need to put some icon in that directory of your project, if you are following along with this example. For the stylesheet, create a file named `styles.css` in that directory, and add the following CSS code:

```css
body {
    background-color: #e0e0e0;
    padding: 15px;
}

h1 {
    background-color : #223388;
    font-size: 1.6em;
    color : #ffcc33;
    padding : 10px;
    margin: 0px;
}

h2 {
    background-color: white;
    margin: 0px;
    padding: 10px;
    font-size: 0.8em;
}

.todolist {
    background-color: white;
    padding: 10px;
    margin: 0px;
}

.todolist fieldset {
    border: none;
```

```
    padding: 0px;
}

.todolist legend {
    color: #223388;
    font-weight: bold;
    font-size: 1em;
}

.todolist p {
    padding: 0px;
    margin: 2px 0px 5px 3px;
    color: gray;
    font-size: 0.8em;
}
```

This is just a sample. The complete CSS file can be found in the sample code for
this book. For the styles to actually work, we need to make a few changes to the
`index.pt` template, to add some classes, and modify the delete button to use an
image. Here's the code again, with some explanations and the changes highlighted:

```
<html>
 <head>
    <title>To-Do list manager</title>
    <link rel="stylesheet" type="text/css"
          tal:attributes="href static/styles.css" />
 </head>
```

First, notice how the link declaration in the document head uses the TAL
`attributes` statement to set the `href` attribute. The word `static` in this case does
not refer to the file system directory itself, but to the special view that finds the file
there and generates a link to the appropriate file. The link is created in this manner
to make it work correctly, no matter where the application is installed, even if we are
using virtual hosting.

```
<body>
 <h1>To-Do list manager</h1>
 <h2>Here you can add new lists and check off all the items that
     you complete .</h2>
 <tal:block repeat="todolist context/todolists">
    <form class="todolist" method="post"
          tal:attributes="action view/url">
       <fieldset>
         <legend tal:content="todolist/title">title</legend>
         <p tal:content="todolist/description">description</p>
```

```
                    <div tal:repeat="item todolist/items"
                        tal:attributes="class python:item['checked'] and
                                        'done' or 'pending'">
                <input type="checkbox"
                        tal:attributes="name
                        string:item_${repeat/item/index};
                        checked item/checked"/>
                <span tal:content="item/description"></span>
                <input type="image" tal:attributes="name
                        string:delete_${rep eat/item/index};
                        src static/bin_closed.png" value="Delete"/><br/>
            </div>
                    <input type="hidden" name="list_index"
                            tal:attributes="value repeat/todolist/index"/>
                    <input type="submit" class="update_button"
                        name="update_list" value="Update list"/><br/>
                    <label for="item_description">New item:</label><br/>
                    <input type="text" size="60"
                        name="item_description"><br/>
                    <input type="submit" class="new_button"
                        name="new_item" value="Add to list"/>
            </fieldset>
          </form>
        </tal:block>
          <form class="add" method="post" tal:attributes="action view/url">
            <fieldset>
                <legend>Create new list</legend>
                <label for="list_title">Title:</label>
                <input type="text" name="list_title" size="40"/><br/>
                <label for="list_description">Description:</label><br/>
                <textarea name="list_description" rows="3"
                        cols="50"></textarea><br/>
                <input type="submit" class="new_button" name="new_list"
                    value="Create"/>
            </fieldset>
          </form>
        </body>
       </html>
```

The class attributes that we added are pretty straightforward, but in the case of list
items, we wanted to have checked items display differently to unchecked items,
so we used the `attributes` statement again to dynamically decide at render time
whether each item is checked (class done) or not (class pending) and use a different
class in each case.

Finally, we switched the input type of the delete button from `submit` to `image` and added a link to an icon using the special `static` name again.

That's it. We don't need to stop the server to see how it looks. Just reload the page and see. The Python code was not even touched, and the template has minimal changes, but the application looks completely different when it uses the CSS, as shown in the following screenshot:

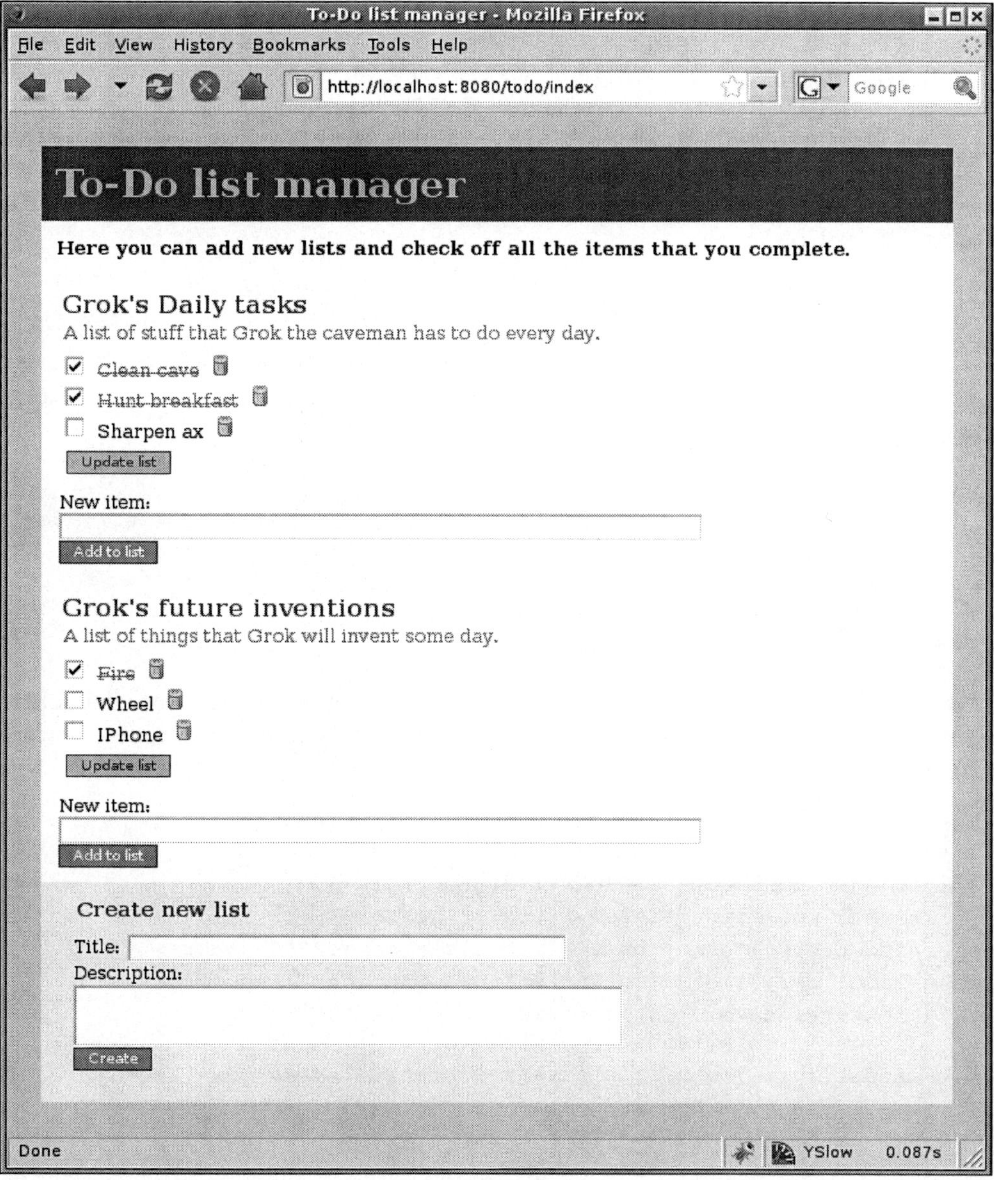

Putting in some JavaScript flourish

Our to-do application looks a lot better now, but there are a few touches that we can also do to make it feel better. Having to press the update button each time that we check off one task is somewhat awkward, and can be easily forgotten. It would be nice if the list is automatically updated whenever we click on a checkbox.

Visually, the input box and button for adding list items are a bit distracting, so maybe we could hide them until they are needed. A final visual touch that we could add would be to move all of the checked-off items to the bottom of the list, so that it's clear what has and hasn't been done.

For hiding the form controls, we have to modify the template to make the new item label clickable, and call a toggle function in JavaScript when the user clicks it. We'll assign the `onclick` attribute dynamically to refer to the unique ID of the `<div>` that contains the controls.

```
<label for="item_description" tal:attributes="onclick
 string:toggleAddControls('add_controls_${repeat/todolist/index}');">
 New item</label><br/>
```

Of course, for this to work we have to wrap the controls in a `<div>` tag and assign the same ID to it:

```
<div class="controls"
    tal:attributes="id string:add_controls_${repeat/todolist/index}">
    <input type="text" size="60" name="item_description"><br/>
    <input type="submit" class="new_button"
           name="new_item" value="Add to list"/>
</div>
```

That does it. In fact, this is so easy that we can do the same for the create list controls. The only thing is that we don't need a dynamic ID here, since there's only one 'create list' form:

```
<legend onclick="toggleAddControls('new_list_controls');">Create new
list</legend>
<div class="controls" id="new_list_controls">
    <label for="list_title">Title:</label>
    <input type="text" name="list_title" size="40"/><br/>
    <label for="list_description">Description:</label><br/>
    <textarea name="list_description" rows="3"
            cols="50"></textarea><br/>
    <input type="submit" class="new_button" name="new_list"
            value="Create"/>
</div>
```

Moving completed items to the bottom does not require us to modify anything in the template. It's all done using JavaScript and the DOM. Skipping the use of the update button, however, is a bit harder, because we will need to use the XMLHTTPRequest object (better known by the word AJAX these days) to call a Grok view from JavaScript.

Earlier, we said that a view usually consists of a template and a class. However, there are cases where a template is not really necessary. What we need here is a simple view that will set the checked state of the checkbox that was clicked on by the user. This view should return just the ID of the affected item, so that we can dynamically change its CSS class to reflect the change.

Adding a view in Grok is very easy, we just need to define a class that inherits from grok.View, and then add the required behavior to this. In this case, we don't even need a template, because we will just be returning the item ID as plain text. Grok allows us to use a render method on a view when we don't want to use a template or need to return something other than HTML. We'll add the new view to app.py:

```python
class Check(grok.View):
    def update(self, list_index, item_index):
        self.div_id = 'div_item_%s_%s' % (list_index, item_index)
        list_index=int(list_index)
        item_index=int(item_index)
        items = self.context.todolists[list_index]['items']
        items[item_index]['checked'] = not items[item_index]
          ['checked']

    def render(self):
        return self.div_id
```

The new view class name is Check, so the view URL will use the word check in lowercase. This view expects to be passed a list index and an item index to toggle the state of some item in the list. In this case, we do not need to examine the form, because we know we'll always require the same parameters. Grok can easily retrieve the parameters from the form for us, by specifying them after self in the update method. An error will occur if one or both of them are not present.

Note that the update method is called first, so we store the item ID in the view attribute div_id so that we can return it later when the template is actually rendered. Then, we use the indexes to find the correct item and toggle its state by using the not operator.

As we mentioned before, we'll return a simple string ID, so no template is needed. That's why this view has a `render` method, which in this case just returns the ID that we stored earlier. In other situations, the `render` method could do much more—for example, generating the HTML for the page, or sending a specific kind of content, such as an image or a PDF file. To do this, in addition to the code to render the desired document, the `render` method must also set the `Content-Type` by using the special `response` object, as in this example of returning XML:

```
self.response.setHeader('Content-Type','text/xml; charset=UTF-8')
```

When we use the `render` method, no template is expected, so if Grok finds a template that should be associated with this view, it will signal an error to avoid ambiguity. In this case, if we put a template named `check.pt` inside the `app_templates` directory, Grok will stop with an error.

Now that we have our new view, we need to call it from the template when the user clicks on a checkbox. We'll use the `onclick` event handler here, too:

```
<div tal:repeat="item todolist/items"
   tal:attributes="class python:item['checked'] and 'done' or 'pending';
     id string:div_item_${repeat/todolist/index}_${repeat/item/index}">
   <input type="checkbox"
     tal:define="check_url python:view.url('check');"
     tal:attributes="name string:item_${repeat/item/index};
     checked item/checked; onclick string:checkItem(
     '${check_url}?list_index=${repeat/todolist/index}&
     item_index=${repeat/item/index}')"/>
     <span tal:content="item/description"></span>
     <input type="image"
           tal:attributes="name string:delete_${repeat/item/index};
                           src static/bin_closed.png"
           value="Delete"/>
     <br/>
  </div>
```

First, we need to assign a unique ID to each item, which we do in the `<div>` tag, by using the `list` and `item` indexes. Then we assign the `onclick` attribute by using the TAL `attributes` statement, so that we can dynamically construct the URL with the `check` view name and the list and item indexes as query parameters. To avoid hardcoding URL information, we use the `url` method from the view class, which, when called with a string as a parameter, returns the view with that name. We use the `define` statement for this.

Now, when the user clicks on a checkbox, the `check` view will be called from JavaScript with a `GET` request, and the JavaScript callback function that gets the return value will use it to set the correct CSS class for the checked state, and rearrange the completed items at the bottom.

The JavaScript code necessary for doing this work is included in the source code for this book. You should study it if you are interested in the details. Explaining that code would be outside the goals of this chapter. The key thing to take away from this example is the ability to have views in Grok that return anything that we want, and not just templates.

Summary

Using our newly acquired knowledge of ZPT, we now have a simple, but complete, Grok application, including a nice design and JavaScript embellishments. As we designed it, we learned what Grok views are and the basics of working with them. In the next chapter, we will see where the data for views comes from: the content objects or models that define Grok applications.

4
Models

In Chapter 3, we learned how to display information on a web page by using views. In fact, as we saw, the view machinery is powerful enough to create complete applications, like our to-do list manager. We'll now turn our attention to where the data for these views comes from: the content objects, or models that define Grok applications. Here's a list of what we'll cover in this chapter:

- What a model is and what relationship it has with views

- How to persist model data on the ZODB

- How to structure our code to maintain the separation of display logic from application logic

- What a container is and how to use one

- How to use multiple models and associate specific views to each

- How to use the Grok introspector to navigate models

Models and applications

Although the views do the actual work of showing our data and handling user interaction, they are just one possible way of displaying the data. In the previous chapter, we started with a very simple view with no styles or client-side scripting, and by the end of the chapter, we had a completely different looking application. What remained constant throughout was the thing we were working with: to-do lists.

Whenever we added lists or list items and checked off items, we were interacting with the model for our application, which in this case was defined with just two lines of code:

```
class Todo(grok.Application, grok.Model):
    todolists = []
```

A Grok application is composed of one or more models. The models can be simple Python objects, but generally use `grok.Model` as a base class. The main model of an application should inherit from `grok.Application` as well, which is what happens in the preceding code.

The model contains the application data and all of the logic that's not directly related to how this data is shown. In the case of our to-do list manager, the model consists of only a `todolists` class attribute that holds all the lists and their items.

Even though this model is so simple, the views work for the model and not the other way around. If we look at the code in both the `index` and `check` views, we'll see that every time something important happens the value of `self.context.todolists` is modified. As we mentioned before, all views have a `context` attribute that refers to their associated model. Through it, views can access all of the attributes of this model.

Storing model data

So far, we can create and manage lists successfully, but once we restart the application we lose all the data. We need a way to persist the information.

For web applications, this usually means creating some tables in a relational database and storing the information by using direct SQL queries or an **Object Relational Mapper (ORM)**. An ORM is a good solution as it takes our objects and transparently stores their attributes in the corresponding tables. Each time we need to work with our objects, the ORM reassembles them from the database once again, without the need for us to worry about SQL.

Grok can store data in relational databases using plain SQL as well as a diverse range of ORMs for Python, such as SQLAlchemy (`http://www.sqlalchemy.org`) or Storm (`https://storm.canonical.com`). However, Grok gives us another interesting option that is a more natural fit for our Python objects, and can work even more transparently than ORMs: the **Zope Object Database (ZODB)**.

The ZODB

We discussed the ZODB in the first chapter, where we mentioned that it is very well integrated with Grok. We'll show a simple example of storing data now, and come back to the details, later.

Right now, the to-do list manager application has its title defined inside the `<h1>` tag on the `index` template. Let's give each application instance a `title` attribute, so that the user can set the title himself. First, we'll replace the simplistic model definition that we have been using so far with more realistic code:

```python
class Todo(grok.Application, grok.Model):
    def __init__(self):
        super(Todo, self).__init__()
        self.title = 'To-Do list manager'
        self.todolists = []
```

We have added an __init__ method that is called when the application is created. Inside this method, we make sure that we call the superclass' __init__ method as well, so that our method extends, rather than replaces the original code. We then define two instance attributes, `title` and `todolists`.

In Python, there are two kinds of objects: **mutable objects**, which can have their values changed, and **immutable objects**, that cannot. For immutable objects, such as strings or numbers, we gain automatic persistence in the ZODB merely by inheriting from `grok.Model`. In the case of the title, now we can transparently store it in the ZODB. The `todolists`, as they are stored inside a list (a mutable object), need a little more work, but we'll get to them later.

Changing the title dynamically

Now that we have a `title` attribute, we can modify the `index.pt` template to show that, instead of the old text. Both the <title> and <h1> tags need a `tal:content` statement, like in the following example:

```html
<h1 tal:content="context/title">To-Do list manager</h1>
```

Now, the template will use whatever title is stored in the application instance. Now we need a way for the user to set the title. Let's create a simple Ajax view that can do this:

```python
class SetTitle(grok.View):
    def update(self,new_title):
        self.context.title = new_title

    def render(self):
        return self.context.title
```

All this does is checks for the key `new_title` in the request, and sets the `title` attribute to its value. As we did with the `Check` view back in Chapter 3, the response does not use a template, but a simple Python code that returns plain text. We just return the `title` attribute that was changed in the `update` method, so that the JavaScript callback function can change it immediately after it's set.

On the client side, we use a couple of JavaScript functions to produce an *edit-in-place* effect, so that the user can click on the title and change it right there. We won't go into the code here, but you can find it in the Chapter 4 directory in the book's code package. You can look at the result in the following screenshot:

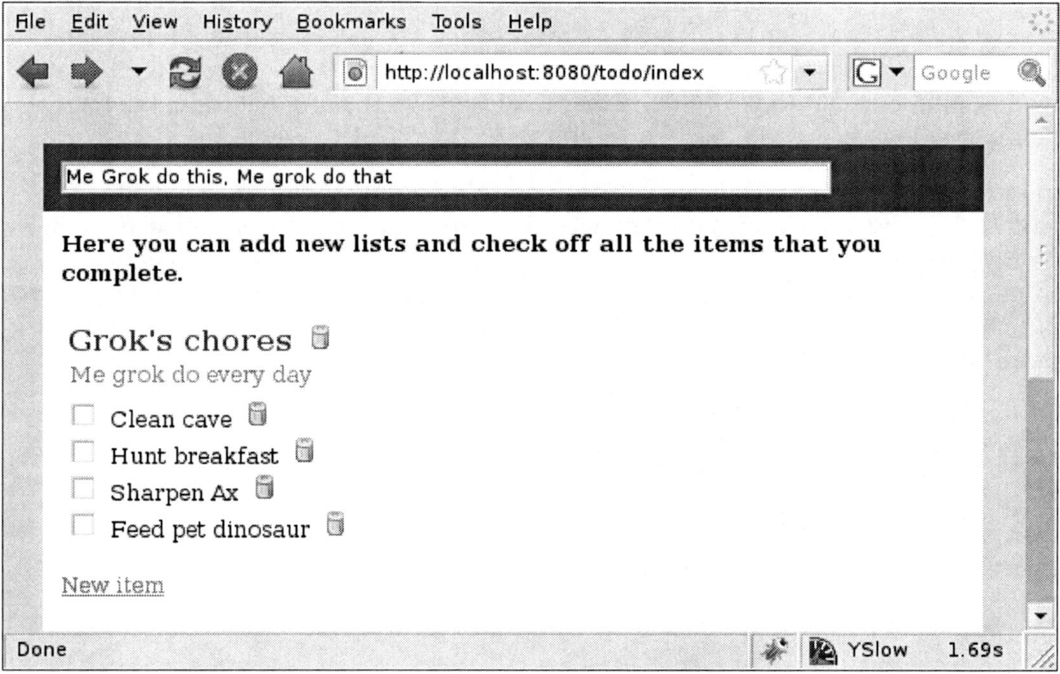

If we run the application now, it will be possible to edit the title, restart the application, and see that its value is saved across server restarts. One word of warning though: because we added an attribute to the application instance inside the `__init__` method, it's necessary to delete any existing application instances before trying this code. That's because the `title` attribute is added at the time of application creation, when the `__init__` method is run, which didn't happen when we created applications in the previous chapter. If we try to use an older application instance, we'll get an attribute error when we try to access the `title` attribute.

The rules of persistence

As we mentioned earlier, the `todolists` attribute will not get persisted to the ZODB that easily. The reason is that whenever changes are made to mutable attributes, the application needs to inform the ZODB that there has been a change. This is done by setting the special `_p_changed` attribute of the instance to `True`.

In the case of the `todolists` attribute, all we have to do is set `_p_changed` to `True` after any modification to the attribute. We'll just need to add this code at the end of the `update` methods in the index and check views:

```
self.context._p_changed_ = True
```

Thankfully, this is the only rule that we have to keep in mind when working with the ZODB in Grok. Well, there are a few more rules, but Grok already follows them, so this is the only one that will require us to modify the code. Let's look at the rules of persistence for the ZODB:

- Inherit from `persistent.Persistent` (a class defined in the ZODB code) or one of its subclasses. The Grok classes, `grok.Model` and `grok.Container` already do this for us, so by extending them we will automatically persist our classes.

- Class instances have to be related to each other in a hierarchical structure. The ZODB has a root object and this object contains other objects, which can in turn contain some other objects, forming a tree.

- When modifying mutable attributes of persistent objects that are not persistent themselves, the persistence machinery has to be notified, by setting the special `_p_changed` attribute of the instance to `True`.

Like we said, Grok follows these rules, so that by using Grok's models and containers we automatically have persistent data storage for our applications. In this way, we can think only in terms of classes and attributes instead of translating them back and forth in our minds (and code) into tables and columns.

That's all we have to do to store the to-do lists inside the ZODB. We almost have a complete application, so now let's focus on how to better structure our code.

Display logic and application logic

We keep talking about the separation of display and application logic, but our code so far is clearly not enforcing this rule. The model only holds the lists and everything else happens inside the views.

The problem with this approach is that our views need to know too much about how the model is implemented, and it becomes very hard to change it without needing to modify some or all of the views.

For example, when we add a list item in the `update` method of our index view, we have to know that list items are stored as dictionaries with `description` and `check` keys . We also have to know that the list of items is stored under the key items in a dictionary representing the list itself. These are too many internal details, and writing view code, which relies on this knowledge may require heavy modifications to it, if the model implementation changes.

Worse, relying on this knowledge makes our code more repetitive than it should be, and forces us to make the same change in multiple places when there are modifications. Look at this line of code from the to-do list manager:

```
items = self.context.todolists[list_index]['items']
```

We only have two views, and this line shows up in both of them. If we add more views and need to look at the items from some list in them, we'll have to repeat this code again. Now suppose we add projects to our application and wish to store the lists inside a project. In this case, we would have to change every occurrence of this line in every view, to reflect the new structure.

This is why separation of display and application logic is so important. It helps to structure our applications and allows us to change the way the data is displayed without modifying its internal representation, or the other way around.

Separating display and application logic

Let's think about how we could restructure the application so that this principle is taken into account. Remember, the model shouldn't know anything about how it is displayed and the views should not depend on any implementation details from the model.

We could start by adding some method to the model to add lists and get all the items from a list, so that we can call these new methods from the view and stop depending on how list data are stored in the main list of the to-do lists. We might be tempted to write something like this:

```python
class Todo(grok.Application, grok.Model):
    def __init__(self):
        super(Todo, self).__init__()
        self.title = 'To-Do list manager'
        self.todolists = []


    def createList(self, title, description):
        self.todolists.append({'title':title,
          'description':description, 'items':[]})
```

```
        self._p_changed = True

    def getListItems(self, index):
        items = self.todolists[index]['items']
        return items
```

However, we must resist the temptation. If we go down this path, our code will be filled with `self._p_changed` lines, and we'll be passing list indexes around like crazy. Having the to-do lists represented as a simple list is really not the way to go. We should instead use a more carefully designed model, and take full advantage of Grok's model classes.

Using containers and multiple models

Up to this point, we are using `grok.Model` as a base class for our application, which mostly buys us nearly transparent ZODB storage, as we have seen. Most non-trivial applications, however, will require more than one type of object to be useful. Also, it's fairly common to organize application data using parent and child relationships, so that one main object is the parent and contains a number of child objects. In our to-do list manager application, the main application is a container of to-do lists and each list in turn can contain a number of items.

Because this is a very common pattern, Grok offers a `grok.Container` class which allows us to store other models and also handles ZODB persistence. Using it, we can structure our code better, simplify it, and also eliminate the need to signal to the framework every time a change is made to a list or one of its items (no more `self._p_changed` lines). Instead of dealing with an ad hoc list structure and keeping track of indexes, we can think about list objects and item objects.

Adding containers to our application

Conceptually, then, our application will consist of a container of lists. A list object will also be a container, where the items will be stored. Let's start by defining the main model:

```
class Todo(grok.Application, grok.Container):

    def __init__(self):
        super(Todo, self).__init__()
        self.next_id = 0
        self.title = 'To-Do list manager'
```

This is not very different from what we had before. The important change is that we now inherit from `grok.Container` instead of `grok.Model`. This will allow the application to store list objects. We also define a `next_id` attribute to create identifiers for the lists. OK, let's define the list model now:

```
class TodoList(grok.Container):

    def __init__(self,list_title,list_description):
        super(TodoList, self).__init__()
        self.next_id = 0
        self.title = list_title
        self.description = list_description
```

A list has `title` and `description` attributes, both mandatory parameters at instance creation. As with the list model, we also define a `next_id` attribute to keep track of individual items. Notice that `grok.Application` is not a base class here, because this is a model that will be used by the application defined earlier. In some cases, we could have a need for more than one application in a project, and technically we could define both in the same file, but generally it's suggested that we use a separate file for different applications.

The `TodoList` class is also a `grok.Container` because it will contain to-do items. These items will not contain other types of models, so the list item class definition will simply be a model:

```
class TodoItem(grok.Model):

    def __init__(self,item_description):
        super(TodoItem, self).__init__()
        self.description = item_description
        self.checked = False
```

The `TodoItem` class just inherits from `grok.Model`. It only has a `description` attribute, which is a mandatory parameter at instance creation.

Adding behavior to the models

Now that we have our application model structured, we should think about which model will perform which actions. We are talking about the different actions, such as list and item creation, that our application performs. However, in the previous version they were crowded inside the `update` method of the `index` view. With a clean model structure we can now separate these actions and put each one where it better belongs.

The main application is the list manager, so the methods for list creation and deletion should be added to the `Todo` class. Let's get going with the code:

```python
def addList(self,title,description):
    id = str(self.next_id)
    self.next_id = self.next_id+1
    self[id] = TodoList(title,description)

def deleteList(self,list):
    del self[list]
```

The `addList` method takes a `title` and `description` and simply creates an instance of `TodoList`. The new list is stored in the container using a key, just like a Python dictionary works (in fact, it supports the same methods, such as keys, values, and items). The key is generated using the `next_id` attribute that we discussed earlier, which is then incremented for the next list creation.

The `deleteList` method is even simpler, as we just need to delete the desired key from the dictionary using the `del` statement. As promised, notice the absence of any code dealing directly with persistence. The lists will be correctly stored in the ZODB without the need for explicit notification.

The TodoList model

Now let's turn our attention to the `TodoList` model. We need a way to add and delete items, similar to what we did with the main application. Also, if we want to keep our non-JavaScript-enabled version of the application working, we need a way to change the `checked` status of multiple items at the same time. Here's the code that we have to add to the `TodoList` class:

```python
def addItem(self,description):
    id = str(self.next_id)
    self.next_id = self.next_id+1
    self[id] = TodoItem(description)

def deleteItem(self,item):
    del self[item]

def updateItems(self, items):
    for name,item in self.items():
        if name in items:
            self[item].checked = True
        else:
            self[item].checked = False
```

The `addItem` method is almost a verbatim copy of the `addList` method that we saw earlier. We use the `next_id` pattern to create the ID, and create a new instance of `TodoItem`. The `deleteItem` method is identical to the `deleteList` method discussed earlier. The `updateItems` method is different because it expects a list of item IDs to mark as checked. We iterate through all of the items in the list and set their `checked` attribute to `True` if they are on the received list, or set it to `False` otherwise.

The `TodoItem` model is the simplest of the three. We can directly set the `checked` attribute to `True` or `False`, so we probably don't need separate methods to do that. We will only add a convenience method to toggle the `checked` state of an item, without requiring us to know the current state. This will be useful for the Ajax-enabled check view that we created earlier:

```python
def toggleCheck(self):
    self.checked = not self.checked
```

The `toggleCheck` method simply sets the value of the `checked` attribute of the `TodoItem` to the opposite of the current value, thus acting as a toggle.

We now have a complete model that uses Grok's features and includes all of the application logic. The views will now be able to perform the display work without messing with the application's internals.

Reorganizing the views

Speaking of views, we need to refactor those, too. So far, we have been doing everything with only one view, but this needs to change. We'd like to keep the application as having one single main view and showing all modifications to the different models on the same page, but method calls to each model's actions should come from the views associated with that model. This is because in this way Grok will take care of setting the context for the view correctly, and we will not have to worry about making sure that we act on the correct model in our code. Remember that earlier we used a hidden `<input>` tag with a list index to tell our `update` method on which list we wanted to operate. We don't need to do this anymore if we associate our views with the right models.

For the main application, then, we will keep the `index` view and the `setTitle` views. We'll also add views for calling the `addList` and `deleteList` methods. The new `TodoList` model will have a view for each of its three actions, which are `addItem`, `deleteItem`, and `updateItem`. For the `TodoItem` model, we'll reuse the existing `check` view, but the one associated with this model instead of the main application.

That's it. So, previously we had a single model with three views, but now we have three models, and each will require a couple of views. How will Grok know which views are associated with which model?

Introducing class annotations

One of Grok's conventions is that all views defined in a module where there's only one model definition will be associated with this model. Grok knows that this is the only possibility, and so automatically sets the `context` attribute on all views to be this model. Now that we have three models, each view that we create has to explicitly tell Grok to which model it belongs.

The mechanism Grok uses to do this is called a **class annotation**. Grok has many conventions that help it decide what to do when no information is available, but we can certainly tell Grok what to do when we need to. A class annotation is just a declarative way of telling Grok something about a class.

To explicitly associate a view with a model, we use the `grok.context` class annotation. This class takes as a parameter the model to which we want to associate a view. Let's redefine our `index` view:

```
class Index(grok.View):
    grok.context(Todo)
```

We use the `grok.context` class annotation to tell Grok that this view will work with the `Todo` model as context. This is in fact all of the code that we need for this view, as we have separated the model responsibilities into three different views. No more gigantic `update` methods full of `if` statements.

Before going on with the other views, let's think a bit about how `index` views work. As we saw in the previous chapter, if a view has the name `index` it will be treated as the default view for a model. We also learned that the name of a view is automatically given by the lowercase version of its own class name. Now, for the case where we have more than one model and for each of them we want to have a default view, how do we name the view classes? There can't be two `Index` classes defined in the same module.

Setting view names explicitly

If you guessed that class annotations would come into play again, you were absolutely right. For cases like these, we have the `grok.name` class annotation, which can be used to explicitly set the name of a view. Right now, we need only one `index` view in our code, but we may need to add default views for the other models later, so we might as well change the code at this point:

```
class TodoIndex(grok.View):
    grok.context(Todo)
    grok.name('index')
```

We change the view class name to `TodoIndex`, which would result in URLs with the name `todoindex`. We then use the `grok.name` annotation to set the view name to `index`, thus allowing us to call the default view without using its name.

Now let's take a look at the action views for this model. First, the `addlist` view, which will be used to add new lists to the application:

```
class TodoAddList(grok.View):
    grok.context(Todo)
    grok.name('addlist')

    def update(self,title,description):
        self.context.addList(title,description)

    def render(self):
        self.redirect(self.url('index'))
```

The `TodoAddList` view is also associated with the `Todo` model, but uses a different name. This view will be called when the user fills the create list form and clicks on the submit button.

Notice in this code how the `update` method is just one line long. We just call the `addList` method of the `context` and pass the two required parameters to it. No need to grapple with form parameters or make `if` checks to see what action is desired.

Redirecting views

In this application we want the index page to show all changes immediately. Therefore, in the `render` method, instead of using a template to produce HTML, or sending a plain text string as we have done before, we perform a redirection to the index view, using the `redirect` method available to the view.

The `deletelist` view is very similar to the `addlist` view. We hadn't implemented this functionality in the initial version of our application, but you'll see it's really cheap to do that now that we have the proper structure:

```
class TodoDeleteList(grok.View):
    grok.context(Todo)
    grok.name('deletelist')

    def update(self,list):
        self.context.deleteList(list)

    def render(self):
        self.redirect(self.url('index'))
```

We just use a different name and call the `deleteList` method of the model, but otherwise the code is the same.

The last view for the `Todo` model is the `setTitle` view that we added at the beginning of this chapter. Here's how it looks:

```python
class TodoSetTitle(grok.View):
    grok.context(Todo)
    grok.name('settitle')

    def update(self,title):
        self.context.title = title

    def render(self):
        return self.context.title
```

In this case, we keep the old behavior of returning the new title when rendering. The only change here is that the association with the model is explicit, and we give it a different name than its class name.

The three views associated to the `TodoList` model are almost carbon copies of the `addlist` and `deletelist` views of the `Todo` model. Let's take a look and talk about what's different:

```python
class TodoListAddItem(grok.View):
    grok.context(TodoList)
    grok.name('additem')

    def update(self,description):
        self.context.addItem(description)

    def render(self):
        self.redirect(self.url(self.context.__parent__,'index'))

class TodoListDeleteItem(grok.View):
    grok.context(TodoList)
    grok.name('deleteitem')

    def update(self,item):
        self.context.deleteItem(item)

    def render(self):
        self.redirect(self.url(self.context.__parent__,'index'))
```

```python
class TodoListUpdateItems(grok.View):
    grok.context(TodoList)
    grok.name('updateitems')

    def update(self,items):
        self.context.updateItems(items)

    def render(self):
        self.redirect(self.url(self.context.__parent__,'index'))
```

Notice how the three of them use the `grok.context` annotation to associate themselves with the `TodoList` model. The `update` methods of all three are very similar to the other ones, and just call the correct `update` method from the `context`, which in this case we know is a `TodoList` instance.

The `redirect` call on the `render` method is a little different, though. As the context is a `TodoList` and we want to show the index view for the `Todo` model, we need to get at the container of this list to pass it to the `url` function of the view, so that it can generate the correct URL. To do this, we use another characteristic of a Grok model object, a `__parent__` attribute, which points to its container. As we know that the list is contained by the `Todo` model, we can get at it in this way. Model objects also have a `__name__` attribute, which stores the key that is used to access the object inside its container. We'll use that in a minute when we see how the index template has to change to accommodate the new model structure.

As for the `TodoItem` model, we just need the `check` view that was already used in the previous version of our application:

```python
class TodoItemCheck(grok.View):
    grok.context(TodoItem)
    grok.name('check')

    def update(self):
        self.div_id = 'div_item_%s_%s' %
        (self.context.__parent__.__name__,self. context.__name__)
        self.context.toggleCheck()

    def render(self):
        return self.div_id
```

There are a few differences. The view is now explicitly associated with the
`TodoItem` model using `grok.context`, obviously. Also, we now call the new
`toggleCheck` method of the `TodoItem` instead of making the change in the view.
Finally, we construct the ID for the `<div>` tag that the view will be returning, by
using the __parent__ and __name__ attributes of the model. In this way, we avoid
the need to have list and item indexes passed as view parameters.

We now have a much better separation of application and display logic in our to-do
list manager application. Let's see how this impacts the code for the `index` view, which
now has to display data from three models instead of one. Look at the code for the loop
that shows the lists and their items. First, note that we now iterate over the lists using
`context/values` instead of the list elements that we had in the old model:

```
<tal:block repeat="todolist context/values">
<div class="todolist">
```

After that, we define the `todo` list form. Notice how we use `view.url()` to generate
the correct URL for posting the form. Remember that this function works by passing
the object for which we want to generate a URL and an optional view name to
append to it. In the following code, the action for the first form is defined by calling
the `view url` method, passing the current `todolist` object and the `updateitems`
view name to it.

```
<form method="post"
    tal:attributes="action python:view.url(todolist, 'updateitems')">
<fieldset>
```

Next, we have the code to delete a list. Take a look at how we use the __name__
attribute to create URLs that include the name of the object that we are interested in.
In this way, methods that expect a key to work will receive it directly from this view.
We don't need to do any list and item index calculations, or add hidden fields with
list data:

```
<legend><span tal:content="todolist/title">title</span>
  <a tal:define="url python:view.url('deletelist')"
     tal:attributes="href string:${url}?list=${todolist/__name__}">
    <img border="0"
         tal:attributes="src static/bin_closed.png" />
  </a>
</legend>
```

The rest of the form has very similar changes, which are mostly the use of __name__
and `view.url`:

```
<p tal:content="todolist/description">description</p>
<div tal:repeat="item todolist/values"
   tal:attributes="class python:item.checked and 'done' or 'pending';
   id string:div_item_${todolist/__name__} _${item/__name__}">
```

```
      <input type="checkbox" name="items:list"
        tal:define="check_url python:view.url(item,'check');"
        tal:attributes="checked item/checked;
        onclick string:getRequest('{check_url}', processReqChange)"/>
      <span tal:content="item/description"></span>
      <a tal:define="url python:view.url(todolist,'deleteitem')"
        tal:attributes="href string:${url}?item=${item/__name__}">
      <img border="0" tal:attributes="src static/bin_closed.png" />
      </a>
      <br/>
  </div>
  <input type="submit" class="update_button" name="update_list"
        value="Update list"/>
  </fieldset>
  </form>
```

Finally, the form for adding list items now also uses `view.url` to generate the
form action:

```
<form method="post"
      tal:attributes="action python:view.url(todolist,'add item')">
  <label for="description"tal:attributes="onclick
    string:toggleAddControls('add_controls_${repeat/todolist/index}');;
    this.form.description.focus();">New item</label><br/>
  <div class="controls"
    tal:attributes="id string:add_controls_${repeat/todolist/index}">
    <input type="text" size="60" name="description">
<br/>
    <input type="submit" class="new_button" name="new_item" value="Add
to list"/>
  </div>
</form>
</tal:block>
```

One would think that having to use three models could complicate things in
the view, but we actually have to use less code this time around. It's also a lot
cleaner. Instead of a big form with multiple submit buttons that all go to the same
`update` method in the same view, we now use several forms, and direct the form
submissions to the respective view by using `view.url()` to generate the correct URL
in each case.

Other than these changes, the code for the template is mostly the same as we already
had, so no big changes are required to make it work.

The Grok introspector

So we now have a fully working application. Play with it a little and create some lists and tasks. Everything will be safely stored inside the ZODB.

We'll now take a quick look at one tool that Grok offers that can be very helpful to understand object relationships and responsibilities when we are dealing with applications developed by someone else (or revisiting applications we wrote years ago).

The Grok introspector is a tool that is accessible from the application list at `http://localhost:8080/applications`. Go there and, under **Installed Applications**, you'll see your instance of the `Todo` application. The application name is a link to run it, but to the right of that name there is a link that says **object browser**. Click on this link and you'll see something similar to the next screenshot:

In this case, we can see the data from the current instance of the `Todo` model. Notice how the parent information used for the `__parent__` attribute is there at the top. Below we can see the base classes of the object, which we know are `grok.Application` and `grok.Container`. Under the **Base classes** section there is an **Interfaces provided** section. We'll have more to say about interfaces later, so for now let's skip that.

Below that you can see a section called **Attributes and Properties**. Under **Attributes**, you'll find the `title` and `next_id` attributes of the `Todo` model, with their current values. Then comes the **Mappings** section, where the values for all of the objects stored in this container are shown. If you click on any of these values, you'll get a page with the data for the corresponding model instance, so you can easily navigate the whole data structure produced by the application and look at the information within.

Finally, the names and documentation strings for all of the methods of the object are shown. Try adding a documentation string to a method of our application, and you will see it reflected in that section (after a server restart, of course).

Summary

In this chapter, we extended our demonstration application using models. The amount of code did not increase greatly from the previous chapter, but we have a much more elegant and better-structured application. The code is also more maintainable and pretty extensible, as we'll learn next when we deal with forms in Grok.

5
Forms

We have seen how easy it is to create a small application, such as the to-do list manager that we have developed over the past couple of chapters. We will now take a look at one of the many ways that Grok can help us develop more complex applications.

Until now, we have been working with simple one-or two-field forms. When we changed our model in the previous chapter, we had to go back and edit the HTML for the forms as well. With a couple of fields this requires little work, but when we have complex models with perhaps a dozen fields or more, it would be great if we didn't have to modify two files whenever we make a change.

Fortunately, Grok has a mechanism for automating the creation and processing of forms. We'll see how it works in this chapter, along with a few other form-related subjects:

- What is an interface
- What is a schema
- How interfaces and schemas are used to generate forms automatically, using Grok's form components
- How to create, add, and edit forms
- How to filter fields and prevent them from appearing in a form
- How to change form templates and presentation

A quick demonstration of automatic forms

Let's start by showing how this works, before getting into the details. To do that, we'll add a project model to our application. A project can have any number of lists associated with it, so that related to-do lists can be grouped together. For now, let's consider the project model by itself. Add the following lines to the `app.py` file, just after the `Todo` application class definition. We'll worry later about how this fits into the application as a whole.

```python
class IProject(interface.Interface):
    name = schema.TextLine(title=u'Name', required=True)
    kind = schema.Choice(title=u'Kind of project',
                         values=['personal', 'business'])
    description = schema.Text(title=u'Description')


class AddProject(grok.Form):
    grok.context(Todo)
    form_fields = grok.AutoFields(IProject)
```

We'll also need to add a couple of imports at the top of the file:

```python
from zope import interface
from zope import schema
```

Save the file, restart the server, and go to the URL `http://localhost:8080/todo/addproject`. The result should be similar to the following screenshot:

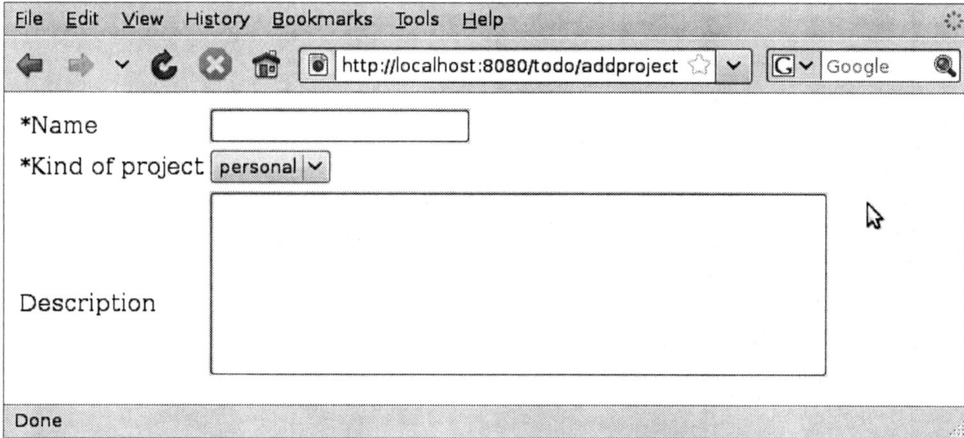

OK, where did the HTML for the form come from? We know that `AddProject` is some sort of a view, because we used the `grok.context` class annotation to set its context and name. Also, the name of the class, but in lowercase, was used in the URL, like in previous view examples.

The important new thing is how the form fields were created and used. First, a class named `IProject` was defined. The interface defines the fields on the form, and the `grok.AutoFields` method assigns them to the `Form` view class. That's how the view knows which HTML form controls to generate when the form is rendered.

We have three fields: `name`, `description`, and `kind`. Later in the code, the `grok.AutoFields` line takes this `IProject` class and turns these fields into form fields.

That's it. There's no need for a template or a `render` method. The `grok.Form` view takes care of generating the HTML required to present the form, taking the information from the value of the `form_fields` attribute that the `grok.AutoFields` call generated.

Interfaces

The `I` in the class name stands for Interface. We imported the `zope.interface` package at the top of the file, and the `Interface` class that we have used as a base class for `IProject` comes from this package.

Example of an interface

An **interface** is an object that is used to specify and describe the external behavior of objects. In a sense, the interface is like a contract. A class is said to implement an interface when it includes all of the methods and attributes defined in an interface class. Let's see a simple example:

```
from zope import interface
class ICaveman(interface.Interface):
    weapon = interface.Attribute('weapon')

    def hunt(animal):
        """Hunt an animal to get food"""
    def eat(animal):
        """Eat hunted animal"""
    def sleep()
        """Rest before getting up to hunt again"""
```

Here, we are describing how cavemen behave. A caveman will have a weapon, and he can hunt, eat, and sleep. Notice that the `weapon` is an *attribute* — something that belongs to the object, whereas `hunt`, `eat`, and `sleep` are *methods*.

Once the interface is defined, we can create classes that implement it. These classes are committed to include all of the attributes and methods of their interface class. Thus, if we say:

```
class Caveman(object):
    interface.implements(ICaveman)
```

Then we are promising that the `Caveman` class will implement the methods and attributes described in the `ICaveman` interface:

```
weapon = 'ax'
def hunt(animal):
    find(animal)
    hit(animal,self.weapon)
def eat(animal):
    cut(animal)
    bite()
def sleep():
    snore()
    rest()
```

Note that though our example class implements all of the interface methods, there is no enforcement of any kind made by the Python interpreter. We could define a class that does not include any of the methods or attributes defined, and it would still work.

Interfaces in Grok

In Grok, a model can implement an interface by using the `grok.implements` method. For example, if we decided to add a project model, it could implement the `IProject` interface as follows:

```
class Project(grok.Container):
    grok.implements(IProject)
```

Due to their descriptive nature, interfaces can be used for documentation. They can also be used for enabling component architectures, but we'll see about that later on. What is of more interest to us right now is that they can be used for generating forms automatically.

Schemas

The way to define the form fields is to use the `zope.schema` package. This package includes many kinds of field definitions that can be used to populate a form.

Basically, a schema permits detailed descriptions of class attributes that are using fields. In terms of a form—which is what is of interest to us here—a schema represents the data that will be passed to the server when the user submits the form. Each field in the form corresponds to a field in the schema.

Let's take a closer look at the schema we defined in the last section:

```
class IProject(interface.Interface):
    name = schema.TextLine(title=u'Name',required=True)
    kind = schema.Choice(title=u'Kind of project',
      required=False,
      values=['personal','business'])
    description = schema.Text(title=u'Description',
      required=False)
```

The schema that we are defining for `IProject` has three fields. There are several kinds of fields, which are listed in the following table. In our example, we have defined a `name` field, which will be a required field, and will have the label `Name` beside it. We also have a `kind` field, which is a list of options from which the user must pick one. Note that the default value for `required` is `True`, but it's usually best to specify it explicitly, to avoid confusion. You can see how the list of possible values is passed statically by using the `values` parameter. Finally, `description` is a text field, which means it will have multiple lines of text.

Available schema attributes and field types

In addition to `title`, `values`, and `required`, each schema field can have a number of properties, as detailed in the following table:

Attribute	Description
`title`	A short summary or label.
`description`	A description of the field.
`required`	Indicates whether a field requires a value to exist.
`readonly`	If `True`, the field's value cannot be changed.
`default`	The field's default value may be `None`, or a valid field value.
`missing_value`	If input for this field is missing, and that's OK, then this is the value to use.
`order`	The `order` attribute can be used to determine the order in which fields in a schema are defined. If one field is created after another (in the same thread), its order will be greater.

In addition to the field attributes described in the preceding table, some field types provide additional attributes. In the previous example, we saw that there are various field types, such as `Text`, `TextLine`, and `Choice`. There are several other field types available, as shown in the following table. We can create very sophisticated forms just by defining a schema in this way, and letting Grok generate them.

Field type	Description	Parameters
`Bool`	Boolean field.	
`Bytes`	Field containing a byte string (such as the python `str`). The value might be constrained to be within length limits.	
`ASCII`	Field containing a 7-bit ASCII string. No characters > DEL (chr(127)) are allowed. The value might be constrained to be within length limits.	
`BytesLine`	Field containing a byte string without new lines.	
`ASCIILine`	Field containing a 7-bit ASCII string without new lines.	
`Text`	Field containing a Unicode string.	
`SourceText`	Field for the source text of an object.	
`TextLine`	Field containing a Unicode string without new lines.	
`Password`	Field containing a Unicode string without new lines, which is set as the password.	
`Int`	Field containing an Integer value.	
`Float`	Field containing a Float.	
`Decimal`	Field containing a Decimal.	
`DateTime`	Field containing a DateTime.	
`Date`	Field containing a date.	
`Timedelta`	Field containing a timedelta.	
`Time`	Field containing time.	
`URI`	A field containing an absolute URI.	
`Id`	A field containing a unique identifier. A unique identifier is either an absolute URI or a dotted name. If it's a dotted name, it should have a module or package name as a prefix.	

Field type	Description	Parameters
`Choice`	Field whose value is contained in a predefined set.	`values`: A list of text choices for the field.
		`vocabulary`: A Vocabulary object that will dynamically produce the choices.
		`source`: A different, newer way to produce dynamic choices.
		Note: only one of the three should be provided. More information about sources and vocabularies is provided later in this book.
`Tuple`	Field containing a value that implements the API of a conventional Python tuple.	`value_type`: Field value items must conform to the given type, expressed via a field.
		`Unique`. Specifies whether the members of the collection must be unique.
`List`	Field containing a value that implements the API of a conventional Python list.	`value_type`: Field value items must conform to the given type, expressed via a field.
		`Unique`. Specifies whether the members of the collection must be unique.
`Set`	Field containing a value that implements the API of a conventional Python standard library `sets.Set` or a Python 2.4+ set.	`value_type`: Field value items must conform to the given type, expressed via a field.
`FrozenSet`	Field containing a value that implements the API of a conventional Python 2.4+ frozenset.	`value_type`: Field value items must conform to the given type, expressed via a field.
`Object`	Field containing an object value.	`Schema`: The interface that defines the fields comprising the object.
`Dict`	Field containing a conventional dictionary. The `key_type` and `value_type` fields allow specification of restrictions for keys and values contained in the dictionary.	`key_type`: Field keys must conform to the given type, expressed via a field.
		`value_type`: Field value items must conform to the given type, expressed via a field.

Form fields and widgets

Schema fields are perfect for defining data structures, but when dealing with forms sometimes they are not enough. In fact, once you generate a form using a schema as a base, Grok turns the schema fields into form fields. A **form field** is like a schema field but has an extended set of methods and attributes. It also has a default associated widget that is responsible for the appearance of the field inside the form.

Rendering forms requires more than the fields and their types. A form field needs to have a user interface, and that is what a widget provides. A `Choice` field, for example, could be rendered as a `<select>` box on the form, but it could also use a collection of checkboxes, or perhaps radio buttons. Sometimes, a field may not need to be displayed on a form, or a writable field may need to be displayed as text instead of allowing users to set the field's value.

Form components

Grok offers four different components that automatically generate forms. We have already worked with the first one of these, `grok.Form`. The other three are specializations of this one:

- `grok.AddForm` is used to add new model instances.
- `grok.EditForm` is used for editing an already existing instance.
- `grok.DisplayForm` simply displays the values of the fields.

A Grok form is itself a specialization of a `grok.View`, which means that it gets the same methods as those that are available to a view. It also means that a model does not actually need a view assignment if it already has a form. In fact, simple applications can get away by using a form as a view for their objects. Of course, there are times when a more complex view template is needed, or even when fields from multiple forms need to be shown in the same view. Grok can handle these cases as well, which we will see later on.

Adding a project container at the root of the site

To get to know Grok's form components, let's properly integrate our project model into our to-do list application. We'll have to restructure the code a little bit, as currently the to-do list container is the root object of the application. We need to have a project container as the root object, and then add a to-do list container to it.

Luckily, we already structured the code properly in the last chapter, so we won't need to make many changes now. To begin, let's modify the top of `app.py`, immediately before the `TodoList` class definition, to look like this:

```python
import grok
from zope import interface, schema

class Todo(grok.Application, grok.Container):
    def __init__(self):
        super(Todo, self).__init__()
        self.title = 'To-Do list manager'
        self.next_id = 0

    def deleteProject(self,project):
        del self[project]
```

First, we import `zope.interface` and `zope.schema`. Notice how we keep the `Todo` class as the root application class, but now it can contain projects instead of lists. We also omitted the `addProject` method, because the `grok.AddForm` instance is going to take care of that. Other than that, the `Todo` class is almost the same.

```python
class IProject(interface.Interface):
    title = schema.TextLine(title=u'Title',required=True)
    kind = schema.Choice(title=u'Kind of project',values=['personal',
      'business'])
    description = schema.Text(title=u'Description',required=False)
    next_id = schema.Int(title=u'Next id',default=0)
```

We then have the interface definition for `IProject`, where we add the `title`, `kind`, `description`, and `next_id` fields. These were the fields that we previously added during the call to the `__init__` method at the time of product initialization.

```python
class Project(grok.Container):
    grok.implements(IProject)

    def addList(self,title,description):
        id = str(self.next_id)
        self.next_id = self.next_id+1
        self[id] = TodoList(title,description)

    def deleteList(self,list):
        del self[list]
```

The key thing to notice in the `Project` class definition is that we use the `grok.implements` class declaration to see that this class will implement the schema that we have just defined.

```
class AddProjectForm(grok.AddForm):
    grok.context(Todo)
    grok.name('index')
    form_fields = grok.AutoFields(Project)
    label = "To begin, add a new project"

    @grok.action('Add project')
    def add(self,**data):
        project = Project()
        self.applyData(project,**data)
        id = str(self.context.next_id)
        self.context.next_id = self.context.next_id+1
        self.context[id] = project
        return self.redirect(self.url(self.context[id]))
```

The actual form view is defined after that, by using `grok.AddForm` as a base class. We assign this view to the main `Todo` container by using the `grok.context` annotation. The name `index` is used for now, so that the default page for the application will be the 'add form' itself.

Next, we create the form fields by calling the `grok.AutoFields` method. Notice that this time the argument to this method call is the `Project` class directly, rather than the interface. This is possible because the `Project` class was associated with the correct interface when we previously used `grok.implements`.

After we have assigned the fields, we set the `label` attribute of the form to the text: **To begin, add a new project**. This is the title that will be shown on the form.

In addition to this new code, all occurrences of `grok.context(Todo)` in the rest of the file need to be changed to `grok.context(Project)`, as the to-do lists and their views will now belong to a project and not to the main `Todo` application. For details, take a look at the source code of this book for Chapter 5.

Form actions

If you carefully look at the screenshot shown in the *A quick demonstration of automatic forms* section, you will see that the form has no submit buttons. In Grok, every form can have one or more actions, and for each action the form will have a submit button. The Grok `action` decorator is used to mark the methods of the form class that will be used as actions. In this case, the `add` method is decorated with it and the value of the text parameter, in this case `Add project`, will be used as the text on the button. To change the text on the button, simply modify the string passed to the decorator:

```python
@grok.action('Add project')
def add(self,**data):
    project = Project()
    self.applyData(project,**data)
    id = str(self.context.next_id)
    self.context.next_id = self.context.next_id+1
    self.context[id] = project
    return self.redirect(self.url(self.context[id]))
```

The `add` method receives all of the filled form fields in the `data` parameter, and then creates a `Project` instance. Next, it sets the attributes of `project` to the values in the form by calling the `applyData` method of the form. Finally, it adds the new project to the `Todo` instance and redirects the user to the project page.

Trying out the application

When you try out the application, there are two things to notice. First, when the add project form is displayed, the `next_id` field, which is used to name the projects, is shown. We could even edit it if we like. Obviously, we don't want this behavior.

Second, once the project has been created and we get redirected to the project page, everything works as before, even though we didn't touch the templates. With the approach that we tried in Chapter 3, using hidden values and list indexes, we would have had to modify the `index.pt` template in lots of places. Now that we have a structure based on models, the views and methods that were registered for them don't need to change, even though the containment hierarchy is different.

Another important thing to notice is that the add project form has no design or styling at all. This is because the form building mechanism uses a common template, which we haven't styled yet.

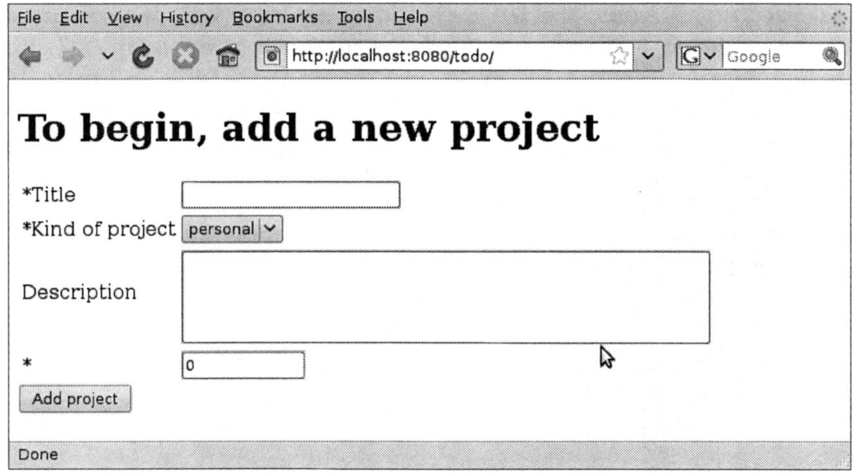

Filtering fields

Remember that currently we have the `next_id` field of the project shown on the form. We don't want it there, so how do we remove it? Fortunately for us, the list of fields generated by the `grok.AutoFields` method can easily be filtered.

We can either select precisely the fields we need, using the `select` method:

```
form_fields = grok.AutoFields(Project).select('title','kind',
  'description')
```

Or we can omit specific fields by using the `omit` method:

```
form_fields = grok.AutoFields(Project).omit('next_id')
```

In both cases, we pass the IDs of the fields as strings to the selected method. Now the `next_id` field is not there anymore, as you can see in the next screenshot.

Filtering fields can be useful not just for removing unwanted fields such as `next_id`. We can also have specialized forms for editing only a part of a schema, or for showing specific fields, depending on user information or input.

Using grok.EditForm

The form that we just made is intended to add a new project to the application, but what if we need to edit an existing project? In this case, we need a form that knows how to get the existing values of all of the fields on the form, and display them when editing. Another difference is that the add project form was assigned to the main Todo application, but an edit form would use as a context the actual project that it would be modifying.

That's why Grok has another kind of form component for editing. Using `grok.EditForm` is even easier than `grok.AddForm`. Here's all the code that we need to add to our application in order to be able to edit projects:

```
class EditProjectForm(grok.EditForm):
    grok.context(Project)
    grok.name('edit')
    form_fields = grok.AutoFields(Project).omit('next_id')
    label = "Edit the project"
```

As mentioned earlier, the context for this form is the `Project` class, which we set by using the `grok.context` class annotation. We give this form the name `edit`, so that it will be possible to just append that word to a project URL to get its edit view. As we discussed in the previous section, it is a good idea to eliminate the display of the `next_id` field from the form, so we use the `omit` method to do that. Finally, we set a label for the form and we are then ready to test it.

Start the application. If you haven't created a project already, please do so. Then, go to the URL: `http://localhost:8080/todo/0/edit`. Edit the project fields and then click on the **Apply** button. You should see a screen similar to the one shown in following screenshot:

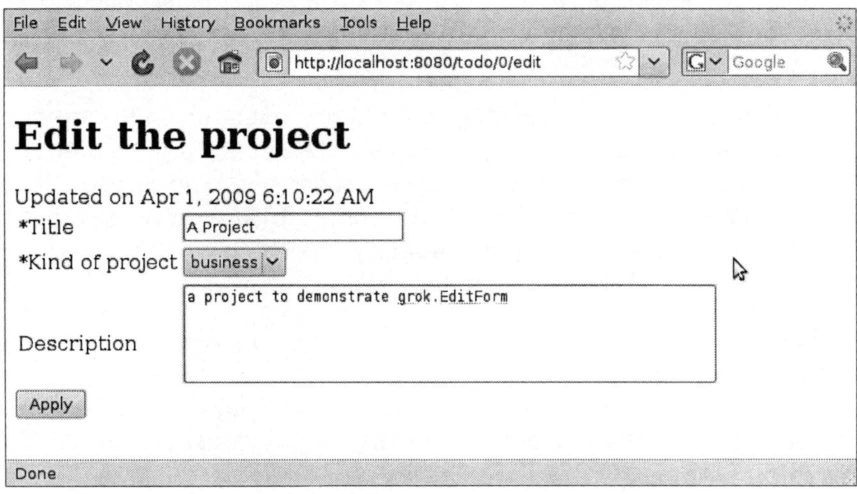

Notice how we didn't include a redirect after rendering the form, so that when we click on the **Apply** button we go back to the same form, but with a message telling us that the object was updated along with the date of modification. If we wanted, we could add an 'edit' action, by using the `action` decorator and a redirect, just like we did for the add form.

Modifying individual form fields

Having the add and edit forms created automatically by Grok is neat, but there are cases where we will need to make small modifications in how a form is rendered. Grok allows us to modify specific field attributes easily to make that happen.

Remember that each form field will be rendered by a widget, which could be thought of as views for specific fields. These views usually accept a number of parameters to allow the user to customize the appearance of the form in one way or another.

Just before being rendered, Grok's form components always call a method named `setUpWidgets`, which we can override in order to make modifications to the fields and their attributes.

In the add and edit project forms, the title of the project, which is of type `TextLine`, has a widget that displays the `<input>` tag used to capture its value with a length of 20 characters. Many project names could be longer than that, so we want to extend the length to 50 characters. Also, the text area for the description is too long for a project summary, so we'll cut it to five rows instead. Let's use the `setUpWidgets` method for this. Add the following lines to both the `AddProjectForm` and `EditProjectForm` classes:

```
def setUpWidgets(self, ignore_request=False):
    super(EditProjectForm, self).setUpWidgets(ignore_request)
    self.widgets['title'].displayWidth = 50
    self.widgets['description'].height = 5
```

Take care to substitute `EditProjectForm` for `AddProjectForm` on the super call when adding the method to its appropriate class. The `setUpWidgets` method is fairly simple. We first call the super class to make sure that we get the correct properties in the form before trying to modify them. Next, we modify any properties that we want for the field. In this case, we access the `widgets` property to get at the widgets for the fields that we defined, and change the values that we want.

Another thing that requires explanation is the `ignore_request` parameter that is passed to the `setUpWidgets` method. If this is set to `False`, as we have defined it, then this means that any field values present in the `HTTP` request will be applied to the corresponding fields. A value of `True` means that no values should be changed during this call.

Restart the application and you will see that the edit and add forms now present the widgets using the properties that we modified.

Form validation

Now we have working forms for adding and editing projects. In fact, the forms can do more than we have shown so far. For example, if we go to the add form and try to submit it without filling in the required `title` field, we'll get the form back, instead of being redirected. No project will be created, and an error message will be visible on the screen, warning us that the field can't be empty.

This validation happens automatically, but we can also add our own constraints by using the `constraint` parameter, when defining a field in the schema. For example, suppose that we absolutely need to have more than two words in the title. We can do that very easily. Just add the following lines before the interface definition:

```
def check_title(value):
    return len(value.split())>2
```

Next, modify the title field definition to look like this:

```
title = schema.TextLine(title=u'Title', required=True,
constraint=check_title)
```

We first defined a function that will receive the field value as a parameter, and must return `True` if the value is valid, or `False` otherwise. We then assign this function to the `constraint` parameter, when defining the field in the interface. This is all very simple, but it allows us to add validations for whatever conditions we need to meet in our form data.

There are cases where a simple constraint is not enough to validate a field. For instance, imagine that what we need is that whenever the kind of the project is 'business', the description can't be empty. In this case, a constraint will not do, as whether or not the description field is valid depends on the value of another field.

A constraint that involves more than one field is known as an **invariant** in Grok. To define one, the `@interface.invariant` decorator is used. For the hypothetical case described earlier, we can use the following definition, which we'll add inside the `Interface` definition:

```
@interface.invariant
def businessNeedsDescription(project):
    if project.kind=='business' and not project.description:
        raise interface.Invalid(
            "Business projects require a description")
```

Now, when we try to add a project of kind 'business', Grok will complain if the description is empty. Look at the next screenshot for reference:

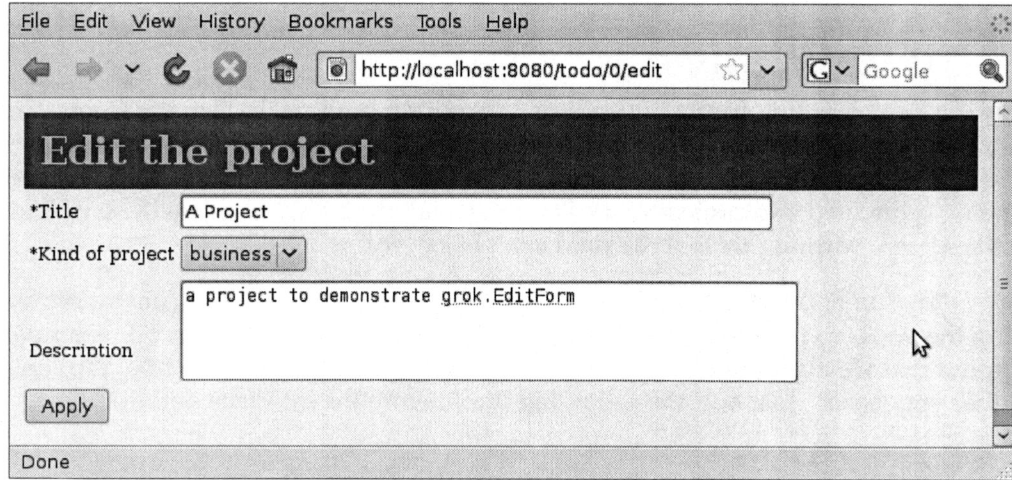

Customizing the form template

Earlier, we commented on the fact that our new project forms have no styling or design applied, and therefore they look markedly different from the rest of our application. It's time to change that.

The disadvantage of using automatic form generation is that the default template must be fairly generic to be useful in multiple applications. However, Grok allows us to set a custom template for editing the form. All we need to do is set the `template` attribute in the form:

```
template = grok.PageTemplateFile('custom_edit_form.pt')
```

Of course, for this to work we also have to provide the named template inside our application directory (not inside `app_templates`). For now, let's just add a stylesheet and a class to the generic edit template that comes with Grok. There is nothing special here, so we will just take the default edit form template and add the same stylesheet that we defined previously. Please look at the source code of this book, if you want to see the rest of the template.

```
<html>
<head>
    <title tal:content="context/title">To-Do list manager</title>
    <link rel="stylesheet" type="text/css"
          tal:attributes="href static/styles.css" />
</head>
```

That's all that's needed in order to have our custom template for editing the form. Take a look at the next screenshot to see how it looks. Of course, we would have to further modify it to get it to look just like we want. We could even leave only the fields that we wanted, placed in an irregular arrangement, but the reason that we used the original template and modified it just a little is so that you can look at it and be careful with the sections where the validation messages are shown and the actions are generated. We'll have more to say about this in future chapters.

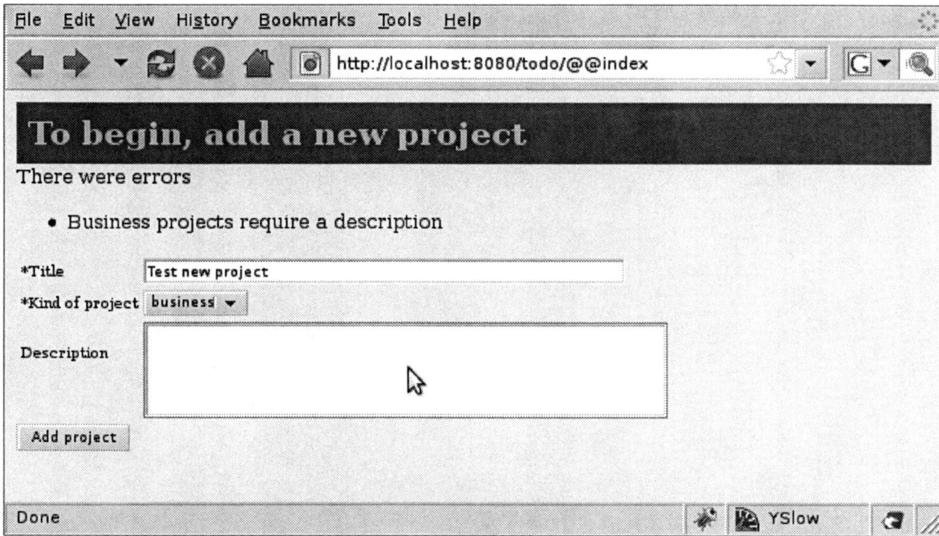

Summary

We have seen how to automatically generate forms by using schemas, and how it's possible to customize their rendering. In addition, we learned a little bit about some Zope Framework libraries, such as `zope.schema` and `zope.interface`.

6
The Catalog: An Object-Oriented Search Engine

We now have an application with multiple projects and lists. As we start adding more lists, there will come a time when we'll need to find a particular list item. We might want to find all items containing a specific word, or maybe all of the items completed on a specific date. Since all of the application data is stored in the ZODB, we need a tool to help us look for specific objects contained therein. This tool comes with Grok by default and is called the catalog.

In this chapter, we are going to learn how to use the catalog. In particular, we will look at the following concepts:

- What a catalog is and how it works
- What indexes are and how they work
- Storing data in the catalog
- Performing simple queries on the catalog
- Creating a search interface for our application

Catalogs and indexes

When we work with small amounts of data, we can always look at all of the elements of a list, for example, to find the ones that we want. However, this approach obviously does not scale up when we are dealing with thousands or millions of objects. A common way of attacking this problem is to use some sort of lookup table that will allow us to quickly and easily find a specific object by using one of its attributes. This is known as an **index**.

A **catalog** is a tool that allows us to manage a collection of related indexes and perform queries against the catalog by using one or more of them. We can add indexes to the catalog that will keep track of a specific attribute of an object. From then on, whenever we create a new object, we can call the catalog to index it, and it will take all of the objects' attributes that have an index setup and includes them in the corresponding index. Once they are there, we can query the catalog by using specific attribute values, and get back the objects that match the query.

Adding a simple search function to the application

The catalog contains references to the actual objects that are stored in the ZODB, and each index is related to one attribute of these objects.

To be able to search for an object in the catalog, the object needs to be indexed by the catalog. This works better if it happens at specific events in the lifetime of the object, so that it gets indexed at creation time and when it gets modified.

Since working with the catalog is the best way of dealing with searches when using the ZODB, Grok comes with a class that allows us to easily hook into the catalog, create indexes, and perform searches. This class is called `grok.Indexes`, and allows us to define indexes and hook our application objects with the appropriate life cycle events, for automatic indexing.

Defining a simple index

Let's define a simple index for the `title` attribute of a project, and show how to perform a search on the catalog by using it:

```
class ProjectIndexes(grok.Indexes):
    grok.site(ITodo)
    grok.context(IProject)
    title = grok.index.Text()
```

We are going to create an index for the `Project` class, so we name our class `ProjectIndexes`. The name is not important, as the key is using `grok.Indexes` as a base for the class. The `grok.site` class annotation is used to signal to Grok which type of object in our application is going to use the indexes defined here.

Next, we need to tell Grok which objects will be automatically indexed when they are modified. This is done by using `grok.context` with either a class or an interface as the parameter. In this case, we select `IProject` as the interface that will mark the objects to be indexed.

Finally, we define the indexes themselves. In this example, we want the whole text of the `title` attribute to be searchable, so we will use a `Text` index. We'll have more to say about the types of indexes shortly. For now, just note that the attribute that will be indexed is the same as the name of the index, which in this case means that the `title` attribute from the project model will be indexed in this catalog. It is possible to have an index named differently than the attribute to be indexed, but then we need to specify the real attribute name with the keyword parameter `attribute`, like this:

```
project_title = grok.index.Text(attribute='title')
```

That's it. Simply by declaring the indexes in this class, Grok will take it upon itself to create the catalog and append the indexes to it, as well as keeping track of when an object needs to be reindexed.

Creating the search view

We will now create the search view that will allow us to see the catalog in action. First, let's take a look at the view code:

```
class TodoSearch(grok.View):
    grok.context(Todo)
    grok.name('search')

    def update(self,query):
        if query:
            catalog = getUtility(ICatalog)
            self.results = catalog.searchResults(title=query)
```

This is a view for the main application, and is named search. The important bit is in the `update` method. We receive a query as a parameter, which represents the text that the user is looking for inside the title of the projects. We then have to get the actual catalog before we can perform a search. Note that the catalog at this point will already contain the indexes that we defined earlier for `Project`. We don't have to do anything else to connect them with the catalog; Grok takes care of all the plumbing.

After we get the `catalog` object, we can search it by using the `searchResults` method, which accepts key/value pairs with index names and query values. In this case, we pass the query that came in the request to the `title` index, so that we get all of the projects that match this query text in their titles, as results.

You might recall that earlier we mentioned that interfaces, besides being useful for documentation and attribute introspection, are very helpful for working with component architectures. Under the hood, Grok contains a registry, which keeps track of all of the interface declarations for objects, so that it's possible to find an object by querying its interface. A catalog always implements the interface `ICatalog`, which is found in the `zope.app.catalog.interfaces` package included with Grok.

As Grok is making our lives simpler by not forcing us to instantiate a catalog and manually add and populate indexes to it, we do not control the code where this happens. So how do we find it? By using the registry, we can query it for an object that implements the `ICatalog` interface and that will be the catalog that we are looking for.

That's precisely what the `getUtility` method from the `zope.component` package does. So, after calling this method we will have the catalog referenced by our `catalog` variable. This might seem to be a roundabout mechanism for getting at the catalog. Why not simply have Grok define a global catalog and use that directly? Well, we can answer that with another question or two: what if we need more than one catalog? Or what if we decide to replace the catalog that Grok creates with our own? When using interfaces and component registration we can cover these cases and the code barely needs to be changed.

Creating a template to display the search results

Once we have the results placed in the view in the last line of the `update` method, we need a template to show this result. Create a template called `todosearch.pt` inside the `app_templates` directory. First comes the header, with our stylesheet:

```
<html>
<head>
    <title tal:content="context/title">To-Do list manager</title>
    <link rel="stylesheet" type="text/css"
          tal:attributes="href static/styles.css" />
</head>
```

Next, we are going to add a search box inside our top header. We use `tal:attributes` to set the text input value to whatever we searched for before, or leave it empty if there was no previous search.

The form action is set to call the search view that we defined earlier:

```
<body>
  <div id="appheader">
    <form id="search"
          tal:attributes="action python:view.url('search')">
      <input type="text" name="query"
             tal:attributes="value request/query|nothing" />
      <input class="new_button" type="submit" value="search" />
    </form>
    <h1 id="apptitle"
        tal:content="string:${context/title}: search">
      To-Do list manager </h1>
  </div>
  <p class="create">
    <a tal:attributes="href python:view.url(context)">
      Go back to main page </a>
  </p>
```

We now come to the heart of the matter. Recall that in the view we performed a search by title, and defined an attribute named `results`. Now we can use those results in the template. First, we need to make sure that we have something to show, and if we don't, we will display a message saying so:

```
<h2 tal:condition="not:view/results|nothing">There were no
   results.</h2>
```

Next, if there are results, we prepare a table with the correct headings, and use `tal:repeat` to loop through the results. The view variable `results` contains all of the projects whose title matched the query, so we iterate through these results and simply show all of their attributes in a table similar to the one that we used for the dashboard.

```
<div class="projects" tal:condition="view/results|nothing">
  <h2>These are the results for
      "<i tal:content="request/query"></i>":</h2 >
  <table>
    <tr>
      <th>Project name</th>
      <th>Kind</th>
      <th>Description</th>
      <th>Created on</th>
      <th>Last modified</th>
      <th>Owner</th>
    </tr>
    <tr tal:repeat="project view/results">
      <td>
        <a href="" tal:attributes="href python:view.url(project)"
                   tal:content="project/title">title</a>
      </td>
```

```
        <td tal:content="project/kind">type</td>
        <td tal:content="project/description">type</td>
        <td tal:content="project/creation_date">type</td>
        <td tal:content="project/modification_date">type</td>
        <td tal:content="project/creator">type</td>
      </tr>
    </table>
  </div>
 </body>
</html>
```

Now we can create a new application instance in the Grok admin UI and define some projects so that we can see how the search works. The reason why we need to define a new application is that indexes only get created when an application is installed. Our `ProjectIndexes` class will actually do nothing if it gets added after the application was created. Take a look at the following screenshot, to see how the search results are displayed:

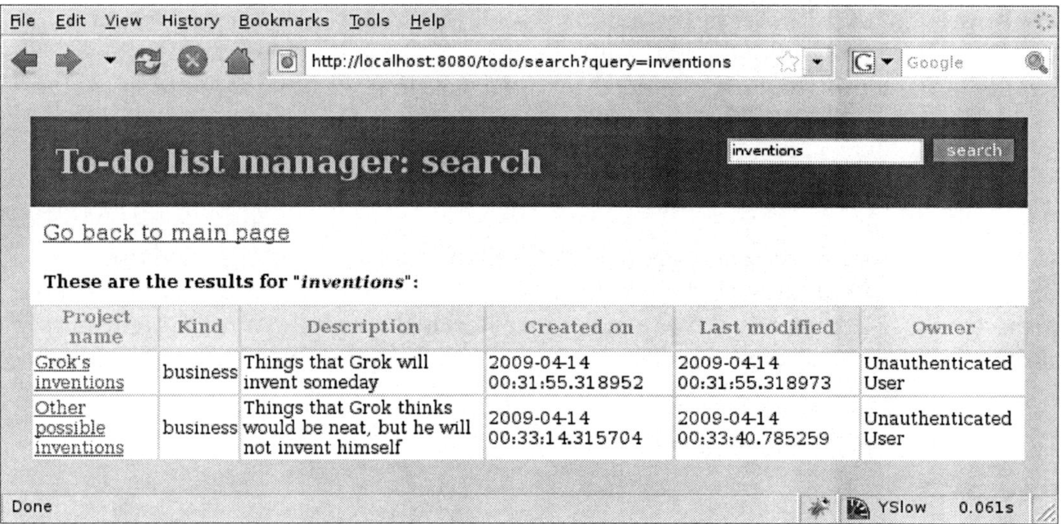

Project name	Kind	Description	Created on	Last modified	Owner
Grok's inventions	business	Things that Grok will invent someday	2009-04-14 00:31:55.318952	2009-04-14 00:31:55.318973	Unauthenticated User
Other possible inventions	business	Things that Grok thinks would be neat, but he will not invent himself	2009-04-14 00:33:14.315704	2009-04-14 00:33:40.785259	Unauthenticated User

A brief diversion: Structuring our application for search

Now that we have experimented with the basics of catalog searches, we'll need to refactor our application a little to play well with the catalog, because our to-do items don't have all the attributes we will likely need to make the search powerful enough. For instance, we are certainly going to be interested in searching for them by date and eventually by user.

Let's pause a bit and reflect on where we want our application to go. If we are going to be managing 'projects', we'll need to add some more attributes to our models. We have not bothered about this until now, but as the complexity of our application grows, it becomes more important to have a clear plan.

The top-level unit of our application will be a project. For our purposes, a *project* is a collection of related to-do lists. We will need to store the project's creation date as well as the last time it was modified. A project is 'done' when all of the items in all of its lists are checked off.

The project can have owners and members. Members are users who have one or more items assigned; owners are members who can also add, edit, or remove lists and items. We haven't seen yet how user management works in Grok, but we will see it in the next chapter, so for now we'll just store the project's creator.

A to-do list can have any number of items. We'll also store the list's creation date. An item will have a completed date as well as a creation date. We'll also keep track of who performed each of these.

In the previous chapter, we worked with forms that were automatically constructed by using interface schemas as a base. At that time, we only added an interface for the `Project` class. Let's finish that work and do the same for the other classes.

We are dealing with different kinds of objects, but surely there will be some attributes that are used in most of them. For example, every project, list, and item will have a creator and a creation date. We'd like to avoid repeating these attributes on every interface definition, so we'll create a general interface for them and make all other classes implement this.

We discussed interfaces briefly before, when working with forms, and saw that a class can promise to implement an interface simply by saying that it does so by using the `grok.implements` class annotation. However, a class is not limited to implementing a single interface. In fact, there's no limit to the number of interfaces that a class can implement. This will be useful for us because all of our classes can implement both the general metadata interfaces as well as their own particular interfaces.

Our refactored models will look like the code below. First, our shared attributes interface:

```python
class IMetadata(interface.Interface):
    creator = schema.TextLine(title=u'Creator')
    creation_date  = schema.Datetime(title=u'Creation date')
    modification_date  = schema.Datetime(title=u'Modification date')
```

The main application class does not need to use the metadata schema; only its own
schema will be used:

```python
class ITodo(interface.Interface):
    title = schema.TextLine(title=u'Title',required=True)
    next_id = schema.Int(title=u'Next id',default=0)


class Todo(grok.Application, grok.Container):
    grok.implements(ITodo)
    title = u'To-do list manager'
    next_id = 0


    def deleteProject(self,project):
        del self[project]
```

We added `title` and `next_id` to the schema and set default values for the class,
after the `grok.implements` call.

Now look at the `Project` class:

```python
class IProject(interface.Interface):
    title = schema.TextLine(title=u'Title', required=True,
        constraint=check_title)
    kind = schema.Choice(title=u'Kind of project', values=['personal',
        'business'])
    description = schema.Text(title=u'Description', required=False)
    next_id = schema.Int(title=u'Next id', default=0)


class Project(grok.Container):
    grok.implements(IProject, IMetadata)
    next_id = 0
    description = u''


    def addList(self, title, description):
        id = str(self.next_id)
        self.next_id = self.next_id+1
        self[id] = TodoList(title, description)


    def deleteList(self, list):
        del self[list]
```

In this case, we define the `Project` schema, and then tell Grok that this class
will use both the schemas — this one and the metadata schema that we defined
earlier. This is fairly simple: we just pass the two interface definitions as arguments
to `grok.implements`.

We'll use the new attributes when a new project is added to the application, like this:

```python
@grok.action('Add project')
def add(self,**data):
    project = Project()
    self.applyData(project,**data)
    id = str(self.context.next_id)
    self.context.next_id = self.context.next_id+1
    self.context[id] = project
    project.creator = self.request.principal.title
    project.creation_date = datetime.datetime.now()
    project.modification_date = datetime.datetime.now()
    return self.redirect(self.url(self.context[id]))
```

After creating a new project and applying the form data to it, we set values for the dates and creator. Keep in mind that interfaces are informative. We are never required to use all of the fields in an interface's schema, but it's very convenient to be able to refer to the schema for documentation purposes. In some cases, it is used to generate a form using one or more fields from it. Incidentally, it's probably very clear what's happening in the date assignments, but the `self.request.principal.title` line may seem a bit odd. A **principal** is a user in Grok, and its title is a string description of who this user is.

That's all there is to know for now about our model restructuring. Here are the final two models:

```python
class ITodoList(interface.Interface):
    title = schema.TextLine(title=u'Title',required=True,
      constraint=check_title)
    description = schema.Text(title=u'Description',required=False)
    next_id = schema.Int(title=u'Next id',default=0)

class TodoList(grok.Container):
    grok.implements(ITodoList, IMetadata)
    next_id = 0
    description = u''

    def __init__(self,title,description):
        super(TodoList, self).__init__()
        self.title = title
        self.description = description
        self.next_id = 0

    def addItem(self,description):
        id = str(self.next_id)
```

```python
            self.next_id = self.next_id+1
            self[id] = TodoItem(description)

        def deleteItem(self,item):
            del self[item]

        def updateItems(self, items):
            for name,item in self.items():
                if name in items:
                    self[item].checked = True
                else:
                    self[item].checked = False

    class ITodoItem(interface.Interface):
        description = schema.Text(title=u'Description',required=True)
        checked = schema.Bool(title=u'Checked',default=False)

    class TodoItem(grok.Model):
        grok.implements(ITodoItem, IMetadata)
        checked = False

        def __init__(self,item_description):
            super(TodoItem, self).__init__()
            self.description = item_description
            self.checked = False

        def toggleCheck(self):
            self.checked = not self.checked
```

Now that we have added the desired attributes and interfaces, let's create a home page template where we can see at a glance all our projects and their attributes, along with links to every project. This will be our application's dashboard. While we are at it, let's add a search box at the top, too. We'll start by adding a view for our dashboard:

```python
    class DashBoard(grok.View):
        grok.context(Todo)
        grok.name('index')
```

Now, for the template, call the `dashboard.pt` file and place it inside `app_templates`. Notice how we use the name `index`, so that this will be the default view for the application:

```html
<html>
<head>
  <title tal:content="context/title">To-Do list manager</title>
```

```
    <link rel="stylesheet" type="text/css"
          tal:attributes="href static/styles.css" />
</head>
<body>
  <div id="appheader">
    <form id="search"
            tal:attributes="action python:view.url('search')">
        <input type="text" name="query" />
        <input class="new_button" type="submit" value="search" />
    </form>
    <h1 id="apptitle" tal:content="context/title">
        To-Do list manager</h1>
  </div>
  <p class="create"><a href="add">Create a new project</a></p>
  <h2 tal:define="projects context/values"
      tal:condition="projects">
    These are your available projects</h2>
  <div class="projects">
  <table>
    <tr>
        <th>Project name</th>
        <th>Kind</th>
        <th>Description</th>
        <th>Created on</th>
        <th>Last modified</th>
        <th>Owner</th>
        <th>Delete</th>
    </tr>
    <tr tal:repeat="project context/values">
        <td>
            <a href="" tal:attributes="href python:view.url(project)"
                        tal:content="project/title">title</a>
        </td>
        <td tal:content="project/kind">type</td>
        <td tal:content="project/description">type</td>
        <td tal:content="project/creation_date">type</td>
        <td tal:content="project/modification_date">type</td>
        <td tal:content="project/creator">type</td>
        <td>
            <a tal:define="url python:view.url('deleteproject')"
               tal:attributes="href
                 string:${url}?project=${project/__name__}">
               <img border="0"
                    tal:attributes="src static/bin_closed.png" />
            </a>
```

```
        </td>
      </tr>
    </table>
    </div>
  </body>
  </html>
```

The template is very straightforward. We just get all of the projects by using the `context/values` call and then iterate through the results showing all of the attributes in a table. The template can be seen in the following screenshot:

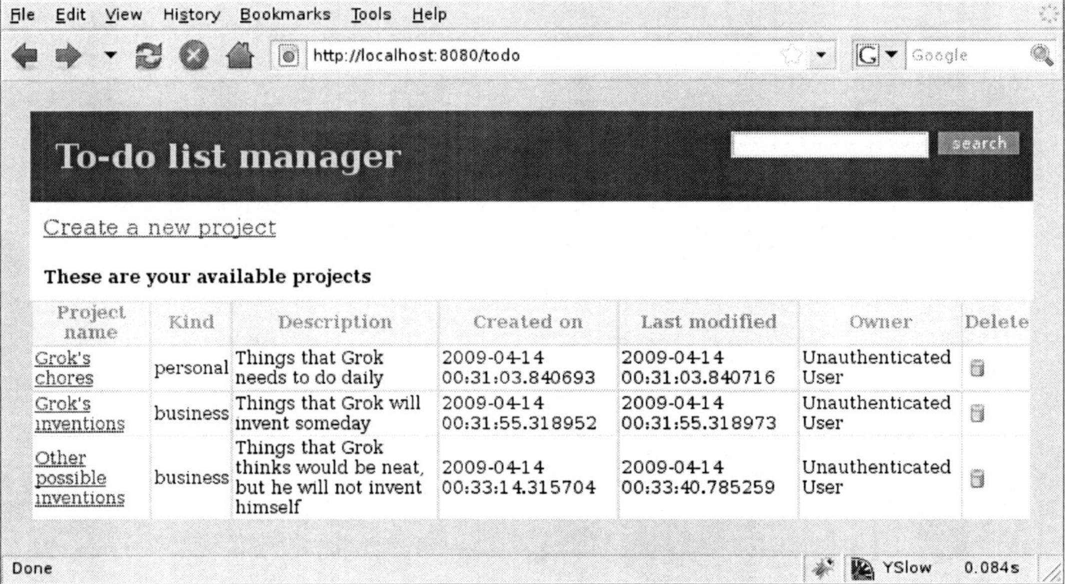

Project name	Kind	Description	Created on	Last modified	Owner	Delete
Grok's chores	personal	Things that Grok needs to do daily	2009-04-14 00:31:03.840693	2009-04-14 00:31:03.840716	Unauthenticated User	
Grok's inventions	business	Things that Grok will invent someday	2009-04-14 00:31:55.318952	2009-04-14 00:31:55.318973	Unauthenticated User	
Other possible inventions	business	Things that Grok thinks would be neat, but he will not invent himself	2009-04-14 00:33:14.315704	2009-04-14 00:33:40.785259	Unauthenticated User	

Back to search: Using multiple indexes

Let's recap briefly where we were with respect to the search before we set out to reorganize our code. The key thing to understand when using the catalog in Grok is that the indexes define the kinds of searches that we can perform. In our example, we used a `Text` index for the `title` attribute and the Grok context for that index was the `Project` model. This means that even if a project has several attributes, we can only search inside the title, at this point.

We are not limited to using only one index, of course. We can add any number of indexes—even one for every attribute of the object. Let's add one for `description`, immediately after the title in the `ProjectIndexes` class:

```python
description = grok.index.Text()
```

Note that the only thing that changes is the index name, which points to the actual attribute to be indexed. To keep things simple for now, we can use the following query:

```python
self.results = catalog.searchResults(title=query, description=query)
```

We pass the `query` parameter to both indexes, because all we have is a text box with room for one parameter. The results will be all of the projects for which both the title and description match the values specified in the query. If we had several parameters, we could pass a different value to each index and we would get back all of the items where all indexes match.

Let's consider how we would like the search box to work in this application. The ideal thing would be for it to be as inclusive as possible, so that we could type a word or two and have the catalog look at different indexes to find results. For example, it would be good if a text search could be performed in such a way that the catalog returns all items that match the query either on the `description` or the `title` indexes. As this is a common situation, Grok offers a solution that is generally useful and also easy to implement. Basically, we can define a method that can collect information from all of the attributes and return the collected information as a single index.

First, we add an empty method definition to our interface. This is done both to document the method and to let the `grok.Indexes` class find the attribute when we declare its name as an index. Remember, the project indexes are connected to the `IProject` interface, so that every attribute or method defined here may be used as an index for searching.

```python
class IProject(interface.Interface):
    title = schema.TextLine(title=u'Title', required=True,
      constraint=check_title)
    kind = schema.Choice(title=u'Kind of project', values=['personal',
      'business'])
    description = schema.Text(title=u'Description', required=False)
    next_id = schema.Int(title=u'Next id', default=0)

    def searchableText():
        """return concatenated string with all text fields to search"""
```

Pay attention to the absence of a `self` parameter inside the method definition. This parameter is not necessary because we are not defining a class, but an interface. It is customary to include a description of the method as a comment in the body of its definition.

We then add this method's name as an index in the `ProjectIndexes` class, like this:

```
searchableText = grok.index.Text()
```

Grok uses the interface definition to find a method or attribute with this name. If it's a method, it will be called at the time of indexing, so what is happening here is that we are informing Grok that the full-text entry for a project will be available by calling its own `searchableText` method. This method is then defined in the `Project` class:

```
def searchableText(self):
    return self.title+self.description
```

The method is extremely simple. We just return the `title` and `description` attributes as a single string, so that the index will actually include both fields. In this way, we can search both of them at the same time by querying the catalog with the new `searchableText` index:

```
self.results = catalog.searchResults(searchableText=query)
```

That's all we need to cover this requirement, but as we can see, this approach can be used to have the `index` method return any kind of content, which gives us enough freedom to create any number of combined indexes that we may need.

Indexing different kinds of objects

So far, we can search the title and description fields of the `Project` class and nothing more. Both lists and items have a description field as well, so it would be nice if the simple search query we are using could also look inside lists and their items.

Right now, we are using `IProject` as the context for the search. The `context` class annotation does not accept more than one parameter, so we can't just pass `ITodoList` and `ITodoItem` and be done. Here is where the concept of interfaces can shine. We can define a general search interface and make all of our objects implement it. They don't even need to provide every attribute:

```
class ISearchable(interface.Interface):
    title = interface.Attribute('title')
    kind = interface.Attribute('kind')
    description = interface.Attribute('description')
    creator = interface.Attribute('creator')
    creation_date = interface.Attribute('creation date')
    modification_date = interface.Attribute('modification date')
```

```python
    checked = interface.Attribute('checked')

    def searchableText():
        """return concatenated string with all text fields to search"""
```

Notice how instead of using a schema for the attribute definition, we simply use the `Attribute` class from the `interface` package. We are not going to generate forms from this interface and it is easy to just describe its attributes without worrying about field properties.

Once we define this interface and include all of the attributes that we want to be indexed in the catalog, we just declare that every model implements it. For example:

```python
class Project(grok.Container):
    grok.implements(IProject, IMetadata, ISearchable)
```

Then, we replace the `context` annotation argument to use it as well. This is very powerful, and means that any of the objects that declare themselves to be searchable via the `grok.implements(ISearchable)` class annotation will be automatically indexed by Grok, or the call to `catalog.searchResults` will take them into account.

```python
class ProjectIndexes(grok.Indexes):
    grok.site(ITodo)
    grok.context(ISearchable)
    title = grok.index.Text()
    description = grok.index.Text()
    searchableText = grok.index.Text()
    creator = grok.index.Field()
    modification_date = grok.index.Field()
    creation_date = grok.index.Field()
    checked = grok.index.Field()
```

Notice how we use `ISearchable` as context now and also create all of the remaining indexes that we could use. As these indexes will contain references to different kinds of models, we add a `content_type` attribute to each model to hold the kind of model it represents. As an example, here is the improved `TodoList` class definition. We add `ISearchable` to the `grok.implements` declaration, and that's enough to make our search view work with todo items as well as projects.

```python
class TodoList(grok.Container):
    grok.implements(ITodoList, IMetadata, ISearchable)
    next_id = 0
    description = u''
    content_type = 'list'
```

```python
def __init__(self,title,description,creator):
    super(TodoList, self).__init__()
    self.title = title
    self.description = description
    self.next_id = 0
    self.creator = creator
    self.creation_date = datetime.datetime.now()
    self.modification_date = datetime.datetime.now()

def searchableText(self):
    return self.title+self.description
```

Again, we are implementing `ISearchable`, which marks the `TodoList` model indexable. Then we define `content_type` with the value `list`, so that when a search result has multiple types of objects, we can find out if one of them is a list just by looking at this attribute. Notice how the rest of the metadata attributes are now assigned some value at creation time, via the `__init__` method, so that the result display is complete.

Finally, the `searchableText` method for full text searches is defined. In this case, the code is the same as for the method of the same name in the `Project` class, but it could be different, as indeed it is in the `TodoItem` class, which is not shown here.

The catalog admin UI

When your catalog begins to grow, it can be useful to find out how many objects it has and how populated each index is. Grok includes a package for performing simple introspection into the catalog, which allows us to take a look inside.

The catalog UI is not integrated into the Grok admin UI. However, we can still access the catalog from the Zope side by using a direct URL. Let's do that. Create some projects and lists in the `todo` application and then point your browser to: `http://localhost:8080/todo/++etc++site/Catalog/@@advanced.html`. The list of project indexes will appear in the browser, along with some statistics, as shown in the following screenshot:

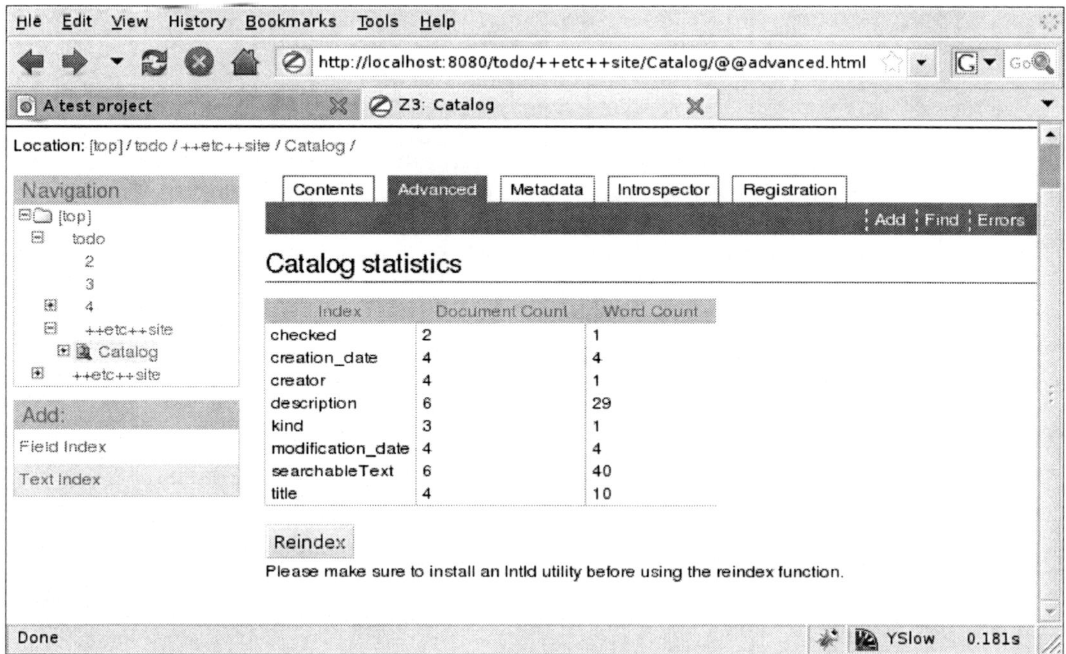

This is the statistics screen of the catalog UI, so we can't do much more here than take a look at the numbers, but it does give us a good sense of how our application data is stored in the catalog.

There are other tabs, the most important of which is the **Contents** tab, from where we can visit the information screens for each of the indexes.

Types of indexes

As we can see from the code of the `ProjectIndexes` class, there is more than one kind of index. So far, we have worked with a `text` index, which allows us to make full-text searches. However, not all searches are equal; text searches allow us to look for words or even fragments of words inside a field value, but there are cases where we would need to match a field value exactly or return no match at all.

Grok offers three ready-to-use index classes, which are summarized in the following table:

Index	Description
Field	Matches against an entire field. Used for indexing orderable values and querying for a range. Supports sorting and limiting the number of results.
Text	Supports full-text searches of a field. Queries can include the 'and' and 'or' Boolean operators. It's also possible to search for fragments of strings by using an asterisk (globbing).
Set	Supports keyword searches of a field. The index allows searches for documents that contain any one set of values; all of a set of values; or between a set of values.

We are not going to add search options for using the other indexes in our application right now, but here are a few examples of how to use them. For the sake of completeness, let's start with the `Text` field:

Finding objects containing the word 'caveman' in the title:

```
results = catalog.searchResults(title='caveman')
```

Finding all objects with either 'spear' or 'club' in their description:

```
results = catalog.searchResults(description='spear or club')
```

Finding objects containing any word starting with 'cave' in their title (caveman, caved, caveat, and so on):

```
results = catalog.searchResults(title='cave*')
```

The `Field` index works differently. It's necessary to always use a tuple for the query, even if we are only interested in a single value. If we want all of the objects created by the user 'Manager':

```
results = catalog.searchResults(creator=(u'Manager', u'Manager'))
```

All objects created between March 31, 2009 and today:

```
from datetime import datetime
results = catalog.searchResults(creation_date=(datetime(2009,3,31),
  datetime.now()))
```

The `Set` index allows us to find matches in lists of values, which is useful for finding objects that share some keywords or tags, but do not necessarily have the same list of keywords or tags applied to them.

Summary

In this chapter, we learned how to use a catalog for searching and categorizing content. We are now able to add indexes and custom search queries to our applications. In the next chapter, we will turn our attention to security.

7
Security

As it stands, our to-do list manager application can be accessed by anyone. Whoever can get to the 8080 port on the Grok server will be able to create, update, and delete projects and tasks.

If we think about what we want the application to do, it would be nice if only authenticated users are able to access it in the first place. For example, it should be possible to install the application inside a company and have only a single department there as the application's users. Users with the correct permissions could create projects and assign tasks to team members.

Grok includes the necessary tools to accomplish this, as we will see in this chapter. Here are the key concepts that we will learn:

- Authentication and authorization
- Principals, permissions, and roles
- What the default security policy is and how it is defined in the `site.zcml` configuration file
- Setting up authentication using `site.zcml` declarations
- Setting up a custom security policy
- Adding and managing users

Authentication and authorization

When speaking about web application security, there are two important concepts to get right before beginning: **authentication** and **authorization**.

In a given application, we might have a number of users who are allowed to log in. To do so, they usually would provide a username and a password. If the username and the password match, the user has been authenticated, so the system assumes he is who he says he is. In this chapter, we will learn how to perform authentication in Grok by using plugins.

Once a user is logged in, he may want to perform a number of actions, from just viewing the application to managing it. The user is authorized to perform some or all of the available actions by giving him specific permissions to carry them out.

Principals, permissions, and roles

In Grok, users are known by the term 'principals'. A **principal** represents any entity that interacts with the application, be it a user or any kind of agent, such as a remote client program. A **group** is a special kind of principal that can contain other principals. In the rest of the chapter, we will mostly use the more familiar term 'user' when talking about principals.

Views in Grok can be protected by permissions, so that only users with the correct permission can access each view. By default, however, Grok allows everybody including authenticated users, to have unrestricted access to all of the views.

Instead of assigning and keeping track of permissions to individual users, it's more efficient to group related permissions together and assign this group to a user. That's what roles do in Grok. For example, the admin user that we have been using for accessing the Grok administration UI has the role `zope.Manager` that grants all existing permissions to this user.

We'll learn about permissions and roles after we introduce security policies in the *Setting up a custom security policy* section of this chapter.

Security policies

A Grok application will thus have a number of principals, permissions, and roles. The collection of these is called a **security policy** and represents the global security decisions for a specific application.

As we mentioned before, Grok applications have a default security policy that gives view permission to everybody. It also defines authenticated and unauthenticated user groups.

Default Grok security policy definition

The security policy that Grok uses by default is defined in the `site.zcml` file, which is inside the `etc` directory. There are several declarations in this file which we will discuss individually.

The following statement is the user representation for unauthenticated users in the system:

```
<unauthenticatedPrincipal id="zope.anybody"
  title="Unauthenticated User" />
```

All of the users who visit the application without authenticating will share this same ID.

The unauthenticated group is assigned to unauthenticated principals:

```
<unauthenticatedGroup id="zope.Anybody"
  title="Unauthenticated Users" />
```

It is useful to have this defined for group operations.

Next, we have a dynamic group that includes all of the authenticated users, irrespective of their permissions or roles:

```
<authenticatedGroup id="zope.Authenticated"
  title="Authenticated Users" />
```

Finally, there is a group that includes all users, authenticated or not:

```
<everybodyGroup id="zope.Everybody" title="All Users" />
```

We now come to the part where users are defined. In this case, there is only one user, the "site manager", with the login "admin":

```
<principal id="zope.manager"
           title="Manager"
           login="admin"
           password_manager="Plain Text"
           password="admin"
           />
```

As you can see, the password is assigned to this manager using plain text. You may recall that the title defined here is what we show in the creator column when listing the projects in the dashboard.

The next two declarations grant the permissions for viewing to the `zope.Anybody` user that represents the unauthenticated principal defined earlier.

```
<grant permission="zope.View"
       principal="zope.Anybody" />
<grant permission="zope.app.dublincore.view"
       principal="zope.Anybody" />
```

Note that in this case there is no separate definition for permission, because a permission is just a name. These declarations allow all unauthenticated users to view, so by default, an application is wide open for viewing.

Next comes the role definitions:

```
<role id="zope.Manager" title="Site Manager" />
<role id="zope.Member" title="Site Member" />
```

A "site manager" role is defined for managing the site. Then, a "site member" role is defined for regular site users, although this role is unused in the default configuration.

Finally, all of the permissions are granted to the `zope.Manager` role by using `grantAll`.

```
<grantAll role="zope.Manager" />
<grant role="zope.Manager"
       principal="zope.manager" />
```

This means that users with the manager role will get all defined permissions. The role is then assigned to the user we defined earlier in the *Principals, permissions, and roles* section.

To recap, a security policy consists of:

- A number of users who can log into the application.
- Groups of users, which can contain any number of users. A user can also belong to several groups.
- Specific permissions for allowing these users to work with parts of the application.
- Roles that can be assigned multiple permissions, so that a user or group can be assigned a role that includes all related permissions for a task. This greatly simplifies permission administration.

Modifying the security policy

So far, we have been accessing the application by using the "manager" user that is defined in the *Default Grok security policy definition* section. Now, close all of the browser windows, reopen the browser, and go to the `todo` application URL directly, without logging in. You are unauthenticated, yet no login window will be shown. Add a project or make some other change and see how the application does it obediently.

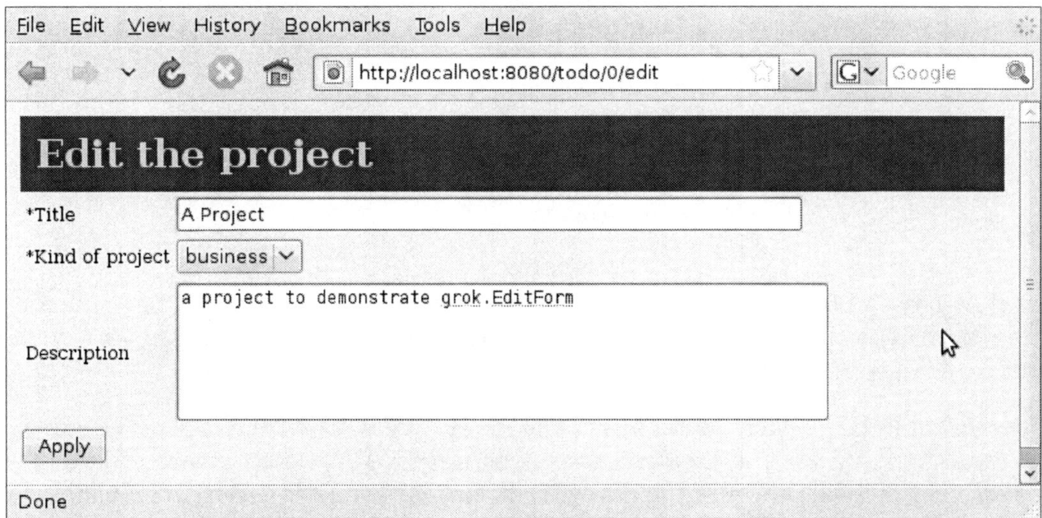

Wait a minute, didn't we say that only the view permission was assigned to the unauthenticated user? Why did Grok allow us to make changes to the projects then?

Well, the thing is, views need to be specifically protected with permissions, if we want to protect them. Until we do so it doesn't matter whether the user is authenticated or not, much less, if he holds the required permissions. Again, all of this is intended by the very open default security policy for Grok applications.

Modifying the default view permissions

Let's change the default security policy a bit to see how it works. In the specific case of the to-do list manager, we would like to keep unauthenticated users away, so let's begin by changing the `grant permission` declarations to look like the following code:

```
<grant permission="zope.View"
       principal="zope.Authenticated" />
<grant permission="zope.app.dublincore.view"
       principal="zope.Authenticated" />
```

Instead of granting view permissions to everybody, we grant them to the `zope.Authenticated` group that we defined earlier, so that only authenticated users are allowed to access the application.

Adding a new user

To test these declarations, we need to add another user to the site, because the "manager" user will get the view permission anyway. Add the following lines to `site.zcml`, after the manager definition:

```
<principal id="todo.user"
           title="User"
           login="user"
           password_manager="Plain Text"
           password="user"
           />
```

We now have a `todo.user` with "user" as the username and password. Save the file and restart Grok. It is necessary to delete and create the application again, as security policies are applied at the moment of application creation.

Now it should be possible to log in as `todo.user`. Try it: Go to the root of the site to get the login window, and then enter the new user's login and password. You will see an error message because the new user does not have permission to manage Grok applications. Ignore the error and go to the application URL. The project dashboard will appear in the browser.

Of course, our new user can create and delete projects and tasks, as the views are not protected. Not only that, but unauthenticated users can still view and edit everything.

Protecting a view

It's time to protect a view and keep unauthenticated users away from it, as intended. Just change the dashboard view to the following:

```
class DashBoard(grok.View):
    grok.context(Todo)
    grok.name('index')
    grok.require('zope.View')
```

To protect a view with a permission, we use the `grok.require` class annotation. Notice how we passed the permission name to it as defined in the `site.zcml` configuration file. Restart the application (no need to re-create it this time), and then close and open the browser to lose the current authentication information. Try to access the application URL without logging in and you should get the login window. Unauthenticated users can't view the dashboard anymore. Enter the `todo.user` credentials, and the dashboard will appear again.

Setting up a custom security policy

Now that we have seen how the security machinery works, we are ready to add our own security policy to the application. Let's begin by creating some permissions, and attaching them to our views.

Creating permissions

Grok offers a very easy mechanism for defining permissions and restricting access. A permission can be defined simply by subclassing from the `grok.Permission` class and adding a name.

To keep things simple, let's define only four permissions for our application—a general permission to view, and specific permissions for adding projects and lists or modifying list items:

```python
class ViewTodos(grok.Permission):
    grok.name('todo.view')

class AddProjects(grok.Permission):
    grok.name('todo.addprojects')

class AddLists(grok.Permission):
    grok.name('todo.addlists')

class ChangeItems(grok.Permission):
    grok.name('todo.changeitems')
```

Permissions are applied to views by using the `grok.require` directive, so to protect each of our views we need to go through our application code and add an appropriate `grok.require` statement to each view. For example:

```python
class DashBoard(grok.View):
    grok.context(Todo)
    grok.name('index')
    grok.require('todo.view')

class ProjectIndex(grok.View):
    grok.context(Project)
    grok.name('index')
    grok.require('todo.view')

class TodoAddList(grok.View):
    grok.context(Project)
    grok.name('addlist')
    grok.require('todo.addlists')

class TodoDeleteProject(grok.View):
    grok.context(Todo)
    grok.name('deleteproject')
    grok.require('todo.addprojects')
```

We protect the dashboard with our view permission, which means no anonymous users will be able to access it. The `TodoAddList` view will require `addlists` permission, and to delete a project, the `addprojects` permission is necessary. In this way, we can protect all of our views with the permissions that we want.

Roles

The views are protected with permissions, but assigning the permissions to actual users is best done by using roles. Let's define three simple roles for the application. *Project members* will be able to view and change list items only. *Project managers* can do all that and also create lists. *Application managers* are the only ones who can create projects.

The `grok.Role` class is useful for defining these roles, as shown by the following code:

```python
class ProjectMemberRole(grok.Role):
    grok.name('todo.ProjectMember')
    grok.permissions('todo.view', 'todo.changeitems')

class ProjectManagerRole(grok.Role):
    grok.name('todo.ProjectManager')
    grok.permissions('todo.view', 'todo.changeitems', 'todo.addlists')
```

```python
class AppManagerRole(grok.Role):
    grok.name('todo.AppManager')
    grok.permissions('todo.view','todo.changeitems',
      'todo.addlists','todo.addprojects')
```

Here, we have created four separate roles for different user levels in our application. Each role is assigned a name and one or more permissions by using the `grok.name` and `grok.permissions` declarations respectively.

As you can see, a **role** is simply a collection of permissions with a name. The benefit of using such a collection instead of assigning each permission individually is that once a role is assigned to a user, it's possible to add or remove permissions from the role without having to grant or remove them from each user individually.

Adding authentication

We now have all of our views protected, but so far there are no users, so nobody can be assigned the roles that we created. We need to add a mechanism for creating and managing users, as well as a way to authenticate them and assign roles to them, so that they can use the different views.

The Pluggable Authentication Utility

The **Pluggable Authentication Utility (PAU)** is a framework for authenticating users. It is a part of the Zope Toolkit and currently Grok offers no built-in mechanisms to work with it, but we'll see that it is not too complex.

PAU uses plugins to do its work, so that it's possible to have plugins for different authentication sources, and easily substitute one for another, or even have them work together.

There are two types of plugins for PAU: "credentials" plugins extract credentials from a request (user and password, for example) and "authenticator" plugins check that these credentials are valid and generate a user for the application to work with, if they are.

Registering PAU with our application

To be able to use PAU in our application, we first need to register it as a local utility. A **utility** is simply a service that an application can provide. Being local means that it can store information and configuration specific to each instance of the application.

Here's how we can register PAU in our main `todo` application definition. First, we import `PluggableAuthentication`, which is a factory that will create the actual PAU object. We also import `IAuthentication`, which is the interface that our PAU utility must provide in order to integrate with the authentication machinery.

```
from zope.app.authentication.authentication import
PluggableAuthentication
from zope.app.security.interfaces import IAuthentication
from auth import setup_authentication
```

When we register a PAU utility, we need to configure it to use the appropriate plugins, which is the purpose of the `setup_authentication` import statement in the preceding code.

Now we register the utility by using the `grok.local_utility` directive and passing to the directive the `PluggableAuthentication` factory, the interface that it's going to provide, and the `setup` function. Keep in mind that this directive is in no way exclusive to PAU—any kind of service can be registered like this:

```
class Todo(grok.Application, grok.Container):
    grok.implements(ITodo)
    grok.local_utility(
        PluggableAuthentication, provides=IAuthentication,
        setup=setup_authentication,
        )
```

That's all we need to do for now in the main `app.py` file. Let's add the `setup_authentication` method, and all of the other security classes and views, in another module. Create the `auth.py` file and add the following lines to it:

```
def setup_authentication(pau):
    pau.credentialsPlugins = ['credentials']
    pau.authenticatorPlugins = ['users']
```

This is a very simple method that just assigns a plugin named `credentials` to the `credentialsPlugins` of our PAU, and assigns another plugin named `users` to the `authenticatorPlugins`. The first will take care of extracting the user's credentials from the browser request and making them available to the application. The `users` plugin will be used for authentication. Of course, these plugins do not exist yet; we need to create them.

Adding a credentials plugin

For the credential extraction service, we are going to use a plugin called
`SessionCredentialsPlugin`, which comes with the Zope Toolkit. As its name
implies, this plugin stores the credentials extracted by requesting the session, so
that the application can easily use this information. As we don't need to store any
application-specific information inside the plugin, let's use a global utility this time.

```python
from zope.app.authentication.session import SessionCredentialsPlugin
from zope.app.authentication.interfaces import ICredentialsPlugin

class MySessionCredentialsPlugin(grok.GlobalUtility,
SessionCredentialsPlugin):
    grok.provides(ICredentialsPlugin)
    grok.name('credentials')
    loginpagename = 'login'
    loginfield = 'login'
    passwordfield = 'password'
```

A **global utility** is simply a service that is not stored in the application data, but
resides in a registry that's available to all application instances in Grok. We will
explain utilities in more detail in Chapter 11.

Notice how we inherit from both `grok.GlobalUtility` and the
`SessionCredentialsPlugin` that we mentioned earlier. The `grok.name` directive
is very important here because it assigns a name to the plugin that we configured
earlier in the `setup_authentication` method for our PAU.

After that comes a few class variables that are used to configure how the plugin
works. `loginpagename` is the name of the view that will be shown whenever a
user attempts to access a protected page. Typically, this points to a login form.
`loginfield` and `passwordfield` are the names of the fields within this form that
will contain the credentials of the user. They will be used by the authenticator plugin
to authenticate the user with the application.

The login form

Now that we have configured the credentials plugin, to look for the login
form when a user wants to access a protected view, we might as well create
the form immediately.

First, we define a form schema by using an interface. The `login` and `password` fields should have the exact same names that we configured in the credentials plugin. We added a `camefrom` parameter that will be used to redirect the user to the page he wanted to view before he logged in.

```
class ILoginForm(Interface):
    login = schema.BytesLine(title=u'Username', required=True)
    camefrom = schema.BytesLine(title=u'', required=False)
    password = schema.Password(title=u'Password', required=True)
```

The `SessionCredentialsPlugin` automatically adds this variable to the request when it redirects the user to the login form, so the name has to be the same. That's why we assign an empty string to the form field `prefix` in the following code—to keep the name intact.

Notice that we use the `grok.require` declaration to assign the permission `zope.Public` to the view. This permission is defined in the Zope Toolkit that powers Grok and is assigned to the views that everyone can see. We use this permission to make it explicit that every visitor to our application can get to the login form.

```
class Login(grok.Form):
    grok.context(Interface)
    grok.require('zope.Public')
    label = "Login"
    template = grok.PageTemplateFile('custom_edit_form.pt')
    prefix = ''
    form_fields = grok.Fields(ILoginForm)
```

We need a `setUpWidgets` method inside this class, so that we can make sure that the `camefrom` field is not displayed on the form, which uses the custom template we created back in Chapter 5. This is done so that it looks integrated with the design that we are using.

```
def setUpWidgets(self, ignore_request=False):
    super(Login, self).setUpWidgets(ignore_request)
    self.widgets['camefrom'].type = 'hidden'
```

Finally, the `handle_login` action redirects the user to the `camefrom` URL, or to the site root if `camefrom` is not available. If the user enters invalid credentials, the login form will be displayed again.

```
@grok.action('login')
def handle_login(self, **data):
    self.redirect(self.request.form.get('camefrom',
      self.url(grok.getSite())))
```

That's it. Look at the form in action, in the next screenshot:

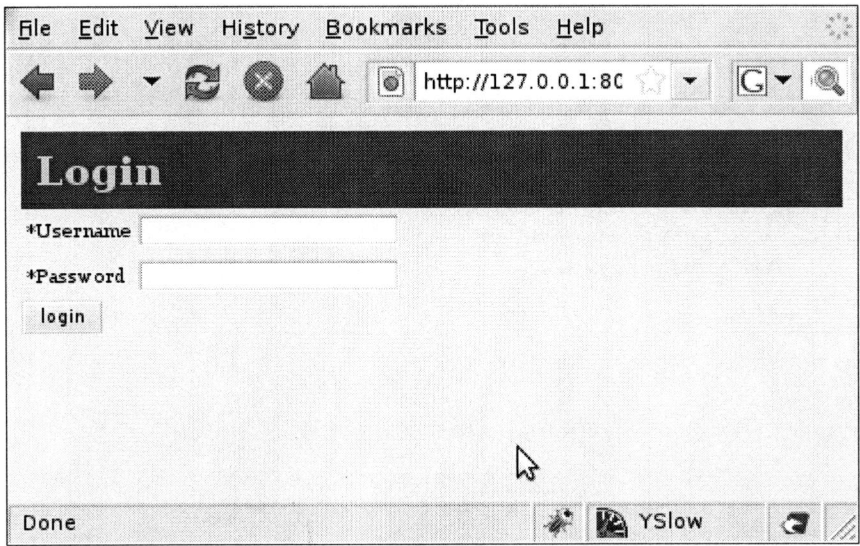

The logout view

We have a login mechanism, so we need a way to finish a session and maybe log in as a different user. We will add a logout view to take care of this requirement:

```python
from zope.app.security.interfaces import IAuthentication,
IUnauthenticatedPrincipal, ILogout

class Logout(grok.View):
    grok.context(Interface)
    grok.require('zope.Public')

    def update(self):
        if not IUnauthenticatedPrincipal.providedBy(
          self.request.principal):
            auth = component.getUtility(IAuthentication)
            Ilogout(auth).logout(self.request)
```

First, we need to determine if the current user is logged in, which we do by getting this information from the request by using `self.request.principal` and checking to see if it provides the `IUnauthenticatedPrincipal` interface. If it does, then we'll know that this user is not authenticated. If it turns out that he is authenticated, we look for our PAU by using `component.getUtility` and calling the `logout` method.

This view needs a template, which we will keep pretty simple for now. Take a look at the next screenshot to see this view in action.

```
<html>
  <head>
    <title>Logged out</title>
  </head>
  <body>
    <p>You are now logged out.</p>
    <p><a tal:attributes="href python:view.url(context)">
       Log in again</a>.
    </p>
  </body>
</html>
```

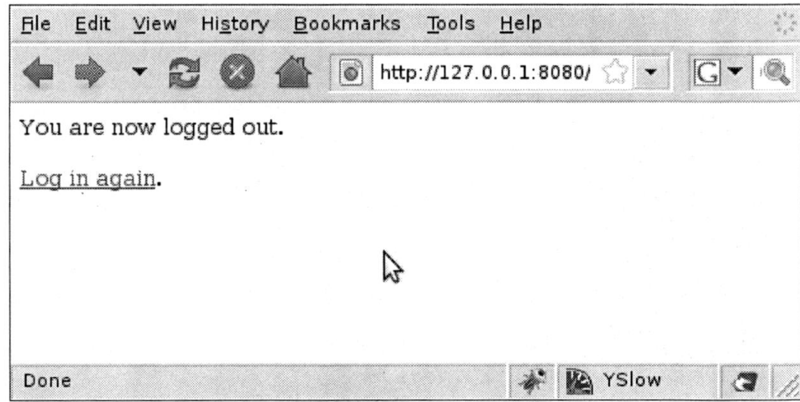

The UserAuthenticator plugin

For the authentication part, we are going to need another local utility because we need to store user information in there. We register the utility in a similar way to the PAU utility, by using the `grok.local_utility` directive. In fact, this code goes just below the PAU declaration in our main application file, `app.py`:

```
from auth import UserAuthenticatorPlugin

grok.local_utility(
    UserAuthenticatorPlugin, provides=IAuthenticatorPlugin,
    name='users',
    )
```

The only difference here is that we pass a `name` parameter that has to correspond to the name that we used for the plugin in the `setup_authentication` method.

We are going to create a Grok container in order to store the user accounts there, so our plugin will know how to create a new user, and to decide if a login attempt has valid credentials for an existing one. Let's look at the authenticator plugin code step-by-step.

First, we need to make some imports, and then comes the plugin definition:

```
from zope.app.authentication.session import SessionCredentialsPlugin
from zope.app.authentication.interfaces import ICredentialsPlugin
from zope.app.authentication.interfaces import IAuthenticatorPlugin
from zope.app.authentication.interfaces import IprincipalInfo

class UserAuthenticatorPlugin(grok.LocalUtility):
    grok.implements(IAuthenticatorPlugin)
    grok.name('users')

    def __init__(self):
        self.user_folder = UserFolder()
```

Notice how we inherit from `grok.LocalUtility` and implement the `IAuthenticatorPlugin` interface. When the utility is initialized (the `__init__` method), we create a user folder and store it there. The user folder is a simple Grok container:

```
class UserFolder(grok.Container):
    pass
```

Now we come to the methods of the plugin itself. The `authenticateCredentials` method is called whenever a login attempt is made. It receives the credentials that the credentials plugin extracted from the request, and then uses the `getAccount` method to try to get a valid account. Next, it calls the account's `checkPassword` method to verify the password against the one from the user's credentials.

```
def authenticateCredentials(self, credentials):
    if not isinstance(credentials, dict):
        return None
    if not ('login' in credentials and 'password' in credentials):
        return None
    account = self.getAccount(credentials['login'])

    if account is None:
        return None
    if not account.checkPassword(credentials['password']):
```

```
        return None
    return PrincipalInfo(id=account.name,
      title=account.real_name,
      description=account.real_name)
```

Notice that the `authenticateCredentials` method returns a `PrincipalInfo` object that contains the account name, the title or display name, and the description for the user. This object implements the `IPrincipalInfo` interface that was imported at the top of the code, which means that you can expect to find similar behavior in other authenticator plugins.

Here's the `PrincipalInfo` class code that is used in this plugin. In addition to the principal information, it holds the credentials and authenticator plugins used to authorize the user.

```
class PrincipalInfo(object):
    grok.implements(IPrincipalInfo)

    def __init__(self, id, title, description):
        self.id = id
        self.title = title
        self.description = description
        self.credentialsPlugin = None
        self.authenticatorPlugin = None
```

The `IAuthenticatorPlugin` interface that we are implementing in this plugin needs to have a `principalInfo` method, which should return the `PrincipalInfo` object that we just defined:

```
def principalInfo(self, id):
    account = self.getAccount(id)
    if account is None:
        return None
    return PrincipalInfo(id=account.name,
      title=account.real_name,
      description=account.real_name)
```

The plugin's most important method is `getAccount`, which tries to find a given user account inside the `user_folder`, and returns that, or `None`, if the user is not found. Right now we are using the Grok ZODB to store the users, but we could easily access a relational database, or an external authentication system instead, by modifying this method.

The implementation is fairly straightforward. We use a Boolean expression to check if the login that was passed into the method is in our `user` folder and if so, return the user object that's inside. Otherwise, we return `None`:

```
def getAccount(self, login):

    return login in self.user_folder and self.user_folder[login]
      or None
```

Adding users

The other important method of our authenticator plugin is `addUser`. This creates an account object with a given username, and then uses this name to assign a role to the user.

```
def addUser(self, username, password, real_name, role):
    if username not in self.user_folder:
        user = Account(username, password, real_name, role)
        self.user_folder[username] = user
        role_manager = IPrincipalRoleManager(grok.getSite())
        if role==u'Project Manager':
            role_manager.assignRoleToPrincipal
              ('todo.ProjectManager',username)
        elif role==u'Application Manager':
            role_manager.assignRoleToPrincipal
              ('todo.AppManager',username)
        else:
            role_manager.assignRoleToPrincipal
              ('todo.ProjectMember',username)
```

After creating a user account inside our `user` folder, the most important bit in this method is the part where we take the role that is passed from the `addUser` form and assign the appropriate role to the new user accordingly.

Observe how we first get the `RoleManager` for the site, as follows:

```
role_manager = IprincipalRoleManager(grok.getSite())
```

Then, when we know what role to apply, we use its `assignRoleToPrincipal` method:

```
role_manager.assignRoleToPrincipal('todo.ProjectMember',username)
```

Here is the account class that we use:

```
from zope.app.authentication.interfaces import IpasswordManager

class Account(grok.Model):
    def __init__(self, name, password, real_name, role):
        self.name = name
```

```
        self.real_name = real_name
        self.role = role
        self.setPassword(password)

    def setPassword(self, password):
        passwordmanager = component.getUtility(IPasswordManager,
          'SHA1')
        self.password = passwordmanager.encodePassword(password)

    def checkPassword(self, password):
        passwordmanager = component.getUtility(IPasswordManager,
          'SHA1')
        return passwordmanager.checkPassword(self.password, password)
```

Account objects need to include the `checkPassword` and `setPassword` methods,
which are used together with a password manager utility. The utility does all of the
heavy work, as the `checkPassword` method simply gets the account password and
passes it, together with the password that the user entered, to the `checkPassword`
method of the `passwordManager`.

The `setPassword` method uses the `encodePassword` method of the `passwordManager`
utility to set the password. You may recall that we saw a 'plain-text' password manager
when we worked with the `site.zcml` declarations at the beginning of this chapter. In
this case, we use a `SHAI` password manager, to be able to store encrypted passwords.

Basic user management

Of course, we need a way to add users to our application. The `addUser` method
of the `UserAuthenticator` is exclusively called by a form that we define using
the interface and schema mechanism for automatic form presentation that were
discussed in Chapter 5. First, we define an interface for the form fields:

```
class IAddUserForm(Interface):
    login = schema.BytesLine(title=u'Username', required=True)
    password = schema.Password(title=u'Password', required=True)
    confirm_password = schema.Password(title=u'Confirm password',
      required=True)
    real_name = schema.BytesLine(title=u'Real name', required=True)
    role = schema.Choice(title=u'User role', values=[u'Project
      Member', u'Project Manager', u'Application Manager'],
      required=True)
```

Then we define the actual `AddUser` form, which uses the fields from the previously defined interface to construct the form. The `handle_add` method uses the Grok `action` decorator to add a button to the form that will call the `addUser` method from the authenticator plugin:

```
class AddUser(grok.Form):
    grok.context(Interface)
    grok.require('zope.ManageApplication')
    label = "Add user"
    template = grok.PageTemplateFile('custom_edit_form.pt')
    form_fields = grok.Fields(IAddUserForm)

    @grok.action('add')
    def handle_add(self, **data):
        users = component.getUtility(IAuthenticatorPlugin, 'users')
        users.addUser(data['login'],data['password'],
          data['real_name'],data['role'])
        self.redirect(self.url(grok.getSite(),'userlist'))
```

Notice how we add a role field that allows the manager to assign one of our defined roles to each user. It's very important to note that this user management view is protected with the `zope.ManageApplication` permission, which is assigned to Zope managers only. If we used one of our own permissions, we would never be able to create a user in the first place. The finished form can be seen in the following screenshot:

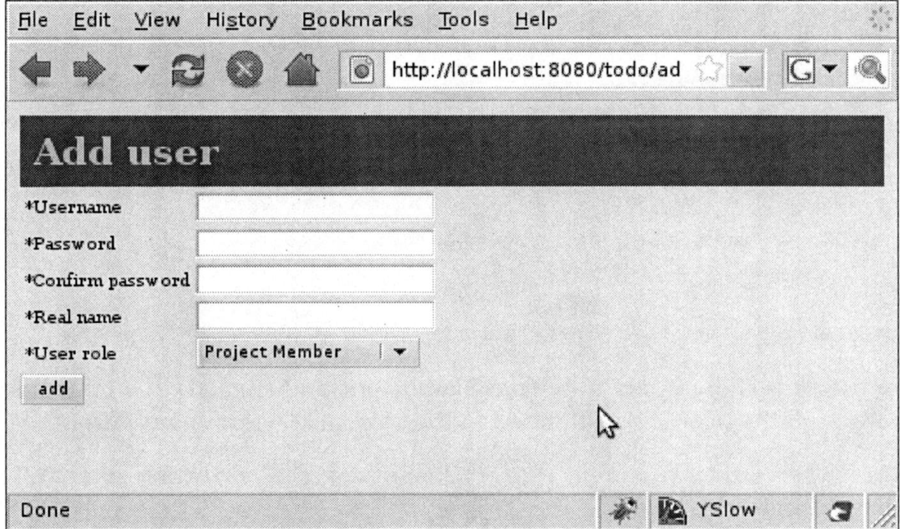

A simple user list view completes the user interface for our user management application:

```
class UserList(grok.View):
    grok.context(Interface)
    grok.require('zope.ManageApplication')

    def update(self):
        users = component.getUtility(IAuthenticatorPlugin, 'users')
        self.users = users.listUsers()
```

Nothing new here. We just get the list of users from the `UserAuthenticator` plugin and pass it on to the view template, which simply lists the users in a table. You should now be familiar with some of this code. First, we insert our stylesheet definition using the static view, to correctly show the URL in the template:

```
<html>
<head>
    <title tal:content="context/title">To-Do list manager</title>
    <link rel="stylesheet" type="text/css"
        tal:attributes="href static/styles.css" />
</head>
```

In the main body of the template, we have the site search form that is a part of the header, and contains the application's title. Then we have a link to add a new user, which points to the form that we just defined.

```
<body>
  <div id="appheader">
    <form id="search"
        tal:attributes="action python:view.url('search')">
      <input type="text" name="query" />
      <input class="new_button" type="submit" value="search" />
    </form>
    <h1 id="apptitle" tal:content="context/title">
        To-Do list manager</h1>
  </div>
  <p class="create"><a href="adduser">Add a new user</a></p>
```

The user listing is shown only if there are any users, and consists of a table that iterates through the user listing defined in the `UserList` view (view/users).

```
<h2 tal:condition="view/users">These are the existing users</h2>
<div class="projects">
<table>
  <tr>
    <th>Login</th>
```

```
        <th>Real name</th>
        <th>Role</th>
    </tr>
    <tr tal:repeat="user view/users">
        <td tal:content="user/name">type</td>
        <td tal:content="user/real_name">type</td>
        <td tal:content="user/role">type</td>
    </tr>
  </table>
  </div>
</body>
</html>
```

That's it. We can now have multiple users with different profiles in our application, as shown in the next screenshot. Create some users and test the permissions and roles to see how it works together.

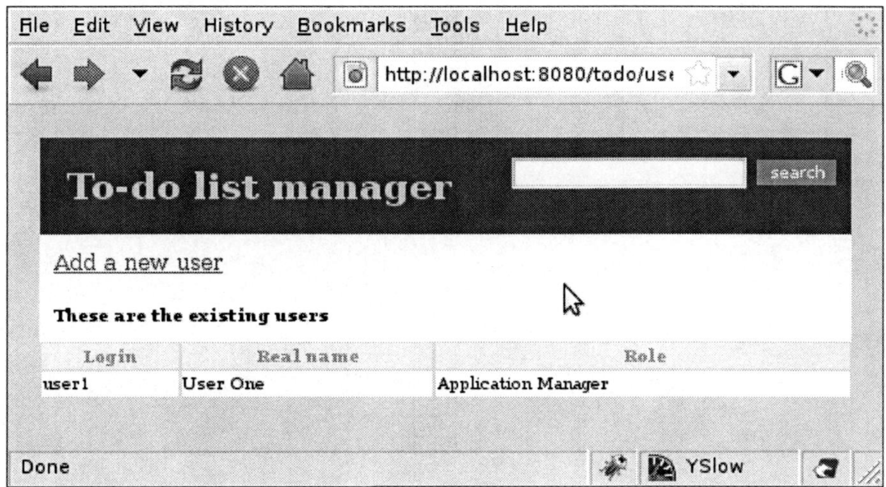

Summary

In this chapter, we learned about Grok's security features, and added authentication and authorization to our application.

8
Application Presentation and Page Layout

Up to this point, we have developed a fairly simple, but a complete application. There are some rough edges that need to be polished, obviously. For example, the templates that we use, all have a different layout, and although they use more or less the same styles and colors, they lack uniformity.

In this chapter, we are going to learn how to lay out an application. Some important points that we will cover include:

- Viewlet managers and viewlets
- Layout definition using viewlets
- Inserting forms into viewlets
- Layers and skins
- Defining an alternative skin for the application

Viewlets and viewlet managers

In a typical web application, there are many parts of its layout that need to be repeated on almost every page. Sometimes these pieces need to be present in different combinations. For example, a login prompt should not appear if the user is already logged in, but a search box should be visible at all times.

Grok solves this problem by allowing the developer to break up web pages into small pieces of HTML called **viewlets**, which can then be assembled as required inside a given view.

Viewlets

Viewlets provide a mechanism for separating the different components of a page into independent pieces, such as header, footer, and navigation. It's possible to further decompose these into HTML snippets, which can be shown on the page or not, depending on contextual information. This concept allows us to have great flexibility in assembling pages.

Unlike a view, which is meant to show a complete page, a viewlet is the representation of an HTML snippet that usually has one clear function.
When using viewlets, we can think of a page as a collection of these snippets.

Viewlet managers

To avoid making a view, keep track of all possible viewlet combinations. Viewlets are assigned to specific viewlet managers. A **viewlet manager** can represent a section of the page layout, such as the header, for instance. Viewlets register with this manager, so that it takes care of their order and rendering. In our header viewlet manager, we could have for example title, login, search box, and main navigation viewlets.

This means that the viewlets are never called directly from a template. Instead, their viewlet manager is called and this, in turn, calls each of its registered viewlets in the desired order and renders them on the page. Viewlet managers have a few other responsibilities:

- Aggregation of all viewlets registered to the manager.
- Applying a set of filters to determine the availability of the viewlets.
- Sorting the viewlets based on an implemented policy. The default is to show them in the order in which they were declared, and Grok can also numerically sort them according to the `grok.order([number])` directive for the viewlets.
- Providing an environment in which the viewlets are rendered.
- Rendering itself, containing the HTML content of the viewlets.

Viewlets can also be tied to specific views, contexts, or permissions, so the overall system is very flexible, and is easier to manage than a collection of macros with conditional tags.

Understanding how the pieces fit together

We now have all of the pieces of how Grok constructs the page layout. When a Grok application serves a page, here's what's going on behind the scenes:

1. The browser makes a request, which contains the desired URL as well as any form input, together with the usual HTTP headers, to Grok.

2. Based on the URL parts, Grok traverses (walks) the site, starting at the root and continuing on to the next part of the URL until it gets to the last model object. This model object is called the **context**.

3. When the model object is found, Grok takes the remainder of the URL and uses it as the name of a view. If there is no URL remainder, the name "index" is used.

4. Once it has the name of the view, Grok finds it and initializes the view, passing to it the context and the request used to find the view.

5. The view usually has a template assigned to it, which is used to render the response to the browser.

6. The template may include calls to a number of viewlet managers, which in turn call their contained viewlets to assemble the HTML that will be returned in the response.

The template is the final result of calling the Grok application, and it represents the rendering of the view. The view, in turn, is associated with a context, which is the model object that has been assigned to that view.

Grok passes a lot of information to the template, in order to let the developer use all of the pieces. This information is in the form of variables that point to the following objects that can be used by the developer to build the template:

*   `request`: The HTTP request that was sent by the browser, including all of the headers.

*   `context`: The model object pointed to by the requested URL. In our application, this could be a project or a to-do list item.

*   `view`: The view that is configured to be used for the context, according to its name. This is the code that is associated with the current template.

*   `viewlet`: Inside a viewlet template, this variable represents the viewlet object.

*   `viewletmanager`: Inside a viewlet template, this variable points to the viewlet manager responsible for the current viewlet.

View methods and attributes

These methods and attributes are a part of the `view` variable, and can be used by the developer, inside the template.

View methods and attributes	Description
`context`	The object that the view is presenting. This is often an instance of a `grok.Model` class, but can be a `grok.Application`, a `grok.Container` object, or any type of Python object.
`request`	The `HTTP Request` object.
`response`	The `HTTP Response` object that is associated with the request. This is also available as `self.request.response`, but the `response` attribute is provided as a convenience.
`static`	Directory resource containing the static files of the view's package.
`redirect(url)`	Redirects to a given URL.
`url(obj=None, name=None, data=None)`	<ul><li>Constructs URL.</li><li>If no arguments are given, constructs the URL to the view itself.</li><li>If only the `obj` argument is given, constructs the URL to `obj`.</li><li>If only `name` is given as the first argument, constructs the URL to context/name.</li><li>If both of the object and name arguments are supplied, constructs the URL to `obj`/`name`.</li><li>Optionally, you can pass a `data` keyword argument that is added to the URL as a `cgi` query string.</li></ul>
`default_namespace()`	Returns a dictionary of namespaces that the template implementation expects to be available always. This method is *not* intended to be overridden by application developers.
`namespace()`	Returns a dictionary that is injected into the template namespace in addition to the default namespace. This method is intended to be overridden by the application developer.

View methods and attributes	Description
`update(**kw)`	This method is meant to be implemented by `grok.View` subclasses. It will be called before the view's associated template is rendered, and can be used to precompute values for the template. `update()` can take arbitrary keyword parameters that will be filled in from the request (in which case they *must* be present in the request).
`render(**kw)`	A view can either be rendered by an associated template, or it can implement this method to render itself from Python. This is useful if the view's output isn't XML/HTML but something computed in Python (such as plain text, PDF, and so on). `render()` can take arbitrary keyword parameters that will be filled in from the request (in which case they *must* be present in the request).
`application_ url(name=None)`	Returns the URL of the closest application object in the hierarchy, or the URL of a named object (`name` parameter) relative to the closest application object.
`flash(message, type='message')`	Sends a short message to the user.

Viewlet methods and attributes

From inside a viewlet template, the following methods and attributes are available to the developer:

Viewlet methods and attributes	Description
`context`	Typically, this is the model object for which this viewlet is being rendered in the context of.
`request`	The `Request` object.
`view`	A reference to the view that the viewlet is being provided in.
`viewletmanager`	A reference to the `ViewletManager` that is rendering this viewlet.
`update()`	This method is called before the viewlet is rendered, and can be used to perform precomputation.
`render(*args, **kw)`	This method renders the content provided by this viewlet.

Viewlet manager methods and attributes

The `viewletmanager` variable is available to developers from inside a viewlet.
These are the methods and attributes that it contains:

Viewlet manager methods and attributes	Description
`context`	This is typically the model object for which this `ViewletManager` is being rendered in the context of.
`request`	The `Request` object.
`view`	A reference to the view in which the `ViewletManager` is being provided.
`update()`	This method is called before the `ViewletManager` is rendered, and can be used to perform precomputation.
`render(*args, **kw)`	This method renders the content provided by this `ViewletManager`. Typically this will mean rendering and concatenating all of the viewlets managed by this `ViewletManager`.

In addition to these methods, the viewlets contained inside the viewlet manager can
be accessed using standard Python dictionary syntax.

To-do list manager layout

For our application then, we will use viewlets to generate the layout. First, let's
define our layout structure, which will be more or less what we have now. Take
a look at the following screenshot:

It's a very simple layout. Each of the three sections (**Header**, **Main**, and **Footer**) represents a viewlet manager and the list of things inside these sections refers to the viewlets that will be needed. To do this in a page template, we need to use a special kind of template expression called a **provider**. This is how our master template will look:

```
<!DOCTYPE html PUBLIC "-//W3C//DTD XHTML 1.0 Transitional//EN"
        "http://www.w3.org/TR/xhtml1/DTD/xhtml1-transitional.dtd">
<html xmlns="http://www.w3.org/1999/xhtml" xml:lang="en"
      lang="en">
<head>
    <tal:headslot content="structure provider:headslot" />
</head>
<body>
  <div id="header">
    <tal:header content="structure provider:header" />
  </div>
  <div id="main">
    <tal:main content="structure provider:main" />
  </div>
  <div id="footer">
    <tal:footer content="structure provider:footer" />
  </div>
</body>
</html>
```

As we are thinking about our application's final presentation, the first thing to note is that we inserted a correct `<DOCTYPE>` declaration. We also removed the `<title>` and `<style>` tags from the header, as they will go inside a viewlet now.

We define four layout areas: headslot, header, main, and footer. The content for each one of those will be provided by a separate viewlet manager. The `provider:name` expression tells Grok to find a viewlet manager with this name, render all of its registered viewlets, and return them in their configured order. As you may recall, the `structure` prefix means to interpret whatever comes from the function call as HTML to be rendered.

Defining viewlet managers in application code

We looked at the template first, to see how it relates to the desired layout, but we actually need to define some viewlet managers and viewlets to make this work. Fortunately, Grok has `Viewlet` and `ViewletManager` classes that we can use for this. First, let's define our viewlet managers:

```
class HeadSlot(grok.ViewletManager):
    grok.context(Interface)
    grok.name('headslot')
```

```
class Header(grok.ViewletManager):
    grok.context(Interface)
    grok.name('header')

class Main(grok.ViewletManager):
    grok.context(Interface)
    grok.name('main')

class Footer(grok.ViewletManager):
    grok.context(Interface)
    grok.name('footer')
```

That's it. We just subclass from `grok.ViewletManager` and Grok will pretty much do it all for us. The key part is the `grok.name` class declaration, as the name we use here is the one that goes inside the provider expressions in the templates. The `grok.context` directive uses `Interface` because it is the most general declaration possible, so doing this will enable the managers in all of our application's views and models.

Registering viewlets

To get the viewlets going, we need to modify our application a bit. Up to now, we have been using separate views to define what goes on on each page and who can see it. As may be apparent from the master template that we just defined, this will now be the responsibility of the viewlets themselves.

To convert our application to use viewlets, the first step is to take the parts that we want to turn into viewlets from the `dashboard.pt` template and put them in their own templates. We'll do the title first, as an example. In the project, create a file named `apptitle.pt` and enter the following code into it:

```
<div id="apptitle">
  <h1 tal:content="context/title">To-Do list manager</h1>
</div>
```

Right now, this contains only the title, but we could eventually include a logo and other similar elements.

To register this viewlet with a viewlet manager, the `Viewlet` class is used as a base, and the `grok.viewletmanager` class is invoked:

```
class AppTitle(grok.Viewlet):
    grok.viewletmanager(Header)
    grok.context(Interface)
    grok.order(2)
```

That's it. This viewlet will be registered with the `Header` viewlet manager defined earlier. Viewlets also require a context, to let the viewlet managers know if they are to be displayed in the current context or not. As is the case for viewlet managers, we use `Interface` as the context, so that the viewlet is enabled everywhere in the application. Also note the `grok.order` directive, which is useful for specifying the order that the viewlet manager should use when rendering the viewlets. If `grok.order` is not used, the viewlets will be rendered in the order that they are defined.

A `Viewlet` class is very similar to a view. It has an `update` method to prepare it for rendering, and a `render` method to do the actual rendering. If these methods are omitted, Grok simply renders the corresponding template, which in this case is `apptitle.pt`.

Now let's go for the other simple viewlets. The template for the head section, `head.pt`, looks like this:

```
<meta tal:attributes="http-equiv string:Content-Type; content
string:text/html;;charset=utf-8" />
<title tal:content="context/title">To-Do list manager</title>
<link rel="stylesheet" type="text/css"
      tal:attributes="href static/styles.css" />
```

The template for the search box, `searchbox.pt`:

```
<div id="searchbox">
  <form id="search"
   tal:attributes= "action python:view.url('search')">
     <input type="text" name="query" />
     <input class="new_button" type="submit" value="search" />
  </form>
</div>
```

The logged in information and logout link, `loggedin.pt`, is as follows:

```
<div id="loggedin">
  <p>
    <span
    tal:content="string:Logged in as ${request/principal/title}">
    </span>
    <a tal:attributes="href python:view.url('logout')">(Log out)</a>
  </p>
</div>
```

And a simple navigational aid, `navigation.pt`, is defined as:

```
<div id="navigation">
  <a tal:attributes="href python:view.url('index')">Go back to main
    page</a>
</div>
```

For the footer, we will use a simple **Powered by Grok** message, along with Grok's logo, which will be defined in `grokpowered.pt`:

```
<div id="grokpowered">
  <a href="http://grok.zope.org">
     <img border="0" tal:attributes="src static/groklogo.png" />
  </a>
  <span id="poweredtext">Powered by Grok!</span>
</div>
```

Now we'll register these viewlets with their managers. We just need to add the appropriate class declarations in `app.py`, as follows:

```python
class Head(grok.Viewlet):
    grok.viewletmanager(HeadSlot)
    grok.context(Interface)

class SearchBox(grok.Viewlet):
    grok.viewletmanager(Header)
    grok.context(Interface)
    grok.order(1)

class LoggedIn(grok.Viewlet):
    grok.viewletmanager(Header)
    grok.context(Interface)
    grok.order(4)

class Navigation(grok.Viewlet):
    grok.viewletmanager(Header)
    grok.context(Interface)
    grok.order(3)

class GrokPowered(grok.Viewlet):
    grok.viewletmanager(Footer)
    grok.context(Interface)
```

This way, the `Header` viewlet manager has four viewlets registered in a specific order. The `Footer` has just one viewlet at the moment.

Modifying existing views to use the master template

We already have several working views in our application. To get them to use the new layout defined in the master template, we need to do two things:

- Make them use the master template
- Create viewlets that show the main parts of the old template

The first part is easy; we just need to use the `grok.template` directive to force each view to use the master template, like this:

```
class DashBoard(grok.View):
    grok.context(Todo)
    grok.name('index')
    grok.require('todo.view')
    grok.template('master')
```

The viewlet itself is very similar to the other ones that we have defined, with the addition of a couple of lines:

```
class DashBoardViewlet(grok.Viewlet):
    grok.viewletmanager(Main)
    grok.context(Todo)
    grok.template('dashboard_viewlet')
    grok.view(DashBoard)
```

We use the `grok.template` directive to force the viewlet to use the `dashboard_viewlet` template. The `grok.view` directive is used next, to make this viewlet show up only in the `DashBoard` view. We have to do this to prevent multiple viewlets that are registered with the `Main` viewlet manager from showing up all at once in every view. In other words, this means that the `DashBoardViewlet` will only be rendered inside the `Main` viewlet manager when the user is browsing the default view of the application, which happens to be the `DashBoard` view.

To make this work, we need an additional step. Currently, we have the template `dashboard.pt` in the `app_templates` directory. We can't keep this name because then the `DashBoard` view would have two possible templates to use and Grok will refuse to guess which one to use. Therefore, we'll change the name to `dashboard_viewlet.pt`, which is what we put in the `grok.template` directive.

The final step is to change the template itself, and remove all of the structure from it. This structure is now included in the `master.pt` template. This is the result:

```
<div id="dashboard">
  <p class="create"><a href="add">Create a new project</a></p>
  <h2 tal:define="projects context/values"
      tal:condition="projects">These are your available projects</h2>
  <div class="projects">
  <table>
    <tr>
      <th>Project name</th>
      <th>Kind</th>
      <th>Description</th>
      <th>Created on</th>
      <th>Last modified</th>
      <th>Owner</th>
      <th>Delete</th>
    </tr>
    <tr tal:repeat="project context/values">
      <td>
        <a href="" tal:attributes="href python:view.url(project)"
                   tal:content="project/title">title</a>
      </td>
      <td tal:content="project/kind">type</td>
      <td tal:content="project/description">type</td>
      <td tal:content="project/creation_date">type</td>
      <td tal:content="project/modification_date">type</td>
      <td tal:content="project/creator">type</td>
      <td>
        <a tal:define="url python:view.url('deleteproject')"
           tal:attributes="href
             string:${url}?project=${project/__name__}">
          <img border="0" tal:attributes="src static/bin_closed.png" />
        </a>
      </td>
    </tr>
  </table>
  </div>
</div>
```

We have to perform the same steps to make the `TodoSearch` and `UserList` views work. We'll end up with `TodoSearchViewlet` and `UserListViewlet` declarations, along with `todosearch_viewlet.pt` and `userlist_viewlet.pt` templates. The `ProjectIndex` view requires extra work, because of its use of JavaScript. We'll see how to fix that later in this chapter.

For now, you can take a look at the next screenshot and see how the layout works:

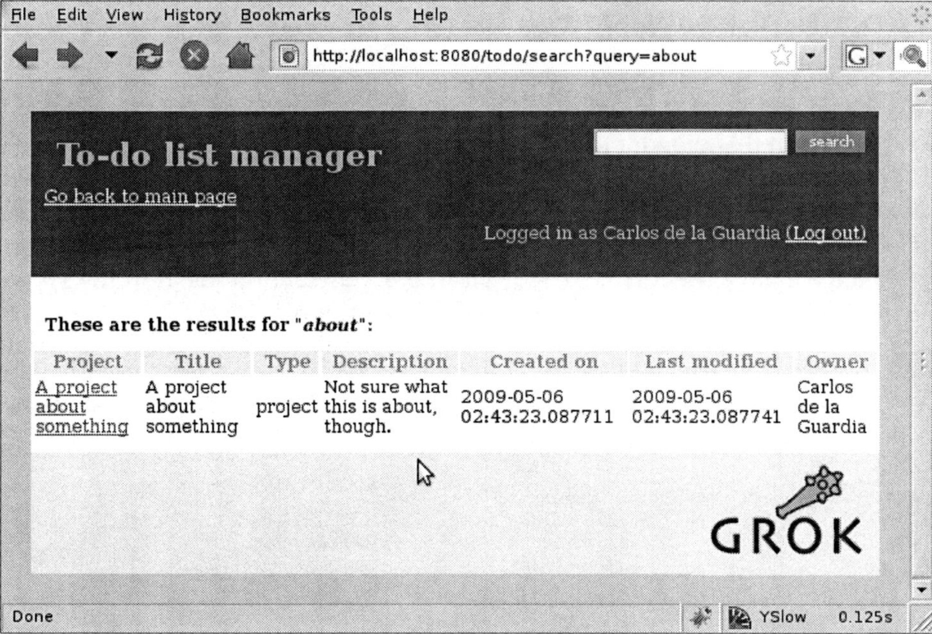

Project	Title	Type	Description	Created on	Last modified	Owner
A project about something	A project about something	project	Not sure what this is about, though.	2009-05-06 02:43:23.087711	2009-05-06 02:43:23.087741	Carlos de la Guardia

Inserting forms into viewlets

As the "add user" and "add project" forms are generated automatically, they are still not using our new layout. We have to put these forms inside a viewlet so that we can take advantage of the layout. This requires a bit more work because the viewlet needs to render the form.

```python
class AddProject(grok.View):
    grok.context(Todo)
    grok.template('master')

class AddProjectViewlet(grok.Viewlet):
    grok.viewletmanager(Main)
    grok.context(Todo)
    grok.view(AddProject)

    def update(self):
        self.form = getMultiAdapter((self.context, self.request),
         name='add')
        self.form.update_form()

    def render(self):
        return self.form.render()
```

We previously defined the `AddProjectForm` and gave it the name "add". This code uses that form directly to render the viewlet. First, we define a view that will use the master template. We keep the same context that the real form uses, which is `Todo` in this case.

Next, we create a viewlet that we register with the `Main` viewlet manager in the same context. We assign this viewlet to the view that was just defined. The trick here is to get hold of the form, which we do by using the `getMultiAdapter` method imported from `zope.component`. We'll have more to say about adapters in Chapter 11, but for now, take it on faith that this call will get us the form named "add" in the current context. Once we have the form, we store it in the viewlet and use it in the viewlet's `render` method in order to pull the rendering from the real form.

That's all there is to it, we just need to change the link in `dashboard_viewlet.pt` to point to "addproject" instead of just "add", and we'll get the result that we want, as shown in the following screenshot:

Using viewlets to insert different static resources

We have almost converted the whole application to use our new layout. The only thing missing is the project view. The problem with this view is that it uses some JavaScript code that is not used elsewhere, so we need to include it in the header, somehow.

As we already have a `headslot` viewlet manager, the easiest way to accomplish this is by registering a viewlet with this manager that will only be applied to the project view. We have done this before. The trick is to use the `grok.view` directive to make the viewlet show only for the selected view:

```python
class ProjectJavascript(grok.Viewlet):
    grok.viewletmanager(HeadSlot)
    grok.context(Project)
    grok.view(ProjectIndex)
```

We can now add a new template named `projectjavascript.pt` that will include our JavaScript calls:

```
<script type="text/javascript" tal:attributes = "src static/todo.js">
</script>
<script tal:define="url python:view.url('settitle')"
 tal:content="string:window.onload = hideControls;;
 settitleurl = '${url}';;">
</script>
```

Now the JavaScript code will work properly in this view and the project viewlet can be seen without problems.

Layers and skins

We have shown how building a flexible layout is possible by using viewlets. Grok allows us to have even more flexibility, by using layers and skins.

The look and feel of our application was created by combining some viewlets and using appropriate CSS styles. The final combination can be thought of as the 'theme' of the application. In Grok, the name we use for this is 'skin'.

A **skin** represents the look and feel of our application. It should be possible to rearrange all of the viewlets and edit the styles to create a totally different look and feel without changing the way that the application works. Thus, having a mechanism to handle skins allows us to easily create themes for our applications or create special skins for other uses, such as mobile browser presentation, views that respond to specific HTTP verbs (known as REST views, which are actually built like this inside Grok), or special power-user skins, depending on who is logged in.

To simplify the creation and use of skins, they are composed of a number of layers, each of which will include only the parts of the look and feel that are different for them. This makes it easy to reuse most of the application UI and focus only on what's particular to the skin in question.

Skins in Grok

In Grok, all views and viewlets have to be assigned to a layer. Up to now, this has been happening in the background because by default there is a layer that all of them use. This is called the **default browser layer**. All applications in Grok have a default skin, which has no name and is composed of only one layer.

However, the difference between a skin and a layer is subtle. In reality they are very similar, but a skin has a name that will be known to the user, whereas a layer is anonymous. The intention is to have skins consisting of a number of layers, and to use the name to refer to the result.

Adding themes to our application

Let's add different themes to our application by using skins. We'll make it very simple for now. We already have a viewlet that includes the `<link>` tag for our stylesheet. To design a theme, we'll simply create a layer that overrides this viewlet and uses a different stylesheet. In this way, we can create a new theme just by adding seven lines of code, a template, and a stylesheet.

We are using blue for the masthead of our application. We'll add a second theme, which uses red, and another one that uses green. As the names will be known to the users, we'll use fancy names: the red theme will be called "martian" and the green theme will be known as "forest".

A layer in Grok needs to inherit from the `IDefaultBrowserLayer` defined in `zope.publisher`. So the first thing we need to do is to import that:

```
from zope.publisher.interfaces.browser import IDefaultBrowserLayer
```

We can now define the skins in `app.py`, as follows:

```python
class MartianLayer(IDefaultBrowserLayer):
    grok.skin('martian')


class ForestLayer(IDefaultBrowserLayer):
    grok.skin('forest')
```

For each skin, we just define a class based on `IDefaultBrowserLayer`, and then use the `grok.skin` directive to name it. This name will be used to browse to the skin.

Overriding a viewlet

Now that we have the skins, we can override the `Head` viewlet, where the stylesheet link is defined. This viewlet is managed by the `HeadSlot` viewlet manager. To override a viewlet, we just have to create another one, with the same name:

```python
class HeadMartian(grok.Viewlet):
    grok.viewletmanager(HeadSlot)
    grok.context(Interface)
    grok.name('head')
    grok.template('head_martian')
    grok.layer(MartianLayer)


class HeadForest(grok.Viewlet):
    grok.viewletmanager(HeadSlot)
    grok.context(Interface)
    grok.name('head')
    grok.template('head_forest')
    grok.layer(ForestLayer)
```

Notice how the `HeadMartian` and `HeadForest` viewlets have exactly the same viewlet manager, context, and name as those used by the `Head` viewlet that they override. The difference is that they will use another template. To make the `HeadMartian` viewlet work only on the `MartianLayer` skin, we add the `grok.layer` directive and pass it to the skin. Keep in mind that `grok.layer` can be used in any viewlet or view that we define, so we could override anything from the application, or create new views or viewlets that appear only when using a specific skin.

In this case, this is all the code that needs to be added to these two themes for our application. We just need to add the templates and styles and we are done. For the martian theme, we directed the viewlet to use the `head_martian` template, so we create a file named `head_martian.pt` and add the following code to it:

```
<meta tal:attributes="http-equiv string:Content-Type; content
string:text/html;;charset=utf-8"/>
<title tal:content="context/title">To-Do list manager</title>
<link rel="stylesheet" type="text/css"
      tal:attributes="href static/styles_martian.css" />
```

The only change is the name of the stylesheet in the `<link>` tag.

For the forest theme, we'll create the `head_forest.pt` file and add the same text, except that we have to change the name of the CSS file to `styles_forest.css` in order to use the correct stylesheet.

All that's left now is to add the new stylesheets. To keep things simple, we'll just copy the `styles.css` file to `styles_martian.css` and `styles_forest.css`, and then make some color substitutions. Using your favorite text editor, change all occurrences of `#223388` to `#883322` in martian and to `#338822` in forest. Other than that, the themes will be exactly the same, but we'll easily be able to see the difference. Feel free to make more style changes if you like.

Using the new skins

To actually see the new skins, we need to tell Grok that a different skin than the default has to be used. The simplest way to do this is to use the special `++skin++` name in the URL, along with the skin name. Grok will see this, and use the correct skin.

For example, we'll see the martian skin if we point the browser to the following URL: `http://localhost:8080/++skin++martian/todo`. Notice how the `++skin++` name goes immediately after the hostname. Grok will signal an error if we put it anywhere else in the URL. To see the forest skin, just change the word `martian` to `forest` in the preceding URL. See the next screenshot to take a look at the martian skin:

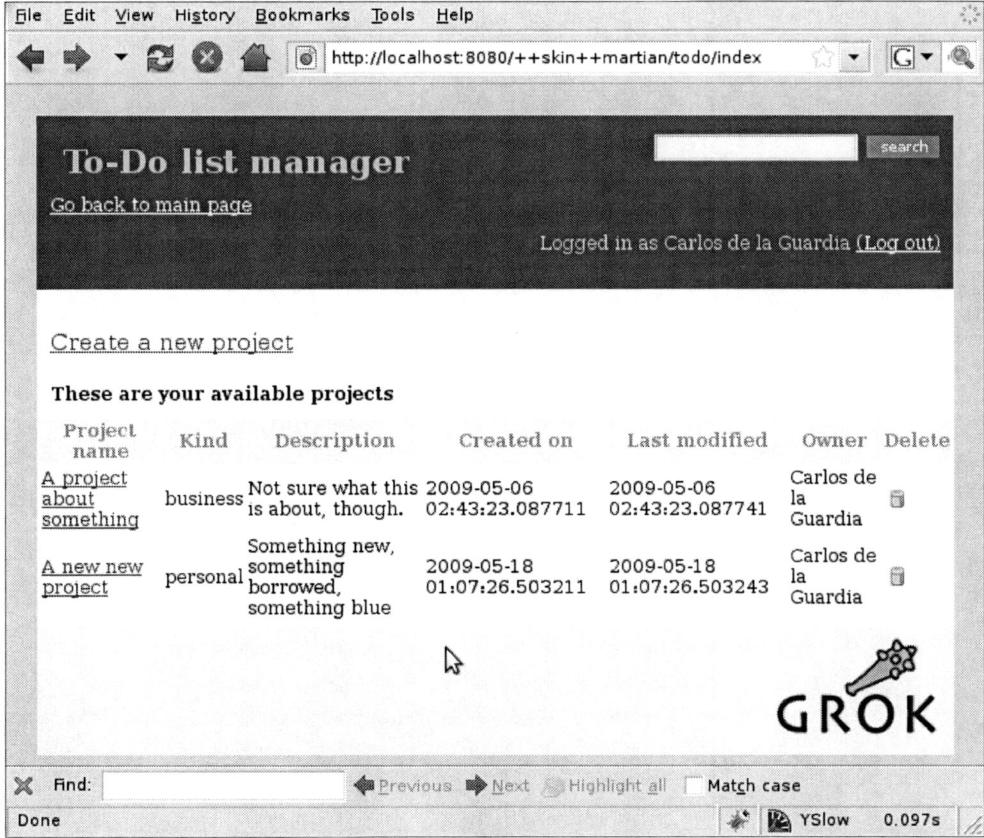

We are done. If we browse through the application, we'll see that all of the pages now show the header with the corresponding background color.

Of course, asking the user to type the name of the skin in the URL will not do for production use. In Chapter 11, we'll see how to let the user choose a skin via a preferences menu, and get Grok to apply the correct skin itself.

Summary

In this chapter, we learned about Grok's layout and presentation facilities, including viewlets, layers, and skins. We modified our application to have a consistent look and feel, by using these tools. We will now go on to learn about the ZODB and how Grok uses it.

9
Grok and the ZODB

As we stressed right from the first chapter, one of the most important pieces of Grok is the ZODB. The capability to store objects transparently has allowed us to create a complete application without having to think about persisting its data.

Although Grok takes care of what little ZODB interaction our application needs behind the scenes, there are a few more things that the ZODB can do, and we will review them in this chapter. In particular, we will see:

- How the ZODB works
- What ZODB storage is
- How to add file attachments to our application by using Blob support
- How to pack the database and why this is recommended
- How to use the ZODB outside Grok

How the ZODB works

Before we get into the details of how to use other ZODB functionality, let's talk a bit more about how ZODB works.

Simply put, the ZODB is a persistence system for Python objects. Its objective is to make persistence as transparent as possible, so that any changes to objects can automatically be saved to disk and read again when they are needed.

ZODB is an object database, which means that instead of partitioning objects into one or more tables according to a data schema, the objects themselves are written to the database in their current state. In a relational database system, once a row of data is read from the database, the program still needs to reassemble the columns of information to get a real object instance. In an object database system, an object instance is immediately there when you fetch it from the database.

Transparency

Because it's possible to store objects directly into the database as they are, very little effort is needed to make an object ZODB aware. In other words, objects are stored transparently. Due to this, although there are some cases where a little more work is needed, objects can generally be persisted in the database simply by meeting one simple requirement: to subclass from the `persistent.Persistent` class provided by the ZODB.

When instances of persistent objects are modified, they are marked by the ZODB mechanisms, and the changes can be written to the database, if the user requests this. Of course, more than one modification could be requested at the same time. A group of one or more changes to stored objects is known as a **transaction**, and when the objects are written, the transaction is said to have been **committed**.

A transaction can also be aborted, so that modifications to objects made since the last commit are forgotten. It's also possible to roll back an already committed transaction, leaving the database in a previous state.

ACID properties

If you have worked with relational databases, all this talk about transactions should be familiar to you. You might also know that transactional systems need to make sure that the database never gets into an inconsistent state, which they do by supporting four properties, known by the acronym **ACID**:

- **Atomicity**:

  Either all of the modifications grouped in a transaction will be written to the database or, if something makes this impossible, the whole transaction will be aborted. This ensures that in the event of a write error or a hardware glitch, the database will remain in the previous state and avoid inconsistencies.

- **Consistency**:

  For write transactions, this means that no transaction will be allowed if it would leave the database in an inconsistent state. For read transactions, this means that a read operation will see the database in the consistent state it was at the beginning of the transaction, regardless of other transactions taking place at that time.

- **Isolation**:

  When changes are made to the database by two different programs, they will not be able to see each other's transactions until they commit their own.

- **Durability**:

  This simply means that the data will be safely stored once the transaction is committed. A software or hardware crash after that will not cause any information to be lost.

Other ZODB features

In addition to being ACID compliant, the ZODB provides several other features that make it a really good option for industrial-strength data management.

- **In memory caching**:

  Every time an object is read from the database, it is kept on a cache in memory, so that subsequent accesses to this object consume less resources and time. The ZODB manages the cache transparently, and automatically removes the objects that have not been accessed for a long time. The size of the cache can be configured, so that machines with more memory can take better advantage of it.

- **Undo**:

  The ZODB provides a very simple mechanism for rolling back any committed transaction, which is possible because it keeps track of the database state before and after every transaction. This makes it possible to undo the changes in a transaction, even if more transactions have been committed after it. Of course, if the objects involved in this transaction that we need to undo have changed in later transactions, it will not be possible to undo it because of consistency requirements.

- **History**:

  As every transaction is kept in the database, it is possible to see an object as it was in previous transactions, and compare it with its current state. This allows a developer to quickly implement simple versioning functionality.

- **Save points**:

  As changes made during a single transaction are kept in memory until the transaction is committed, memory usage can skyrocket during a transaction where lots of objects are modified at the same time (say, a `for` loop that changes a property on 100,000 objects). Save points allow us to commit part of a transaction before it has finished, so that changes are written to the database and the memory that the changes had occupied is released. These changes in the save points are not really committed until the whole transaction is completed, so that if it is aborted, any save points will be rolled back as well.

- **Blobs (Binary large objects)**:

  Binary large objects, such as images or office documents, do not need all of the versioning facilities that the ZODB offers. In fact, if they were handled as regular object properties, blobs would make the size of a database increase greatly, and generally slow things down. That's why the ZODB uses a special storage for blobs, which makes it feasible to easily handle large files up to a few hundred megabytes without performance problems.

- **Packing**:

  As we have seen, the ZODB keeps all versions of the objects stored in it. This means that the database grows with every object modification and can reach really large sizes, which may slow it down. The ZODB allows us to remove old revisions of stored objects via a procedure known as *packing* the database. The packing routine is flexible enough to allow only objects older than a specified number of days to be removed, keeping the newer revisions.

- **Pluggable storages**:

  By default, the ZODB stores the database in a single file. The program that manages this is called a **file storage**. However, the ZODB is built in such a way that other storages can be plugged in without needing to modify it. This feature can be used to store ZODB data in other media or formats, as we'll see later in more detail.

ZEO

ZEO stands for **Zope Enterprise Objects** and is a network storage for the ZODB. By using ZEO, any number of Grok instances can connect to the same ZODB. ZEO can be used to provide scalability, because the load can be distributed between several ZEO clients instead of only one.

We'll learn more about ZEO in Chapter 14.

Using the ZODB

To store objects, the ZODB makes use of a root object, which is basically a container for other objects. Contained objects, in turn, can also act as containers, which means that the ZODB structure can be expressed using a tree.

The rules of persistence

Not all object modifications can be automatically detected and transparently written to the database. As we saw earlier in this book, there are some rules about how to make an object persistent and what conditions require additional work:

- Inherit from `persistent.Persistent` (a class defined in the ZODB code) or one of its subclasses.

- Class instances have to be related to each other in a hierarchical structure. The ZODB has a root object, and this object contains other objects, which can in turn contain further objects, thereby forming a tree.

- When modifying mutable attributes of persistent objects that are not persistent themselves, the persistence machinery has to be notified, by setting the special `_p_changed` attribute of the instance to `True`.

Traversal

To get to a particular object inside the database, the ZODB always starts with the root object and recursively goes inside any containers until it finds the object. This is called **traversal**, because every containing object in the visited object's path has to be touched to get to it.

This means that a unique object can be identified by its path within the database. By design, URL paths can be mapped pretty well to a ZODB structure, so when we have a URL in Grok, every element of its path usually represents an object that has to be traversed to get to a specific object. The exception is sometimes the last element of the path, which can also represent a view.

How Grok uses the ZODB

We haven't had to do anything directly with the ZODB so far, because Grok has already set up everything to take advantage of the ZODB's transparency. Grok's models and containers already inherit from `persistence.Persistent`, so modifications to any of our model objects are automatically saved to the database.

In addition, Grok's URL-resolving mechanism uses traversal to get to the persisted objects, so we don't have to keep track of where we put what, in order for Grok to get us the correct object.

However, Grok can't help us avoid the ZODB requirement to signal the persistence machinery about changes to mutable objects. Remember, whenever changes are made to mutable attributes, the application needs to inform the ZODB that there has been a change. This is done by setting the special _p_changed attribute of the instance to True:

```
self.context.p_changed_ = True
```

If you use regular Python mutable objects, such as lists and dictionaries, you have to remember this rule, which is not a lot to ask for, but still can be easy to forget. For precisely this reason, the ZODB package includes a couple of replacements for these built-in Python types:

```
From persistent.list import PersistentList
From persistent.dict import PersistentDict
```

These two types are exact equivalents of the built-in Python types, except they take care of setting p_changed when needed. Consider using them if you need a list or a dictionary in your applications.

Adding Blob support to our application

Many applications need to allow external files to be uploaded and stored, be it office documents, images, multimedia, or other kinds of files. As processing these files by using the ZODB can prove costly in terms of resources and bandwidth, it's better that we show how to take advantage of the ZODB Blob support now.

Adding messages to projects

Right now, the projects in our application have only tasks. This was enough when we had a single-user application, but now that multiple users can log in and have different roles, a mechanism for communicating with other users about the state of the tasks would come in handy.

Let's add a **messages** tab to the project view, where anyone can post a message. A message will have a title, the message text, and optionally will allow users to upload a file.

The megrok.form package

We could add some code to enable a Grok form field to use blobs, but sometimes, it's a lot easier to find a package that already does what we need, and then integrate that into our project instead.

As Grok uses the Zope Toolkit, there are hundreds of packages available to choose from. There are also many packages that have been created specifically for Grok. Just go to the Python Package Index (PyPI) page and you will see that there are a lot of packages ready for downloading.

In this case, there is a package that does exactly what we need, which is to make the use of blobs easy. This package is called `megrok.form`, and we are going to integrate it into our project. It is available at `http://pypi.python.org/pypi/megrok.form`.

Adding an external package to our project

Integrating a package from the PyPI is fairly easy with Grok. The first step is to add it to the project install requirements, which are specified inside the `setup.py` file at the root of our project. Find this file, and change the `install_requires` assignment to look like this:

```
install_requires=['setuptools',
                  'grok',
                  'grokui.admin',
                  'z3c.testsetup',
                  'megrok.form',
                  # Add extra requirements here
                  ],
```

Next, run `bin/buildout` from the command line. The `megrok.form` package and its dependencies will be downloaded and installed into the project. In this case, we added `megrok.form`, but of course, we could pick any other package from PyPI and add it to our project in the same way.

How blob support is configured in Grok

By default, Grok is preconfigured to use the blob storage, so it's simple to take advantage of it. You can see how this configuration is done if you take a look at the `zope.conf` file in the `parts/etc/` directory of our project. The relevant section looks like this:

```
<blobstorage>
<filestorage>
  path /<your directory>/todo/parts/data/Data.fs
</filestorage>
  blob-dir /<your directory>/todo/parts/data/blobs
</blobstorage>
```

The messaging class and schema

Now that we have the supporting packages and configuration that we need, let's get the **messages** tab going. We'll go through the code quickly, as most of the concepts have been used earlier in our application.

First, we add a `Message` class that will store the messages and their attachments. The context of this class will be the `Project` class, as we want messages to be stored by project. Of course, we start by defining the interface for the class:

```
class IMessage(interface.Interface):
    subject = schema.TextLine(title=u'Subject')
    message = schema.Text(title=u'Message text')
    attachment = BlobFile(title=u'Attachment',required=False)
```

We keep it simple, by adding only `subject`, `message`, and `attachment` fields. Note that the field where we'll store the attachment is declared as a `BlobFile`. For this declaration to work, we of course need to include the following import at the top of the file:

```
from megrok.form.fields import BlobFile
```

Now, find the actual class definition, where we just implement the interface, and add a `searchableText` method, to allow messages to appear in search results:

```
class Message(grok.Model):
    grok.implements(IMessage, IMetadata, ISearchable)
    subject = u''
    message = u''
    content_type = 'message'

    def searchableText(self):
        return self.subject+self.message
```

We need a form for creating the messages and uploading the attachment, so that's our next step. This will create an `add_message` form that will require the `todo.changeitems` permission to be used. The fields come from the interface defined earlier, and we use the template for custom edit forms that we created in Chapter 5.

```python
class AddMessageForm(grok.AddForm):
    grok.context(Project)
    grok.name('add_message')
    grok.require('todo.changeitems')
    form_fields = grok.AutoFields(IMessage)
    label = "Add a new message"
    template = grok.PageTemplateFile('custom_edit_form.pt')
```

The key part of the form is the add action, where the message is created and its properties are set with the values from the form. Notice that both messages and lists use the same `next_id` counter for their name, so the `content_type` class attribute becomes very important. This will be used to get only messages or only lists, depending upon the view:

```python
@grok.action('Add message')
def add(self,**data):
    message = Message()
    message.creator = self.request.principal.title
    message.creation_date = datetime.datetime.now()
    message.modification_date = datetime.datetime.now()
    message.project = self.context
    message.project_name = self.context.__name__
    self.applyData(message,**data)
    id = str(self.context.next_id)
    self.context.next_id = self.context.next_id+1
    self.context[id] = message
    return self.redirect(self.url('messages'))

def setUpWidgets(self, ignore_request=False):
    super(AddMessageForm,self).setUpWidgets(ignore_request)
    self.widgets['subject'].displayWidth = 50
    self.widgets['message'].height = 12
```

You can see this form in action in the following screenshot:

The message viewlet

Next, we create the view and viewlet for showing the messages. The view performs a catalog search by using the content type. Of course, we first need to add to our `ProjectIndexes` class (from Chapter 6), so that it gets indexed, as now there are two different kinds of objects that can be stored inside a project (messages and lists). We also have to change the catalog search of `todo` lists to use this new index. Here is the view code:

```
class ProjectMessages(grok.View):
    grok.context(Project)
    grok.name('messages')
    grok.require('todo.view')
    grok.template('master')
```

```python
def update(self):
    catalog = getUtility(ICatalog)
    self.messages = catalog.searchResults
      (content_type=('message','message'),
        project_name=(self.context.__name__,self.context.__name__))
```

For the viewlet, we simply define a template and set the view to the one that we just created:

```python
class ProjectMessagesViewlet(grok.Viewlet):
    grok.viewletmanager(Main)
    grok.context(Project)
    grok.template('projectmessages_viewlet')
    grok.view(ProjectMessages)
```

The message list template

The project messages viewlet uses a new template named `projectmessages_viewlet`. We will show a couple of links at the top that will function more or less like tabs, for switching between list and messages views:

```html
<div id="project">
  <h1 id="apptitle" onclick="editTitle();"
      tal:content="context/title">To-Do list manager</h1>
  <ul id="project-tabs">
    <li><a tal:attributes="href python:view.url('index')"
           title="Project lists">Lists</a></li>
    <li><a tal:attributes="href python:view.url('messages')"
           title="Project messages">Messages</a></li>
  </ul>
  <h2>Here you can add new messages relating to this project.</h2>
  <p class="create"><a href="add_message">Create a new
    message</a></p>
```

After that, we show the messages and their contents by using a "repeat" structure. The most important part of the template for the purposes of this chapter is the link for downloading the attachment, which uses the `view.url` method to point to the download view. Note that a message may not include an attachment, which is why the paragraph with the link has a condition for either showing it or not:

```html
<tal:block repeat="message view/messages">
  <div class="message">
    <h3><span tal:replace="message/subject">subject</span>
      <a tal:define="url python:view.url('deletemessage')"
         tal:attributes="href
            string:${url}?message=${message/__name__}">
         <img border="0"
         tal:attributes="src static/bin_closed.png" /></a>
    </h3>
```

```
        <p class="message_info"
           tal:content="string:By ${message/creator},
             on ${message/creation_date}">
        info
        </p>
        <p tal:content="message/message">text</p>
        <p tal:condition="message/attachment">
           <a tal:attributes="href python:view.url(message,'download')">
             Download attachment
           </a>
          ( <span tal:replace="message/attachment/filename">filename
            </span>,
            <span tal:replace="message/attachment/size">size</span>
            bytes )
        </p>
      </div>
    </tal:block>
  </div>
```

Some CSS styles were added to the project as well. These are not shown here.
Please check the source code for this book to see what they are.

Downloading an attachment

The last step is to add a view for downloading an attachment. We do not need
to show a template here; we have to return the file. This is how it is done:

```
class Download(grok.View):
    grok.context(Message)
    grok.require('todo.changeitems')

    def update(self):
        self.data = self.context.attachment.data
        self.filename = self.context.attachment.filename

    def render(self):
        self.response.setHeader('Content-Disposition',
          'attachment; filename=%s;' % self.filename)
        return self.data
```

First, we get the filename and the file data from the attachment in question, in the
`update` method. Then, in the `render` method, we set the `Content-Disposition`
`response` header to `attachment` and pass the filename to it, so that the browser will
know which file to download by using its original name, directly. Finally, we return
the file data.

Testing the Blob support

We are now ready to run the application. The following screenshot shows the way it should look. Try adding a few messages and files, and then take a look at the contents of the `blob` directory that you specified in the `zope.conf` file. You should see a `blobs` directory containing one directory for each file that you uploaded.

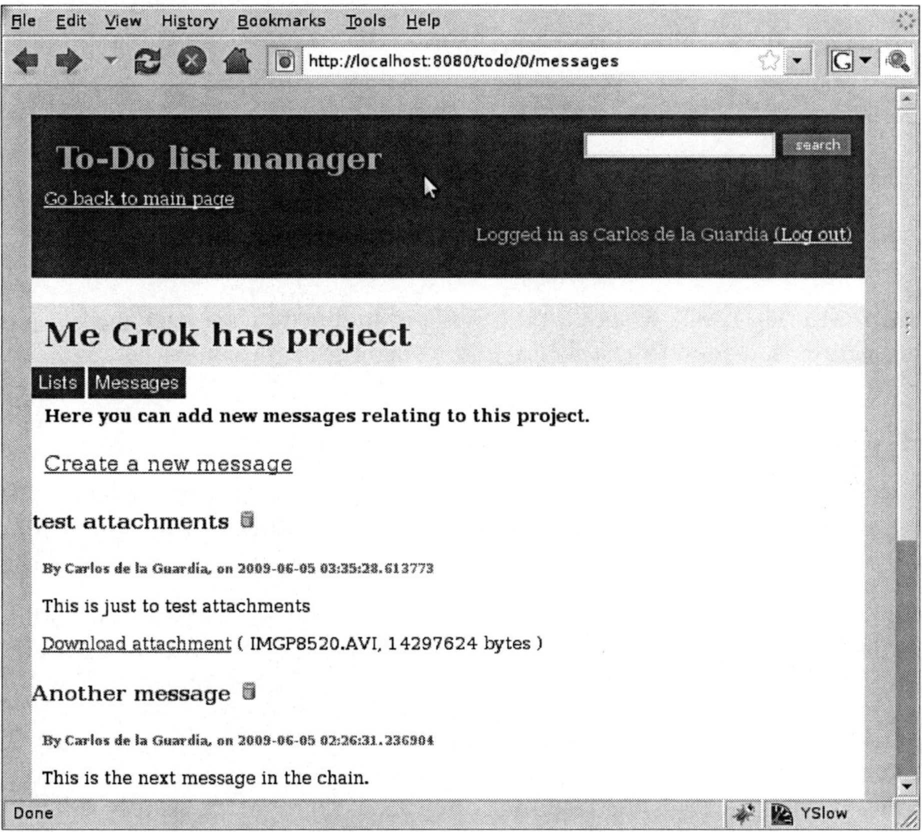

Taking advantage of transactions

We have been saying from the beginning of this chapter that the ZODB is transactional, but so far we haven't seen the benefits that we get from this. Possibly the most important benefit is the ability to roll back, or undo, a transaction.

Using zope.app.undo

As Grok handles the transaction commits for us, we haven't had the chance to show it, but we'll now see how to undo and even redo transactions. The easiest way to show this is to use the `zope.app.undo` package available in the PyPI. We will add it to the project in the same way that we inserted `megrok.form`, earlier in this chapter. Edit the `setup.py` file at the root of the project and add the following code to it:

```
install_requires=['setuptools',
                  'grok',
                  'grokui.admin',
                  'z3c.testsetup',
                  'megrok.form',
                  'zope.app.undo',
                  # Add extra requirements here
                  ],
```

Now rerun `bin/buildout` to let Grok download and install the package. No other action is needed to enable it—just restart the application.

Testing the undo functionality

Create an instance of the todo application, and add a project. Then add a list inside that project, with the title `test undo`. Now delete the list that you have just created. You will see an empty project once again.

To undo the transaction, we'll have to use the Grok management interface, which we used earlier, when learning about the catalog, in Chapter 6. Point your browser to the following URL: `http://localhost:8080/todo/@@undoMore.html`.

You should see a list of transactions, similar to the one in the next screenshot. The screen shows the last ten transactions for the todo application instance visited. The transaction at the top is the last one committed. To revert it, simply select the checkbox to its left, and then click on the **Undo** button at the bottom of the screen.

Now go back to your project. The list that you deleted is magically back there. If you go back to the list, you'll notice that the undo operation itself is now listed as a transaction, so you can "redo" the old transaction, by undoing the transaction that is now at the top.

"Undo" is a powerful feature, and the one that can make you look like a hero in the eyes of your application users. It's also possible to undo multiple transactions at the same time. However, a transaction can only be undone if the objects on which it operated have not been modified by a later transaction. This means that undoing a mistake is something that has to be done quickly, before new transactions can complicate things.

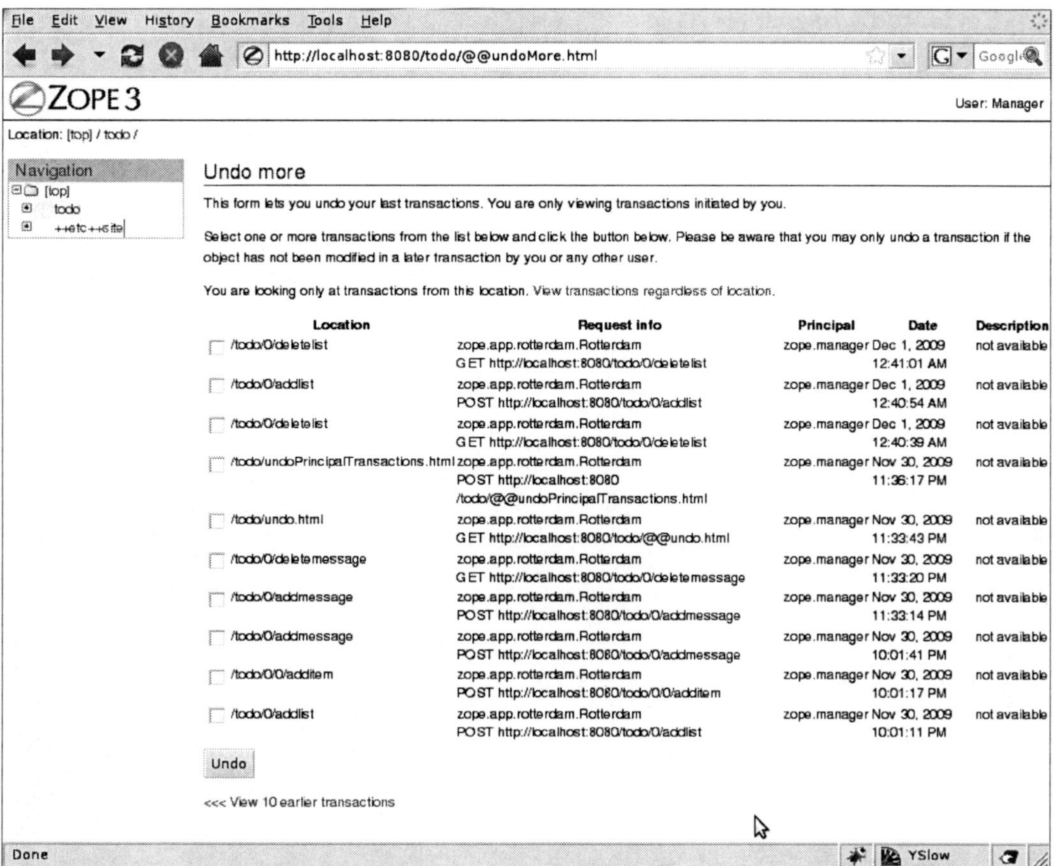

ZODB maintenance

As with any other database system, the ZODB needs some maintenance, from time to time. The main thing that can happen is that the database size will grow to occupy a large amount of disk space, causing some tasks to become slower.

File storage

As we mentioned before, the ZODB keeps track of all of the versions of a stored object, which makes ZODB grow every time an object changes. Packing allows the ZODB to get rid of older versions of objects, thus reducing the database size.

The database is usually contained in a file named `Data.fs`, which is located under `parts/data` in our `project` directory.

Packing is a process that can take some time, and thus it runs on a separate thread. A backup copy of the database file is created before the packing starts, in case something goes wrong, so be aware that you will need to have at least as much free disk space as the current size of the ZODB, in order to be able to pack it.

In Grok, the easiest way to pack the database is to go to the administration interface and click on the **Server Control** link. This will take you to a control panel where the option to pack the current database is shown (see the next screenshot). To pack the database, simply select the number of days beyond which object revisions should be removed. The packing process will be started, and when it's finished, there will be a message at the top of the control panel notifying you of this.

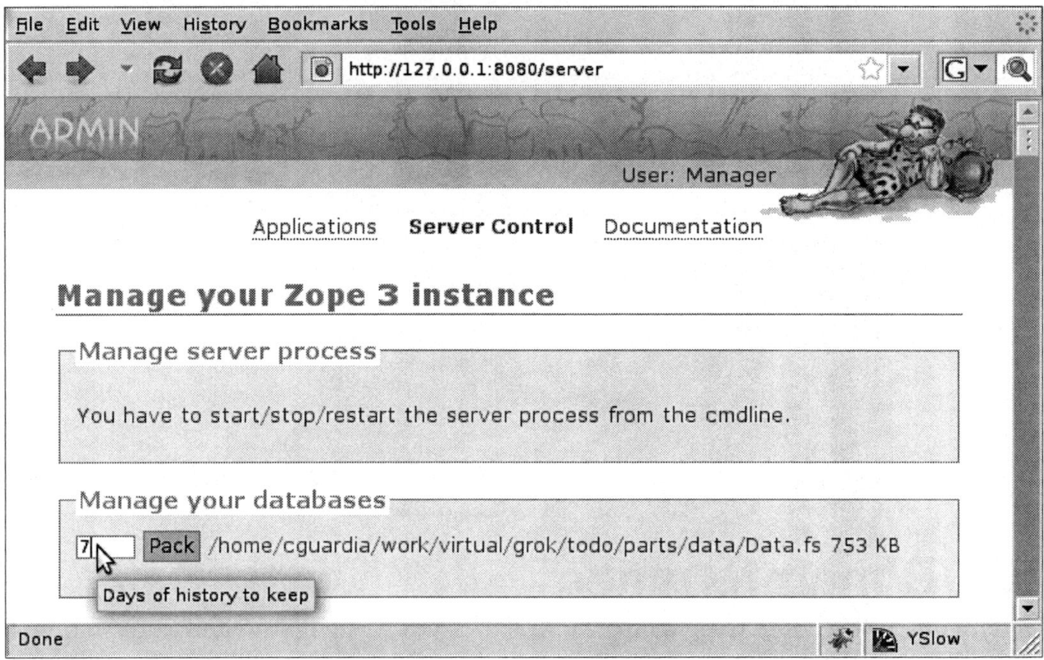

Automatic packing

In most cases, packing will be a good thing to do frequently, unless for some reason you absolutely need to keep track of every revision of every object, ever. Packing the database once a week, for example, could be a good way to keep the database size in check and also to make tasks such as backing up, easier and faster.

Of course, manually packing the database every time could be a burden to an administrator, and is easily forgotten, so an automatic way of performing the packing comes in handy.

Packing is an expensive operation, and doing it from outside Grok requires a separate database connection, which is why using ZEO is a good idea, even if our scalability demands do not call for it. As ZEO allows multiple connections, packing can be done from another ZEO client, without needing to stop the regular service.

This task is so necessary that the Grok installation already makes a script available to pack the ZODB by using ZEO. It's called `zeopack`, and can be found under the `bin` directory of the main Grok installation. To use it, simply make sure that the ZEO server is running, and then call the script with the host and port of the site:

```
$ bin/zeopack -h localhost -p 8080
```

This script call could be added to a UNIX cron script to perform the task weekly, or as frequently as needed.

Backing up

As with all important data handling services, backups are greatly encouraged when using the ZODB. Exactly how often to make backups can vary depending on the type of application, but it should be done regularly.

The Grok installation includes a script, called `repozo`, to facilitate backups. This script allows incremental or full backups to be taken, and can be used both for backing up and restoring a `Data.fs` file. To backup our database, we can first create a directory, called `backups` inside our Grok main directory and then use:

```
$ bin/repozo -B -r backups  -f todo/parts/data/Data.fs
```

The `-B` option means to perform a backup action. The `-f` options gives the path to the `Data.fs` file that we want to backup. The first time, `repozo` will make a full backup to the `backups` directory (specified by the `-r` option). Further calls will result in incremental backups unless the database has been packed after the last backup.

To recover a `Data.fs` file from a `repozo` backup, we use the `-R` option:

```
$ bin/repozo -R -r backups -o RecoveredData.fs
```

This command will recover the latest backup and output the recovered file to `RecoveredData.fs` (specified by the `-o` option). It's also possible to recover a backup from a specified date, by using the `-D` option with a date in the format "yyyy-mm-dd".

Using the ZODB without Grok

The ZODB is a very powerful package, and there is no reason why we couldn't use it on regular applications outside Grok, too. In fact, many simple applications that are usually developed by using a relational database (mainly because that's what most developers are used to) can be even simpler if the ZODB is used.

To show how easy it is to work with the ZODB from Python, we'll show a simple example. All that's needed to follow along is to have Python installed, and to use `easy_install` to get the ZODB3 egg, or download the ZODB package from `http://pypi.python.org/pypi/ZODB3`.

Create a file named `zodb_demo.py`. First, let's create a small class that will take care of opening and closing the connection to a `FileStorage`. Add the following code at the start of your `zodb_demo.py` file:

```python
from ZODB import FileStorage, DB
import transaction

class ZODBHandler(object):
  def __init__(self, path):
    self.storage = FileStorage.FileStorage(path)
    self.db = DB(self.storage)
    self.connection = self.db.open()
    self.dbroot = self.connection.root()

def close(self):
  self.connection.close()
  self.db.close()
  self.storage.close()
```

First, we make a few imports. `FileStorage` is needed to define the file where the database will be stored, `DB` is the actual ZODB library, and `transaction` is used for committing changes to the database.

Next, we create a class named `ZODBHandler` that will take a file path and initialize a file storage for our ZODB. If the file passed in the path exists, it will be used as the database; if it does not exist, it will be created. Either way, we don't have to worry about this, as `FileStorage` takes care of it for us. With this, we have a storage that we can pass to the `DB` class on the following line. After that, we can open a connection and once this is done, we get the root object of the database and store it in `dbroot`. From there, we can work with the database, as we will see shortly.

The other thing that our ZODB handler does, is close the connection and storage when we have finished using them, by means of a `close` method that we can call when we want.

We can now initialize a database, and start writing data to it:

```python
if __name__ == _'__main__':
    db = ZODBHandler('./Data.fs')
    dbroot = db.dbroot
    dbroot['pi'] = 3.14159265358979323
    dbroot['planet'] = 'Earth'
    dbroot['primes'] = [1, 2, 3, 5, 7, 11]
    dbroot['pycon'] = { 2009: 'Chicago', 2010: 'Atlanta' }
    transaction.commit()
```

We pass our handler a path that will create a file named `Data.fs` in the current directory. Next, we get the root object of the database that is stored there. We then add several objects, just to show that any Python object that is pickable can be stored in the database. Finally, we need to commit the transaction, in order to actually save the changes.

To fetch an object from the database, we simply need to refer to it by its key, much like a dictionary works:

```python
print dbroot['primes']
```

Deleting an object is also quite easy:

```python
del dbroot['planet']
transaction.commit()
```

Of course, most applications will not use built-in Python objects, but will create their own classes that subclass from `persistent.Persistent`. Insert the following class definition before the `if` statement, above:

```python
from persistent import Persistent
class Project(Persistent):
    def __init__(self, title, kind, description):
        self.title = title
        self.kind = kind
        self.description = description
```

We can now store projects transparently in our database. Append the following lines at the end of the program:

```
dbroot['project 1'] = Project('test project', 'business',
 'A simple test project')
dbroot['project 2'] = Project('another project', 'personal',
 'a personal project')
transaction.commit()
print dbroot['project 1'].title
dbroot['project 1'].title = 'new title'
transaction.commit()
```

This is a very simple example, but hopefully you can see the potential for creating interesting ZODB-backed applications. No SQL is needed, just plain Python objects.

Summary

In this chapter, we have learned more about the ZODB, and learned how to take advantage of its features, such as blob handling. We also learned a bit about ZODB maintenance and the need to pack the database frequently. Finally, we tried our hand at using the ZODB outside Grok, as a regular Python library.

10

Grok and Relational Databases

So far, we have been using the ZODB for data storage. As we saw in the last chapter, this is a fine solution. Grok developers truly love the ZODB and would like to see it used a lot more across the Python world. Furthermore, Grok takes excellent advantage of its power and features.

Having said that, relational databases are currently the most commonly used persistence mechanism for web applications. For one thing, they are reliable, efficient, and scalable. They are also fairly well understood, and many novice web developers already happen to know a thing or two about SQL.

The fact that relational databases are used consistently for non-web-development projects also makes them more likely to be needed in web applications where access to existing information is required.

In other words, the ZODB is great, but a good web framework needs to offer ample support for working with relational databases. Of course, Grok is such a framework, so in this chapter, we'll find out what facilities Grok has for relational database access. Here are some specific things that we will cover:

- Why is it important that Grok allows developers to use relational databases easily
- What an Object Relational Mapper is
- How to use SQLAlchemy with Grok
- How to change our authentication mechanism to use a relational database instead of the ZODB

Object Relational Mappers

Python is an object-oriented language, and Grok uses this object orientation heavily. In practice, this means that we define models with properties and methods, and each model instance represents an object. Thus, we have project or to-do list objects, and our views work with them, and access their properties and call their methods, freely.

When it's time to save our objects, the ZODB comes in handy because we just grab the whole object and stuff it in there, which is why it's called an object database. Relational databases, on the other hand, work in a very different way. They store everything using tables and columns, usually dividing an object into several related tables.

Obviously, we can't just take one of our to-do list objects and put it into a relational database; some translation is needed, even if there's only one table involved. Relational databases use the SQL language to receive read and write commands for a table or tables, so we could take our object's properties one-by-one, generate a SQL statement as a string, and send it to the database. We would then reverse the process to assemble the object again from the database columns. This doesn't really scale well, so the usual solution is to use a library specifically designed for disassembling objects into tables and assembling them back when queried, transparently generating the required SQL to make it work. These libraries are known as **Object Relational Mappers**, or **ORMs** for short.

ORMs are also very good at keeping the code independent of the database used, because the developer performs operations in terms of objects, and the ORMs generate a SQL specific for a database, behind the scenes. This makes it a lot easier to switch databases in a project without getting into time-consuming syntax changes in the SQL used.

SQLAlchemy

There are many ORMs for Python, but perhaps the most popular one is **SQLAlchemy**. One of the reasons for its popularity is that SQLAlchemy, in addition to being a powerful ORM, offers a data abstraction layer for constructing SQL expressions in a platform-independent way. This gives the developer ample flexibility to work with the model objects without worrying about database or SQL details, but still have the ability to get down to the SQL level if needed, for performance or other reasons.

SQLAlchemy supports a dozen databases, including SQLite, Postgres, MySQL, Oracle, and MS-SQL. It organizes pending operations into queues and flushes them all in one batch, providing efficiency and transaction safety. SQL clauses can be built by using Python functions and expressions, thus allowing the complete range of language constructs to be used. It also takes care of connection pooling, helping to optimize the use of system resources.

Including SQLAlchemy in our Grok project

We already saw in the previous chapter how to include a Python package from the PyPI in our project. Just add the package to the `install_requires` variable in the project's `setup.py` file:

```
install_requires=['setuptools',
                  'grok',
                  'grokui.admin',
                  'z3c.testsetup',
                  'megrok.form',
                  'SQLAlchemy',
                  # Add extra requirements here
                  ],
```

After that, rerun the buildout and the package should be included:

$ bin/buildout

Once we've done that, SQLAlchemy is ready to use.

Using SQLAlchemy

To get a feel of how SQLAlchemy operates by itself, let's try it directly from the Python prompt first. Go to the top directory of the project and type:

$ bin/python-console

This will start the Python interpreter in the command line. As we already ran the buildout with the SQLAlchemy package, we should be able to import from it:

>>> from sqlalchemy import create_engine

>>> engine = create_engine('sqlite:///:memory:',echo=True)

The `create_engine` method is used to tell `sqlalchemy` which database to interact with. The first parameter is called a **connection string** and contains all the information required to connect to the database, such as database name, username, and password. In this example, we use SQLite, which is a lightweight database included with Python since version 2.5. SQLite allows us to work in memory instead of creating a database on disk. As we are just testing, we can use this feature.

The `echo` parameter is passed a value of `True` so that we can see the SQL generated by SQLAlchemy in the console output.

Now we'll do a few more imports:

```
>>> from sqlalchemy import Column, Integer, String
>>> from sqlalchemy.ext.declarative import declarative_base
>>> Base = declarative_base()
```

The `Column` class is used to define a table column. `Integer` and `String` are column data types. We'll use them to define our table.

Next, we import `declarative_base`, which allows us to create a base class for use with our object models. To use it, we have to call it and assign the result to the variable that will act as a base class for our model.

We are now ready to create a model:

```
>>> class User(Base):
...         __tablename__ = 'users'
...         id = Column(Integer, primary_key=True)
...         name = Column(String)
...         realname = Column(String)
...         role = Column(String)
...         password = Column(String)
...         def __init__(self, name, real_name, role, password):
...             self.name = name
...             self.real_name = real_name
...             self.role = role
...             self.password = password
```

In this example, we create a `User` class for storing user data. We have to use the `Base` class that we just created with `declarative_base` for SQLAlchemy to be able to work transparently with this model. A `__tablename__` attribute is needed as well to designate the name of the table in the database that will store the model's information.

Next, the columns are defined using the `Column` class and the types we imported earlier. Note the use of the `primary_key` parameter to make `id` the primary key for this table.

Last, we need to define an `__init__` method to set the column values on creation. After this is done, SQLAlchemy can create the table:

```
>>> metadata = Base.metadata
>>> metadata.create_all(engine)
2009-06-30 03:25:36,368 INFO sqlalchemy.engine.base.Engine.0x...5ecL
PRAGMA table_info("users")
2009-06-30 03:25:36,368 INFO sqlalchemy.engine.base.Engine.0x...5ecL ()
2009-06-30 03:25:36,381 INFO sqlalchemy.engine.base.Engine.0x...5ecL
CREATE TABLE users (
    id INTEGER NOT NULL,
    name VARCHAR,
    realname VARCHAR,
    role VARCHAR,
    password VARCHAR,
    PRIMARY KEY (id)
)
```

The table metadata is stored in the `metadata` attribute of the `Base` class and it can be used to create the table, via the `create_all` method. This method needs to be passed to the engine that we created earlier, to know what dialect of SQL to use and how to connect to the actual database. Notice how the generated SQL is displayed immediately after an SQLAlchemy method call. You can see that the name of the table is the one that we defined by using the `__tablename__` attribute earlier.

Once the table is created, we can populate it with our `User` objects. To do so, we first need to create a session:

```
>>> from sqlalchemy.orm import sessionmaker
>>> Session = sessionmaker(bind=engine)
>>> session = Session()
```

The `sessionmaker` method works in a way similar to that of `declarative_base` and produces a class that we can call to create the actual session. Session creation is done in this way to allow SQLAlchemy to create a specific `Session` class for an engine definition, which is passed to `sessionmaker` by using the `bind` parameter. Once we have a `sessionmaker` tailored to our engine, we can create the database session, and we are ready for our first object instance:

```
>>> grok_user = User('grok','Grok the Caveman','todo.
ProjectMember','secret')
>>> session.add(grok_user)
```

We create an instance of the `User` class, which represents the user 'grok'. To put it in the session queue, we use the `add` method. At this point, the `User` object is ready to be written to the database:

```
>>> session.commit()
2009-06-30 03:30:28,873 INFO sqlalchemy.engine.base.Engine.0x...5ecL
BEGIN
2009-06-30 03:30:28,874 INFO sqlalchemy.engine.base.Engine.0x...5ecL
INSERT INTO users (name, realname, role, password) VALUES (?, ?, ?, ?)
2009-06-30 03:30:28,874 INFO sqlalchemy.engine.base.Engine.0x...5ecL
['grok', None, 'todo.ProjectMember', 'secret']
2009-06-30 03:30:28,875 INFO sqlalchemy.engine.base.Engine.0x...5ecL
COMMIT
```

We use the `commit` method to save the changes to the database. Once again, we can look at the generated SQL in the console output. Now we can query the database by using Python constructs and use the data as we please:

```
>>> for user in session.query(User):
...         print user.name, user.real_name
...
2009-06-30 03:32:18,286 INFO sqlalchemy.engine.base.Engine.0x...5ecL
BEGIN
2009-06-30 03:32:18,287 INFO sqlalchemy.engine.base.Engine.0x...5ecL
SELECT users.id AS users_id, users.name AS users_name, users.realname
AS users_realname, users.role AS users_role, users.password AS users_
password
FROM users
2009-06-30 03:32:18,288 INFO sqlalchemy.engine.base.Engine.0x...5ecL []
grok Grok the Caveman
```

In the preceding example, we use the `query` method of the session to get all of the stored `User` objects, which right now are exactly one. We then print the `name` and `real_name` attribute values of the result.

Once we are finished, we should close the session:

```
>>> session.close()
```

Of course, there's a lot more that the SQLAlchemy can do, but giving an in-depth explanation goes beyond the purpose of this book. There's ample documentation available at the project's website, including a tutorial.

Using a relational database for authentication

We have seen how to use SQLAlchemy by itself, so now we can try to do something with it in our project. One area where relational database connectivity usually comes in handy for a web application, is the authentication process. This is because most of the time, in real enterprise settings, web applications are not isolated but form a part of a series of tools that a company can use in its daily work. It's quite common to have a single database to store all of the company users instead of having a separate database per application.

We will show how to turn our authentication database from a ZODB folder into a relational database table by using SQLAlchemy. To begin, add the following lines to the top of `auth.py`, just after the imports:

```python
from sqlalchemy import create_engine
from sqlalchemy import Column, Integer, String
from sqlalchemy.ext.declarative import declarative_base
from sqlalchemy.orm import sessionmaker


engine = create_engine('sqlite:///todo.db',echo=True)
Base = declarative_base()
Session = sessionmaker(bind=engine)
```

We used these imports and the engine setup statements in the previous section. The only difference is that instead of using an in-memory database, we will now use a file to keep our data. SQLite allows us to pass a relative path in the connection string to create a file for the database. In this case, the file will be named `todo.db` and will be stored in the same directory as the root of the project.

As we are now going to store user data in the database, we don't need the user folder anymore, so we delete its definition from the code. Remove these two lines:

```python
Class UserFolder(grok.Container):
    pass
```

With that out of the way, the next step is to modify the definition of the `Account` class:

```python
class Account(Base):
    __tablename__ = 'users'
    id = Column(Integer, primary_key=True)
    name = Column(String)
    real_name = Column(String)
    role = Column(String)
    password = Column(String)
```

```
def __init__(self, name, password, real_name, role):
    self.name = name
    self.real_name = real_name
    self.role = role
    self.setPassword(password)

def setPassword(self, password):
    passwordmanager = component.getUtility(IPasswordManager,
      'SHA1')
    self.password = passwordmanager.encodePassword(password)

def checkPassword(self, password):
    passwordmanager = component.getUtility(IPasswordManager,
      'SHA1')
    return passwordmanager.checkPassword(self.password, password)
```

Instead of using `grok.Model` as the base class, we switch to the `Base` class from
`declarative_base`. Then, we define the columns, using the same names as in
the already existing properties as declared in the `__init__` method. Note that all
of the other methods of the class remain unchanged from the `grok.Model`-based
`Account` class.

Now that we have an SQLAlchemy-based `Account` class, we can use any
SQLAlchemy functionality that we may need in the code. In this case, we have to
change the `UserAuthenticatorPlugin` implementation to access the database for
user listing, user creation, and user deletion.

Here's the new implementation. Notice that the `authenticateCredentials` and
`principalInfo` methods have not changed from the previous definition, so they are
not included:

```
class UserAuthenticatorPlugin(grok.LocalUtility):
    grok.implements(IAuthenticatorPlugin)
    grok.name('users')

    def __init__(self):
        metadata = Base.metadata
        metadata.create_all(engine)
```

The `__init__` method uses the `metadata.create_all` method with the predefined
engine to create the database table when the plugin is initialized.

```
def getAccount(self, login):
    session = Session()
    result = session.query(Account).filter_by(name=login).first()
    return result
```

To get an account, we start a session and then query the Account class by using the filter_by method, which returns only the database rows that match the login passed. SQLAlchemy allows chaining of query results, so we use the first method on the filtered results to get either the first (and only) match, or None, if there is no such user.

```python
def addUser(self, username, password, real_name, role):
    session = Session()
    result = session.query(Account).filter_by(|
     name=username).first()
    if result is None:
        user = Account(username, password, real_name, role)
        session.add(user)
        session.commit()
        role_manager = IPrincipalRoleManager(grok.getSite())
        if role==u'Project Manager':
            role_manager.assignRoleToPrincipal(
                'todo.ProjectManager',username)
        elif role==u'Application Manager':
            role_manager.assignRoleToPrincipal(
                'todo.AppManager',username)
        else:
            role_manager.assignRoleToPrincipal(
                'todo.ProjectMember',username)
```

To add a user, we first check if the login exists, using the same filter_by call from the getAccount method. If the result is None, we create the user account and add it to the session. We immediately commit to save the results.

```python
def deleteUser(self, username):
    session = Session()
    result = session.query(Account).filter_by(
     name=username).first()
    if result is not None:
        session.delete(result)
        session.commit()
```

One thing that we didn't do when we covered authentication back in Chapter 7 was to give administrators the ability to delete users. The deleteUser method above does just that. We again use the filter_by call to see if a user with the passed login exists. If it does, we call session.delete to remove it from the database and commit.

```python
def listUsers(self):
    session = Session()
    results = session.query(Account).all()
    return results
```

Finally, on `listUsers`, we simply call the `all` method to return every row in the table.

This is all that is needed to change authentication from using a `grok.Container` in the ZODB to using a table in a relational database (refer to the next screenshot). To use a different database, we just need to change the engine definition to whatever database we want to use. Be aware, though, you have to install any drivers required by the database in your system, as well as add the corresponding Python driver to the project's `setup.py`. Check the SQLAlchemy documentation for more information.

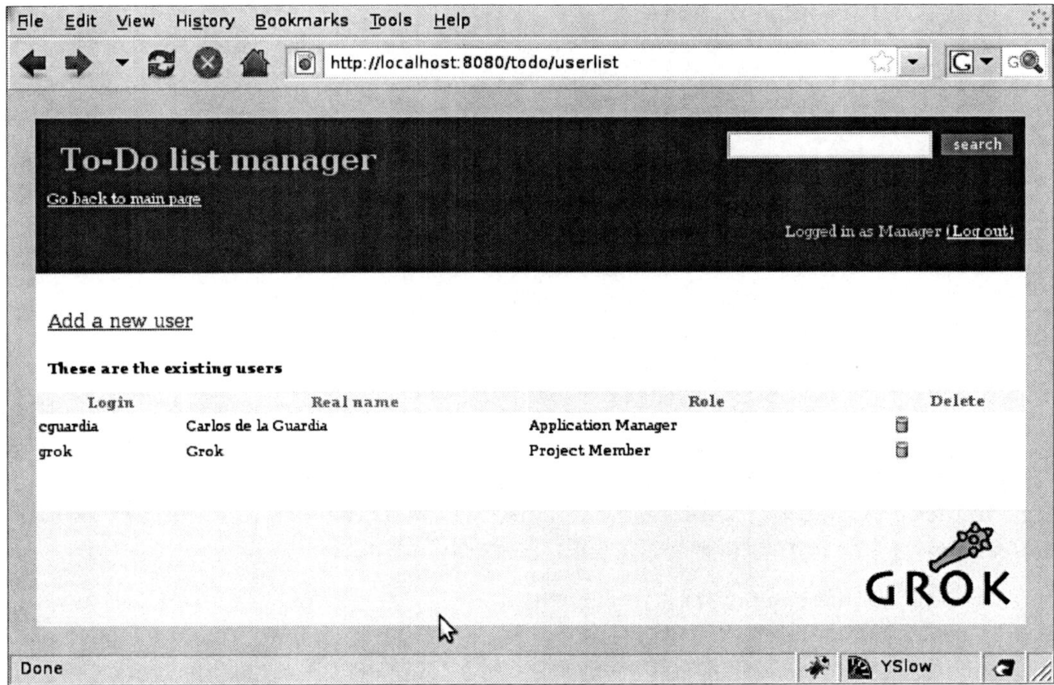

Handling database transactions securely

So we now have relational database authentication with very little work. However, there is a subtle problem with our code, especially in the `addUser` method. Grok has a transaction machinery, as we have seen, but so does a relational database.

Right now we are calling `session.commit()` right after adding the user to the database. At that moment, the user data is saved to disk. The problem is that after saving this change, we immediately set the appropriate role for the user by using Grok's permission machinery, which is ZODB based.

Now, if some error occurs when calling `assignRoleToPrincipal`, the Grok transaction will be aborted, meaning that the role will not be set for the new user. Meanwhile, the database transaction has been committed, so we end up with a user that exists in the database but who can't access the application features because it has no roles set.

This is what we call an inconsistent state for the database and users would call it a bug. In this case, we could move the `session.commit()` call after the role changes and we would at least guarantee that a database error would then result in an aborted transaction in Grok. But clearly there could be more complicated cases where careful placement of the `session.commit()` call would not be enough.

What is needed is a way to synchronize both, the Grok and the SQLAlchemy transactions, so that we don't have to control them separately. Fortunately, the huge collection of packages available for Grok via the Zope Toolkit has the right tool for this job.

The package that we need is called `zope.sqlalchemy` and it can be found on the PyPI, which means that it can be easily added to our project using `setup.py`. You know the dance by now, add it to the `install_requires` and rerun the buildout:

```
install_requires=['setuptools',
                  'grok',
                  'grokui.admin',
                  'z3c.testsetup',
                  'megrok.form',
                  'SQLAlchemy',
                  'zope.sqlalchemy',
                  # Add extra requirements here
                  ],
```

The `zope.sqlalchemy` package has a single purpose: to provide a transaction manager for integrating Grok and SQLAlchemy transactions. To use it, we first have to add a couple of imports at the top of `auth.py`:

```
from sqlalchemy.orm import scoped_session
from zope.sqlalchemy import ZopeTransactionExtension
```

`scoped_session` is a special SQLAlchemy session manager that makes sure that any calls to `Session()` during the same transaction will return the same session object. `ZopeTransactionExtension` will create the object that is responsible for tying up Grok and the SQLAlchemy sessions.

The engine and `Base` declarations at the top of the module remain unchanged, but we have to drop the line where the `Session` class is defined and use the following line of code in its place:

```
Session = scoped_session(sessionmaker(bind=engine,
    extension=ZopeTransactionExtension()))
```

This will initialize a scoped session and integrate the two transactions by using the `ZopeTransactionExtension`. All that is required now is to substitute all of the `session.commit()` calls with `transaction.commit()` calls and our application will enjoy secure transaction handling. Here's a look at the resulting `addUser` method:

```
def addUser(self, username, password, real_name, role):
    session = Session()
    result = session.query(Account).filter_by(
     name=username).first()
    if result is None:
        user = Account(username, password, real_name, role)
        session.add(user)
        role_manager = IPrincipalRoleManager(grok.getSite())
        if role==u'Project Manager':
            role_manager.assignRoleToPrincipal(
              'todo.ProjectManager',username)
        elif role==u'Application Manager':
            role_manager.assignRoleToPrincipal(
              'todo.AppManager',username)
        else:
            role_manager.assignRoleToPrincipal(
              'todo.ProjectMember',username)
```

As you can see, committing the `db` transaction is no longer necessary, as we are using the Grok transaction manager now, instead of the SQLAlchemy session object. The database transaction will be automatically committed when Grok commits the transaction for us, and the Grok machinery will make sure that either both transactions succeed or both fail. Less work and no data inconsistencies.

Creating database-backed models and containers

We have shown how easy it is to access and use data from a relational database. Very few lines of the program had to be modified and not a line of SQL was used. Of course, authentication is a functionality that is somewhat peripheral to the main application. What if we need to store all the data generated by our application in a relational database?

Grok's `Model` and `Container` classes store information in the ZODB, so if we want to use a relational database, we need to create our own model and container implementations, right? This seems like a lot of work. Fortunately, someone has already done that work for us.

The megrok.rdb package

It turns out that the `megrok.rdb` package provides the Grok developer with `Container` and `Model` classes that work similarly to Grok's own classes, but store all information in a relational database. What's more, `megrok.rdb` also uses SQLAlchemy, so it goes hand in hand with what we have done in this chapter so far.

This package is available from the PyPI, as you might have guessed. Hopefully, by this time you know that `megrok.rdb` should be added to the `install_requires` section of `setup.py` and the buildout needs to be run once again. This way the `megrok.rdb` package will be ready for use.

Making an application database backed

Converting our whole application to use `megrok.rdb` requires more work than is realistic for this introductory chapter, so let's just imagine, how we would design the application if we had a relational database planned for storage from the very beginning.

As this is just an exercise, we will show only the code that would be needed for getting the `Project` class working, along with its contained to-do lists. First, we need some imports from `sqlalchemy`, similar to those we used earlier. Of course, we have to import the `rdb` module from `megrok.rdb` as well:

```
from sqlalchemy import Column, ForeignKey
from sqlalchemy.types import Integer, String
from sqlalchemy.orm import relation
from megrok.rdb import rdb
```

For now, we'll dispense as well with the database connection setup. Just assume that we have created a database as we have done earlier in this chapter. However, we do need a special `metadata` object instead of the one provided by SQLAlchemy. We'll get it from the `rdb` module that we just imported:

```
metadata = rdb.MetaData()
```

We can now create the models. Remember, this code is just for illustration purposes, do not add it to our project.

```python
class TodoLists(rdb.Container):
    pass

class Project(rdb.Model):
    id = Column(Integer, primary_key=True)
    title = Column(String(50))
    kind = Column(String(50))
    description = Column(String(140))
    todolists = relation('TodoList', backref='project',
     collection_class=TodoLists)

class TodoList(rdb.Model):
    id = Column(Integer, primary_key=True)
    title = Column(String(50))
    description = Column(String(140))
    project = Column('project_id', Integer, ForeignKey('project.id'))
```

We define the to-do lists container first. It's just an empty class. Then, we define a `Project` model and its columns by using regular SQLAlchemy declarations. We have a `todolists` container as a property on the project, connected with the container that we defined earlier by using the SQLAlchemy relation declaration. This is necessary for having Grok-style containers in our relational database application.

For the `TodoList` class, we use the `rdb.Model` base class and add its columns as well, but here, we use a foreign key to relate the to-do list with a project.

Once this is done, we can generate the database structure, which will usually be done at an application's creation time. We have also done this in the previous section, so let's assume that we have everything ready, and start creating content:

```python
session = rdb.Session()
project_x = Project(title='Project X',kind='personal',
  description='My secret project')
session.add(project_x)
```

First, we create a session. After that, we create a new `Project` and add it to the session, just like regular SQLAlchemy usage. Next, we define some to-do lists:

```python
planning = TodoList(title='Planning',description='Define steps for
master plan')
execution = TodoList(title='Execution',description='Perform plan
flawlessly')
world_domination = TodoList(title='World Domination',
description='Things to do after conquering the world')
```

This is again just regular SQLAlchemy syntax, but now we come to the part where we use the container that we defined inside the `Project` class to store the to-do lists. This is what makes it possible for us to have Grok container-like functionality for our database objects:

```
project_x.todolists.set(planning)
project_x.todolists.set(execution)
project_x.todolists.set(world_domination)
```

The `set` method takes care of 'adding' the list to the container and lets the database set the key for each row. We could now call Grok container methods, such as `items()` on the `project_x.todolists` container and get the expected results, just like using `grok.Container`.

There are other things that can be done with `megrok.rdb`, so if you are interested in having a Grok-like database-backed application, you should consult the documentation.

When to use the ZODB versus a relational database

Because it's fairly easy to use relational databases with Grok, people who are used to working with relational applications may wonder why they should use the ZODB at all. As comfortable as it is, to go with what we know best, no database technology is ideal for every kind of project.

A relational database is a flat entity. When working with object-oriented languages such as Python, it's usually necessary to take a complex hierarchy of interrelated objects and "flatten" it to fit into several tables. Sometimes it's a lot easier and faster to simply store the objects exactly as they are, like an object-oriented database does.

Which one is best for your application? The key words here are *flat* and *hierarchy*. If your application will handle flat information structures, such as customers, products, records, orders, and so on, or if you need to do heavy reporting and data manipulation, a relational database is most likely your best bet. Online stores are a good example of an application that is well suited for relational database use. The user management part of our application which we just did is also a good fit here.

If you have complex, hierarchical structures of objects, it might be better to use the ZODB and persist the hierarchies in their natural form. Content management applications, where you need to model structures resembling folders and pages that can be nested several levels deep, are ideally suited to an object-oriented database.

In the end, it's usually just a matter of preference, but in any case, Grok will let you use either one or even both of these mechanisms in a simple way, which gives you maximum flexibility.

Summary

In this chapter, we saw:

- How Grok makes it very easy to use the existing Python relational database packages and ORMs. We also learned to use the more advanced `megrok.rdb` package to transparently turn our models into ORM mappings.

- How to integrate relational database transactions with ZODB's transaction support.

- How to use `megrok.rdb` to turn our models into ORM mappings.

11
Key Concepts Behind Grok

In the first chapter of this book, we discussed the features of Grok, placing a strong emphasis on the importance of the **Zope Toolkit (ZTK)** and the **Zope Component Architecture (ZCA)**. We also mentioned that Grok offers an agile way of using these.

Throughout the preceding chapters, we used several ZTK packages and employed many ZCA patterns, introducing and explaining them, whenever needed. We also saw how agile Grok can be, as we grew our application bit by bit, while having a fully functional application from the very beginning.

With the material that we have covered so far, it's possible to create fairly complex applications, but to really get the most out of Grok, the concepts behind the ZCA and the tools that provide Grok's agility have to be explained at a more detailed level.

Although a full explanation of the ZCA and its patterns is beyond the scope of this book, this chapter will at least discuss its more important concepts and show their utility through small additions and extensions to our to-do list application. The author believes that it's easier to understand these concepts once we have seen practical examples of their use at work, which we can refer to when explaining them.

In this chapter, we will look at these concepts in detail. In particular, we'll discuss:

- What the ZCA is
- Interfaces
- Adapters, utilities, and events
- Application extension through events
- Application extension through adaptation

The Zope Component Architecture

Many agile web application frameworks were designed specifically to allow a quick turnaround from idea to working application. This is a good thing, but sometimes the emphasis on fast development cycles results in a little less attention being paid to things such as extensibility and code reuse. In contrast, Grok is based on a set of patterns whose primary concern is the maintainability and extensibility of applications. In fact, Grok applications can be extended even from the outside, without the need to touch their code. The set of patterns that allows this is known as the **Zope Component Architecture**.

Even though the word "Zope" is in its name, the ZCA is a set of general Python packages that can be used to create component-based applications, independent of the Zope web application server or the ZTK. In fact, we could use the ZCA to create any kind of Python application, and it's especially suited to the development of large systems.

The ZCA works by encapsulating the functionality of a Python object into an entity called a **component**, which has a well-defined behavior that can be described by using a separate object, known as an **interface**. The interface helps the developer to find out how to use a given component, or even replace it wholesale by implementing all of the functionality expressed therein.

Because the concept of breaking up the functionality of a system into multiple components requires the developer to keep track of a potentially large number of components, the ZCA offers a registry that can register and retrieve components based on their interfaces. This is truly the key part of the Zope Component Architecture, as working with it mainly consists of interacting with the registry in various ways.

Interfaces

We introduced 'interfaces' in Chapter 5, when we used them for automatically generating forms. In that chapter, we explained that an interface is used to document the external behavior of objects.

An object that has its functionality defined in an interface is said to *provide* this interface. The interface defines what an object can do, but how the object internally complies with this contract is entirely decided by the implementor.

Interfaces in the ZCA are used to register and find components in the registry. This allows us to find components on the basis of what they do, and easily replace, extend, or override a specific functionality in an application.

When a class includes the functionality described in an interface, it is said to *implement* that interface. The interface is independent of the class, though. One specific interface may be implemented by any number of classes. In addition, a class can implement any number of interfaces.

Let's take a look at the interface that we defined in Chapter 6, to make the projects, lists, and items searchable:

```python
class ISearchable(interface.Interface):
    title = interface.Attribute('title')
    kind = interface.Attribute('kind')
    description = interface.Attribute('description')
    creator = interface.Attribute('creator')
    creation_date  = interface.Attribute('creation date')
    modification_date  = interface.Attribute('modification date')
    checked = interface.Attribute('checked')
    content_type = interface.Attribute('content type')
    project_name = interface.Attribute('project name')

    def searchableText():
        """return concatenated string with all text fields
        to search"""
```

An interface is a class that subclasses the `Interface` class defined in the `zope.interface` package. The `ISearchable` interface describes the attributes and methods that a searchable object must provide. Similar to our to-do list application, we may have several different content types, but as long as all of their class definitions promise to implement `ISearchable`, we can use the same search code on them without problems.

Notice how the `searchableText` method definition does not contain the `self` parameter that is used in Python classes. That's because although the interface documents the methods, it will never be instantiated itself, and so `self` is not required here.

Once we have defined an interface, we can create the classes that implement it. In our application, the `ISearchable` interface is implemented by several classes. For example, here's how the `Project` content type declares its intention of abiding by the `ISearchable` contract:

```python
class Project(grok.Container):
    grok.implements(IProject, IMetadata, ISearchable)
```

In Grok, we use the `implements` class annotation to declare that a class implements one or more interfaces. We can see that, in addition to `ISearchable`, the `Project` class also implements `IProject` and `IMetadata`.

Once we create an actual `Project` object, it is said to *provide* `ISearchable`, which means that classes implement interfaces, and instances of those classes provide them.

An interface can also be used to define schemata for form generation. We have used this a lot throughout our application's code. Here's an example:

```
class ITodoList(interface.Interface):
    title = schema.TextLine(title=u'Title', required=True,
      constraint=check_title)
    description = schema.Text(title=u'Description', required=False)
    next_id = schema.Int(title=u'Next id' ,default=0)
```

We already saw that by using the `grok.AutoFields` directive, we can turn this schema definition into HTML controls on a form.

Because interfaces are used as keys in the component registry, it's possible to find all of the objects that implement an interface. This comes in handy for finding objects belonging to some type, but can also be used for more interesting things, such as creating methods that work only with objects that provide an interface, or components that extend the functionality of any class that implements it.

This is generally useful when no special functionality needs to be defined for some interface, so sometimes we can come across empty interface definitions, known as **marker interfaces**. They basically mark an object as belonging to a certain type, which allows the registry to find them and register other components to work with them. We have not needed them so far in our application, but they can be a very useful addition to our arsenal.

Adapters

One of the principles of the ZCA is to use components instead of inheritance for extending application behavior, so that we can interconnect different components with each other to get the desired result.

This approach requires three things:

- Well-defined components, which is why we use interfaces. They mark a component as providing a specific behavior and also offer a sort of blueprint or contract for that functionality.

- An easy way to keep track of multiple components. We already mentioned that the ZCA has a registry, and that interfaces are used as keys to retrieve the components according to their defined functionality. This also makes possible the complete replacement of a component for an entirely different one as long as it implements the same interface.

- A way to make disparate components work together even if they have completely different interfaces. That's where adapters come in.

An **adapter** is simply a piece of code that takes an object with a certain interface and makes it provide an additional interface. In other words, it adapts the component, so that it offers new behavior, without requiring any change in its code.

Real-world adapters

It may be helpful to think of this in terms of real-world objects. Nowadays, cellphones are ubiquitous, and many people depend on them for their communication needs. However, they have a pretty short battery life and need constant recharging. When we buy a new cellphone, we usually get an AC adapter, which allows us to plug the phone into any wall outlet and charge it. In some cases, we may not have access to a wall outlet, for example, during a long car trip. In such a situation, we can of course get a car adapter to charge the phone by using the vehicle's power outlet.

Adapters for the ZCA are very similar to these phone adapters. They adapt a power source, be it the car or the wall outlet, and make it present in a different interface that can be used by the phone to get charged. Neither the power source nor the phone are changed in the least, or even need to know anything about the specific adapter used, as long as they conform to the established power and phone connection interfaces (now you see where the terminology came from).

Defining and using an adapter

Up to now, we have not explicitly defined or used an adapter, so let's take a quick look at how we would do this in Grok. Suppose that we want to show the number of days elapsed since the last modification to any content in our to-do list application. If we add the methods to each content type, we'll have a lot of repeated code, and any change to one method's logic would require making a change to all of the content types. By using an adapter, we get all of the code in one place, as shown below:

```python
import datetime
class IDayCalculations(Interface):
    def daysOld():
        "number of days since the content was created"
    def daysFromLastModification():
        "number of days since the last modification"

class DaysOld(grok.Adapter):
    grok.implements(IDayCalculations)
    grok.adapts(ISearchable)
```

```
def daysOld(self):
    return (datetime.datetime.now() -
      self.context.creation_date).days
def daysFromLastModification(self):
    return (datetime.datetime.now() -
      self.context.modification_date).days
```

First, we define the interface for our 'day' calculation methods. We'll keep it simple, for demonstration purposes. The `grok.Adapter` component is used to define an adapter. We create one, and use the `grok.implements` directive to signal that it will implement the methods that we just defined in our interface.

All of the content in our application already implements the `ISearchable` interface, so to make every to-do application object provide this interface, we use the `grok.adapts` directive. Thus, `DaysOld` is an adapter that takes any object that provides `ISearchable`, and provides `IDayCalculations` for it.

The adapter instance will have both the `context` and the `request` attributes. This is because an adapter always receives, as parameters, the things that it adapts, in order to be able to get at their properties and use them in the implementation. In this example, `self.context` refers to the adapted `context` object, which can be a `TodoList`, a `Project`, a `TodoListItem`, and so on. As all of these objects implement `ISearchable`, we know that `modification_date` and `creation_date` will be available for the calculations.

We could use this adapter inside any view for one of our content types, in the following way:

```
class ProjectView(grok.View):
    grok.context(Project)

    def update(self):
        self.days_old = IDayCalculations(self.context).daysOld()
        self.days_modified = IDayCalculations(
          self.context).daysFromLastModification()
```

In this example, we use the `update` method to insert the `days_modified` and `days_old` properties into the view, so that they will be available to the view template, when it's rendered. To get the adapter from the registry, we call the `IDayCalculations` interface itself, with the `context` object as parameter, which in this case is a `Project`. Once we have the adapter, we can simply call its methods, and it will behave as if these methods are a part of the `Project` component.

When first getting to know them, adapters might seem to be sort of a roundabout way of getting to the component that we need, but bear in mind that this whole system is designed for easy expansion and evolution. By using adapters, we could override components from within other packages and still have the system work fine without needing to modify the original code in any way.

Adapters that we have used in our application

For adapters to be used in Grok, they first need to be registered with the ZCA. Grok itself performs a number of registrations when the application is started. In fact, we have used these already in our code. In Chapter 7, we added authentication to our application and we decided to add specific roles to every new user that was created, to simplify permission management.

A Grok site knows nothing about role assignment, so to be able to define roles for a principal, it uses a role manager. This **role manager** is an adapter that enables the site to provide the role manager interface. Take a look at the code that we used:

```
def addUser(self, username, password, real_name, role):
    session = Session()
    result = session.query(Account).filter_by(name = username).first()
    if result is None:
        user = Account(username, password, real_name, role)
        session.add(user)
        role_manager = IPrincipalRoleManager(grok.getSite())
        if role==u'Project Manager':
            role_manager.assignRoleToPrincipal('todo.ProjectManager',
                username)
        elif role==u'Application Manager':
            role_manager.assignRoleToPrincipal('todo.AppManager',
                username)
        else:
            role_manager.assignRoleToPrincipal('todo.ProjectMember',
                username )
        transaction.commit()
```

Here, we are adding a new user, and immediately after that, we are assigning a role to the user. As we mentioned earlier, the site delegates this responsibility to a role manager. The role manager is an adapter that is registered as implementing the `IPrincipalRoleManager` interface for Grok sites, so we need to query the registry with this information to get the actual manager. The line that does this is:

```
role_manager = IPrincipalRoleManager(grok.getSite())
```

The interface itself performs the registry lookup, asking for a component that is registered for providing it to objects that implement the Grok site interface. Note that the Grok site itself is passed in as a parameter and not its interface, but the ZCA is smart enough to find the correct component, if it's registered.

In this case, the query gets us a role manager object that implements the `IPrincipalRoleManager` interface, so that we know that the `assignRoleToPrincipal` method will be available to assign the correct role to our new user.

Adapters can be named, so that we could use its name to get a specific `IPrincipalRoleManager` component. Also, it's possible for an adapter to adapt more than one component at the same time, in which case, it's called a **multiadapter**. For example, all of the views in Grok are multiadapters for a request and a context:

```
class TodoListUpdateItems(grok.View):
    grok.context(TodoList)
    grok.name('updateitems')
    grok.require('todo.changeitems')
```

The context is specified in the class body by using the `grok.context` directive, and the request refers to the current browser request. In the preceding code, `TodoListUpdateItems` is a multiadapter for a request and a `TodoList`. It uses the name `updateitems`. This multiadapter/view will be called by Grok only when the user requests the `updateitems` view while browsing through a `TodoList` object.

We have also used multiadapters explicitly in our to-do list manager code:

```
class AddProjectViewlet(grok.Viewlet):
    grok.viewletmanager(Main)
    grok.context(Todo)
    grok.view(AddProject)

    def update(self):
        self.form = getMultiAdapter((self.context, self.request),
         name='add')
        self.form.update_form()

    def render(self):
```

In Chapter 8, we showed how to get a form that is rendered inside a viewlet, and saw that we needed to get at the specific component that creates that specific form. Here, the registry lookup is performed by the `getMultiAdapter` method, which is imported from `zope.component`. We specifically want the 'add form' for a project, because we want to render the `AddProjectViewlet`. We know that we have a request and that the context is a `Todo` application, due to the `grok.context` directive above, so if we call `getMultiAdapter` and pass the request and the context along with the name of the required form, the ZCA machinery will find it for us.

Utilities

As we have seen, the component registry mainly consists of adapters that are registered to specific interfaces. In some cases, it's also useful to register components that do not adapt anything, but provide some sort of service that we need to be able to override or replace. A database connection, an authentication backend, and a user source are examples of this.

The ZCA has the concept of a utility to cover this case. A **utility** is simply a component with a declared interface, which may also have a name. Utilities in the ZCA can be either local or global.

Global utilities

A **global utility** is the one that is created and registered when Grok is started, but which is not persistent (that is, its state is not saved in the ZODB). Examples of global utilities that we have used include database connections and session credentials.

Let's take a look at the utility that we added in Chapter 7, when we integrated authentication services into our application:

```python
class MySessionCredentialsPlugin(grok.GlobalUtility,
SessionCredentialsPlugin):
    grok.provides(ICredentialsPlugin)
    grok.name('credentials')

    loginpagename = 'login'
    loginfield = 'login'
    passwordfield = 'password'
```

To define a global utility, we inherit from the `grok.GlobalUtility` component and declare the interface provided by the component, by using the `grok.provides` directive. Named utilities also need to use the `grok.name` directive to register their names.

To get a global utility from the registry, we use the `getUtility` function defined in `zope.component`. In this case, the `credentials` utility is not called directly by our code, but by the authentication mechanism itself. However, if we wanted to use this utility, we would get it as follows:

```
from zope.component import getUtility
credentials_plugin = getUtility(ICredentialsPlugin, 'credentials')
```

Local utilities

A **local utility** is very similar to a global utility, but it gets saved in the database, so that its state and configuration are persistent. The Zope Toolkit catalog and the pluggable authentication mechanism used in our application are both examples of local utilities.

We can take a look at the `UserAuthenticatorPlugin` that we defined in Chapter 7, to see how to define a local utility:

```
class UserAuthenticatorPlugin(grok.LocalUtility):
    grok.implements(IAuthenticatorPlugin)
    grok.name('users')
```

We can see that this works exactly the same way as a global utility does, except that we inherit from `grok.LocalUtility` instead. However, we can't actually use a local utility until we explicitly add it to a `grok.Container` component. Take a look at the main application component for the `Todo` application:

```
class Todo(grok.Application, grok.Container):
    grok.implements(ITodo)
    grok.local_utility(
        UserAuthenticatorPlugin, provides=IAuthenticatorPlugin,
        name='users',
        )
    grok.local_utility(
        PluggableAuthentication, provides=IAuthentication,
        setup=setup_authentication,
        )
```

Our application contains two local utilities. There is a `UserAuthenticatorPlugin` utility, which is named, as we may want to work with several user sources. There is also a `PluggableAuthentication` utility, which will handle all of the authentication needs for our site, and thus does not need to be differentiated from other similar utilities by name.

In fact, our application also contains a third local utility, the "Catalog", which is added automatically by Grok upon application creation. The Catalog is not a named utility.

To work with any of these utilities, we use the same `getUtility` function that we used for our global utility:

```
users = component.getUtility(IAuthenticatorPlugin, 'users')
auth = component.getUtility(IAuthentication)
```

One very important thing to keep in mind about local utilities is that, because they are added at an application's creation time and stored in the database, changing the initialization code of one will have no effect once the application is created. The easiest way to get a modified local utility to work, in this case, is to delete the application instance and create it again.

Events

The Zope Toolkit defines a series of life cycle events that are fired whenever certain operations are performed on an object, such as creation or modification. An **event** can have one or more subscribers, which are called whenever the subscribed event takes place. These subscribers are known as **event handlers,** and Grok offers an easy way of defining them.

Here are some of the events that we can subscribe to by using Grok:

Event	Description	Event attributes
`IObjectModifiedEvent`	An object has been modified. This is a general event that encompasses any change to a persistent object, such as adding, moving, copying, or removing objects.	`object` `descriptions`
`IContainerModifiedEvent`	The container has been modified. Container modifications are specific to addition, removal, or reordering of subobjects. Inherits from `grok.IObjectModifiedEvent`.	`object` `descriptions`

`IObjectMovedEvent`	An object has been moved.	`object`
		`oldParent`
		`oldName`
		`newParent`
		`newName`

Event	Description	Event attributes

`IObjectAddedEvent`	An object has been added to a container.	`object`
		`oldParent`
		`oldName`
		`newParent`
		`newName`

`IObjectCopiedEvent`	An object has been copied.	`object` `original`
`IObjectCreatedEvent`	An object has been created. This event is intended to happen before an object has been made persistent, that is, its location attributes (`__name__` and `__parent__`) will usually be `None`.	`object`

`IObjectRemovedEvent`	An object has been removed from a container.	`object`
		`oldParent`
		`oldName`

`IBeforeTraverseEvent`	The publisher is about to traverse an object.	`object` `request`

We can define an event handler in Grok by using the `grok.subscriber` decorator:

```python
@grok.subscribe(Project, grok.IObjectAddedEvent)
def handler(obj, event):
    "New project added: %s." % obj.title
```

This code will be executed every time a new `Project` is added to a container. The handler receives two parameters—`obj`, which contains the object involved, and `event`, which contains the attributes that are listed in the preceding table.

As the subscription is really a kind of adapter, the first parameter to the `grok.subscribe` decorator can be any interface, thus allowing us to make the subscription as general or specific as we like. In the earlier example, we passed `Project` as a parameter, so the handler will be executed only when a `Project` is added, but we could pass `Interface` instead, in order to get all of the occurrences of the event, regardless of the object type. There can be additional subscribers to the same event, but the order in which they are called cannot be known in advance, so never depend on it.

Extending a Grok application from the outside

Without a doubt, one of the nicest features of the Zope Component Architecture is that it makes it very easy to extend or override the functionality of an application without having to touch its code.

Many Grok components, such as views and utilities, are ready to be overriden without the developer having to do anything special. Other objects, such as viewlets, may need small modifications to add new functionality.

In this section, we are going to show, how easy it is to extend a Grok application from the outside, simply by creating an independent package that adds new functionality to our to-do application. The knowledge that we just obtained about the ZCA will come in handy for this task, so that hopefully we understand it a little better when our add-on is ready.

Preparing the original application

This demonstration will, of course, be more convincing if we keep modifications to the original application to a minimum. Fortunately, we need to make only one small addition to the `app.py` module, and a simple modification to the `navigation.pt` template.

Add the following two lines at the top of `app.py`, just below the `import` statements:

```
master_template = grok.PageTemplateFile('app_templates/master.pt')
form_template = grok.PageTemplateFile('custom_edit_form.pt')
```

This will allow us to use the master page and the form templates in the new application, by using a simple `import` statement.

The only other change that we will make is to add an extra viewlet manager to the navigation viewlet, so that other applications can easily insert navigation options there. To do this, we need to add the viewlet manager definition to `app.py`, as shown below:

```
class ExtraNav(grok.ViewletManager):
    grok.context(Interface)
    grok.name('extranav')
```

We also need to modify the navigation template to take into account the new viewlet manager. Change `app_templates/navigation.pt` to look like this:

```
<div id="navigation">
  <a tal:attributes="href python:view.application_url('index')">
    Go back to main page</a>
  <tal:extranav content="structure provider:extranav" />
</div>
```

The only thing that we added here is the "provider" line, to insert new viewlets after the link, to go back to the main page.

This is all that we need to do in order to leave the to-do application ready for extension by third-party packages. Of course, we could have added this code there from the beginning, but it's instructive to show how little code you have to add, even if you didn't think in terms of extensibility from the start.

The to-do plus package

Imagine that we just found the to-do application somewhere on the net, and we think that it satisfies almost all of our requirements for a list manager, if only it had a couple of more features.

The code is available, so we could just extend the application directly. However, as we don't control its development, we basically are forking the code, which means that any new features added to the application by their original developers would need to be merged into our code in order for us to take advantage of them. Also, the code style for the original application might be different to the one that we are comfortable with, and we don't want to have mixed styles.

What would be best for us is to create a completely independent package that extends the original application, and is under our complete control. If we really don't need to modify the original application heavily, this is the way to go. Let's create a "to-do plus" package that adds a few features to the existing "to-do" package, which we'll declare as a dependency.

Creating the new package

In real life, the to-do package would be available as an "egg" that we could use in a new Grok project, but as we are still in the development stage here, we'll just add a new package to our project, instead of creating another one.

The `buildout` created by the grokproject script that we used to initialize our project has a `src` directory to which we can add our new package. Go into that directory, and type the following command:

```
$ ../bin/paster create -t basic_package todo_plus
```

This script will ask a few questions, but for now, you can just press the *Enter* key after every question, to accept the default values. A new directory, called `todo_plus` will be created. This directory will contain our new package.

First, we need to make sure that this package gets grokked at startup time, so we include `grok`, and grok the current package. As this package depends on the existence of the original `todo` application, we have to make sure that its dependencies are grokked as well. Create a `configure.zcml` file inside the `todo_plus/todo_plus` directory, with the following contents:

```
<configure xmlns="http://namespaces.zope.org/zope"
           xmlns:mail="http://namespaces.zope.org/mail"
           xmlns:grok="http://namespaces.zope.org/grok">
  <include package="grok" />
  <includeDependencies package="." />
  <grok:grok package="." />

</configure>
```

Notice that, unlike the `todo` package created for our original project, the `todo_plus` package has two subdirectory levels, so be careful to create this file inside the second level `todo_plus` directory.

Next, create the `app_templates` and the `static` directories that are used by Grok applications:

```
$ mkdir todo_plus/todo_plus/app_templates
```

```
$ mkdir todo_plus/todo_plus/static
```

Also, you must add the `todo` package to the `requires` section in the `todo_plus/setup.py` file, as follows:

```
install_requires=[
    'todo',
]
```

Finally, the `buildout.cfg` file needs to be updated to include the new package. This is how the top of the file should look after the `todo_plus` package has been added in the required parts (`buildout` will be discussed in more detail in Chapter 14):

```
[buildout]
develop = .
          src/todo_plus
parts = eggbasket app i18n test data log
newest = false
extends = versions.cfg
# eggs will be installed in the default buildout location
# (see .buildout/default.cfg in your home directory)
# unless you specify an eggs-directory option here.

find-links = http://download.zope.org/distribution/

versions = versions


[app]
recipe = zc.recipe.egg
eggs = todo
       todo_plus
       z3c.evalexception>=2.0
       Paste
       PasteScript
       PasteDeploy
interpreter = python-console
site.zcml = <include package="todo_plus" />
```

In the `develop` line, we are telling `buildout` that, in addition to the package in the current directory (that is, the `todo` package itself), we'll be adding our new `todo_plus` development package. This will create a development "egg" for `todo_plus`, which should be added below the eggs line in the `[app]` section, right under the original todo package.

Now we can rerun the `buildout` and our package will be ready to work:

```
$ bin/buildout
```

Adding a skin chooser form to the application

In Chapter 8, we added themes to our application, although the only way to look at a different theme than the default was to use the ugly `++skin++` traversal helper in the URL. As we had mentioned then, we don't want the user to do that, so a way to select the desired skin from a form would be neat.

Let's make that the first feature our `todo_plus` package will add to the to-do list application. The objective is to have a form where we get a list of available screens, pick one, and then save it. After that, Grok should automatically use the chosen skin when we navigate through the to-do application.

Adding a new skin

First, we'll have our package include its own skin layer to add to the three skins available in the original application. Of course, there are a few things we need to import from the to-do application, but it's all very straightforward. Create a file named `app.py` inside the `src/todo_plus/todo_plus` directory, and add the following lines of code to it:

```python
import grok
from zope.interface import Interface
from zope.publisher.interfaces.browser import IBrowserSkinType,
IDefaultBrowserLayer
from todo.app import ITodo, IProject, Todo, HeadSlot, ExtraNav, Main,
master_template, form_template

class PlusLayer(IDefaultBrowserLayer):
    grok.skin('plus')

class HeadPlus(grok.Viewlet):
    grok.viewletmanager(HeadSlot)
    grok.context(Interface)
    grok.name('head')
    grok.template('head_plus')
    grok.layer(PlusLayer)
```

Because we need to add a viewlet to the `HeadSlot` for this skin layer, we have to import it from `todo.app`. Everything else that we need, we already did in Chapter 8. We add a new layer and turn it into a skin by using the `grok.skin` directive. After that, we add a viewlet and register it with the name 'head' for this layer, overriding the original viewlet from the default skin. Of course, we need a template for the new viewlet. Add the following code to `app_templates/head_plus`, at the top:

```html
<meta tal:attributes="http-equiv string:Content-Type;
    content string:text/html;; charset=utf-8" />
<title tal:content="context/title">To-Do list manager</title>
<link rel="stylesheet" type="text/css"
    tal:attributes="href static/styles_plus.css" />
```

Finally, we can copy the `styles.css` file from the original app and save it as `styles_plus.css`. To keep it simple, as we did in Chapter 8, make some obvious modifications, such as changing the header background color, and leave it at that for now.

Restart the to-do application normally, by using paster and then navigate to `http://localhost/++skin++plus/todo/index`, and you'll see the new skin. That's it. Not bad for a simple warm-up. Working from a completely separate package, we have added a new skin that transparently integrates with the to-do application.

The skin chooser form

Now, we are ready to add the form. We need a drop-down list with the names of all of the available skins, which currently are Basic (the default), martian, forest, and plus. We can use a `schema.Choice` field and pass these values to it, but then, if the original application adds a new skin or a third party comes up with another add-on package that has new skins, our skin list will be outdated. We need a dynamic way to specify the skin name values, so that we don't have to keep track of all of the skin names in the code.

Fortunately, as we will frequently find out when we want to add new functionality to a Grok application, the Zope Toolkit already has a package called `zc.sourcefactory` that can help us in this situation. We can use this package by adding it to the `install_requires` section of the `src/todo_plus/setup.py` file, as follows:

```
install_requires=[
    'todo',
    'zc.sourcefactory',
]
```

Rerun the `buildout` and the package will be downloaded and installed, as usual. We can now use it to define a dynamic choice field:

```
from zope import schema
from zope.component import getAllUtilitiesRegisteredFor,
getMultiAdapter, getUtility
from zc.sourcefactory.basic import BasicSourceFactory


class SkinNameSource(BasicSourceFactory):
    def getValues(self):
        values = ['Basic']
        skin_tag = 'grokcore.view.directive.skin'
        skin_names = [s.getTaggedValue(skin_tag)
          for s in getAllUtilitiesRegisteredFor(IBrowserSkinType)
          if skin_tag in s.getTaggedValueTags()]
```

```
        values.extend(skin_names)
        return values

class ISkinChooser(Interface):
    skin_name = schema.Choice(source=SkinNameSource(),
            title=u'Skin Name',
            description=u'Name of the new default skin')
```

A **source** is simply a method that returns a list of values to be used inside a schema field, instead of static lists. The `BasicSourceFactory` subclass is used to define a source.

We have created a form schemata earlier, so the only new thing in the `ISkinChooser` schema definition is the `source=SkinNameSource()` parameter in the `Choice` field. This tells Grok to use a source factory named `SkinNameSource` to provide the skin name values.

To create a source, we just subclass from `BasicSourceFactory`, and add a `getValues` method that will return a list of the skin names. To get the skin names themselves, we have to use the component registry. In Zope, a skin is registered as a named utility with the interface `IBrowserSkinType` and the skin name.

How do we get all of the utilities registered for this interface? The `zope.component` package includes a function called `getAllUtilitiesRegisteredFor` that does this. To distinguish them from the Zope skins, Grok adds a tag to its skin components that identify them as Grok layers. This tag is the `grokcore.view.directive.skin` assigned to `skin_tag` in the preceding code. To get the Grok skin names, we start with a list with the value 'Basic' in it, to account for the default skin, which is not tagged by Grok. We then go through every registered skin and check if it has `skin_tag` on it. If it does, we add it to the list.

In this way, each time a new skin layer is added from a Grok package, it will automatically be listed in our 'skin chooser' form. The component registry takes care of the available skins for us.

Now we need to add the form, and also a `SkinChooser` view and a viewlet that includes the form on it. We have done all of this in Chapter 8, so it should seem familiar:

```
from zope.app.session.interfaces import Isession

class SkinChooserForm(grok.Form):
    grok.context(ITodo)
    grok.name('skin_chooser_form')
    form_fields = grok.AutoFields(ISkinChooser)
    label = "Set the default skin for the To-Do list manager"
    template = form_template
```

```python
    def setUpWidgets(self, ignore_request=False):
        super(SkinChooserForm,self).setUpWidgets(ignore_request)
        session = ISession(self.request)['todo_plus']
        self.widgets['skin_name'].setRenderedValue(session.get(
          'skin_name''Basic'))

    @grok.action('Choose skin')
    def choose(self, **data):
        session = ISession(self.request)['todo_plus']
        session['skin_name'] = data['skin_name']
        return self.redirect(self.url('skin_chooser'))

class SkinChooser(grok.View):
    grok.context(ITodo)
    grok.name('skin_chooser')
    grok.require('todo.changeitems')

    def render(self):
        return master_template.render(self)

class SkinChooserViewlet(grok.Viewlet):
    grok.viewletmanager(Main)
    grok.context(ITodo)
    grok.view(SkinChooser)

    def update(self):
        self.form = getMultiAdapter((self.context, self.request),
                                    name='skin_chooser_form')
        self.form.update_form()

    def render(self):
        return self.form.render()
```

The `SkinChooserForm` inherits from `grok.Form`, because we want a content-independent form. Its context is `ITodo` to make it show up only at the root application level. We use the fields defined in the `ISkinChooser` interface that we created earlier.

We need a way to store the skin selection so that it is available when the user navigates through the application. For this, we'll use the session mechanism that is defined in the `zope.app.session` package (yeah, the Zope Toolkit to the rescue, again). The session is an adapter for the request, so we can get it by issuing an `ISession(self.request)`. We use the `todo_plus` package name as a session key to avoid namespace clashes with other session objects.

In the `updateWidgets` method of the form, we try to get the value for `skin_name` from the session ('Basic' is returned, if `skin_name` has not been initialized). With this value, we can show the currently selected skin on the form by calling `setRenderedValue` on the choice widget.

Finally, in the form action, we set the `skin_name` key of our session to the value returned in the form data submitted by the user, and redirect the user to the 'skin chooser' view.

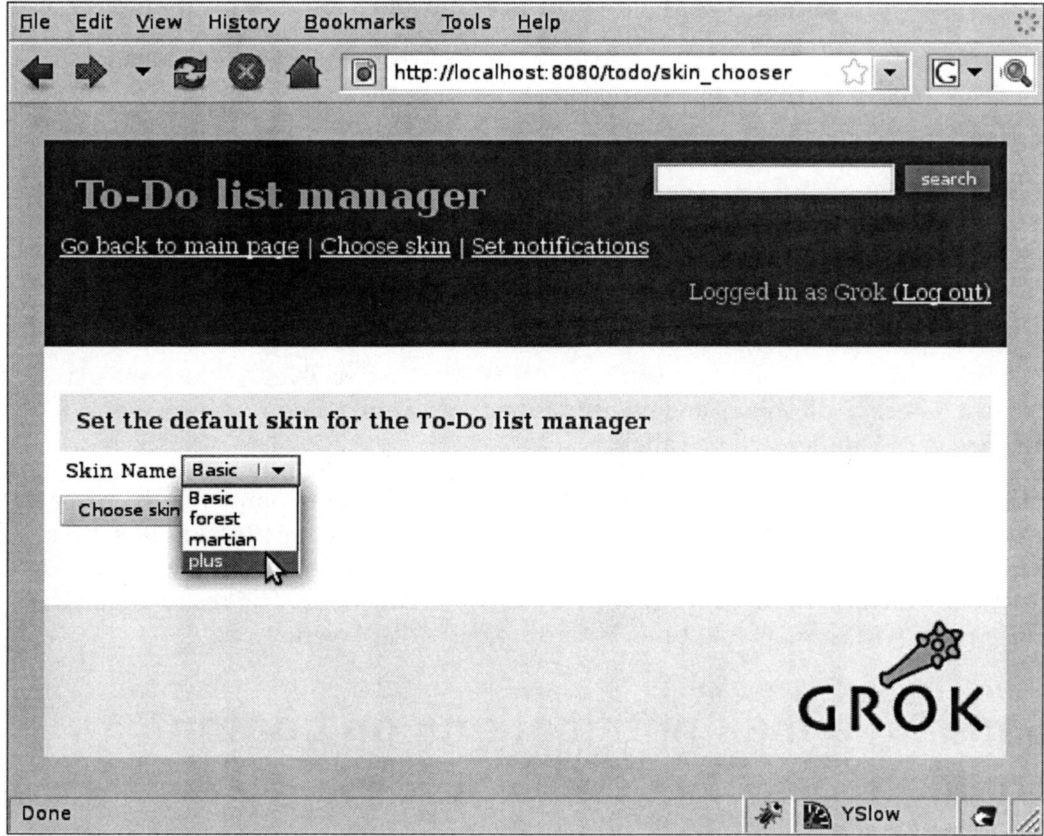

The view and viewlet definitions contain nothing new, but notice how we use the components imported from the original to-do application to perform our registrations. The view is assigned `ITodo` as its context, and the viewlet is registered with the Main viewlet manager from that package.

Using events to show the selected skin

So far, we have a `skin_chooser` form that can save the chosen skin name in the current session, but we still need to use that name to set the skin automatically on every page view. To do this, we will take advantage of Grok's event functionality, which is discussed in *The Zope Component Architecture* section of this chapter.

The ZCA provides an event registered with the interface `IBeforeTraverseEvent` that we can use to set the skin on every request. Grok has a very convenient `grok.subscribe` decorator that allows us to easily add a handler for this event:

```python
from zope.app.publication.interfaces import IbeforeTraverseEvent
from zope.publisher.browser import applySkin

@grok.subscribe(ITodo, IBeforeTraverseEvent)
def choose_skin(obj, event):
    session = ISession(event.request)['todo_plus']
    skin_name = session.get('skin_name','Basic')
    skin = getUtility(IBrowserSkinType,skin_name)
    applySkin(event.request, skin)
```

We register the `ITodo` interface with the `IBeforeTraverse` event, which means that just before Grok shows a view inside the to-do application instance, our `choose_skin` handler will be called.

Inside the handler, we get the session object and find the skin name that is currently selected for that browser session. We then use the `getUtility` function to get the actual skin object by using this name, and then set the skin by using the `applySkin` function, which is imported from `zope.publisher.browser`. The result is that the chosen skin will be set just in time, before a page is displayed.

Sending e-mail notifications on content creation

One feature that is usually requested in multiuser systems, where users can act on other users' content, is e-mail notification of changes. Our to-do plus package will surely earn its 'plus' moniker if we add such a feature to it.

We'll need a form for setting the notification properties, such as the destination e-mail and message subject. Of course, to keep the site layout consistent, we must also do our usual form-inside-a-viewlet registration dance. These are things that we already know how to do. More interesting is how we'll set up our e-mail handler by using an event subscription, and how the actual e-mail will be sent. Let's get going.

For now, this feature will send notification messages to a specified list of e-mails, whenever a project is created. For this, we first need an interface definition for the form schema:

```
class ISetNotifications(Interface):
    enabled = schema.Bool(title=u'Enable notifications',
      description=u'Email will only be sent if this is enabled')
    sender = schema.TextLine(title=u'Sender email',
      description=u'Email address of sender application')
    emails = schema.TextLine(title=u'Notification emails',
      description=u'One or more emails separated by commas')
    subject = schema.TextLine(title=u'Message subject')
    message = schema.Text(title=u'Message introduction')
```

The `enabled` field will allow the manager to turn notifications on or off. If they are turned on, an e-mail with the specified message and `subject` field information will be sent to the list of e-mails specified in the `emails` field.

Object annotations

Before we proceed with the form definition, we need to decide how to store the notification properties. We can't use the session, as we did with the skin chooser, because the notification properties will be global for the application. In fact, they could be considered as a part of the `Todo` instance itself, so the ideal thing would be to store them there. But that would require changing the original code to add these properties, right?

Well, no. Grok offers a special component called `annotation` that can be used to store information inside a specific context object, without needing to alter it directly. This is accomplished by using a persistent adapter registered for the context object. That is, behind the scenes, there is an `IAnnotation` interface that provides this writing service to any objects in the registry that implement the `IAnnotatable` interface.

As usual, Grok simplifies the setup with a convenient component that we can subclass, called `grok.Annotation`. As discussed earlier, let's register our `annotation` component to the main application's `ITodo` interface:

```
class SetNotificationsAnnotation(grok.Annotation):
    grok.implements(ISetNotifications)
    grok.context(ITodo)
    sender = 'grokadmin@example.com'
    emails = ''
    subject = 'New project created'
    message = ''
    enabled = False
```

The `grok.context` directive indicates that annotations will be added to a component with the `ITodo` interface, which we know is the main application object. The `grok.implements` directive tells Grok to register this annotation adapter with the `ISetNotifications` interface, which is how we'll find it in the registry. Notice that this interface is the same as the one that we'll use in the 'notification properties' form. The variables defined after that represent the default values for the stored properties.

Creating the form

As we now know where the properties will be stored, we can go ahead and create the form. The code for the form definition looks like this:

```python
class SetNotificationsForm(grok.Form):
    grok.context(ITodo)
    grok.name('set_notifications_form')
    form_fields = grok.AutoFields(ISetNotifications)
    label = 'Set email notification options'
    template = form_template

    def setUpWidgets(self, ignore_request=False):
        super(SetNotificationsForm,self).setUpWidgets(ignore_request)
        todo_annotation = ISetNotifications(self.context)
        self.widgets['sender'].displayWidth = 80
        self.widgets['emails'].displayWidth = 80
        self.widgets['subject'].displayWidth = 50
        self.widgets['message'].height = 7
        self.widgets['emails'].setRenderedValue(
          ','.join(todo_annotation.emails))
        self.widgets['enabled'].setRenderedValue(
          todo_annotation.enabled)
        self.widgets['sender'].setRenderedValue(
          todo_annotation.sender)
        self.widgets['message'].setRenderedValue(
          todo_annotation.message)
        self.widgets['subject'].setRenderedValue(
          todo_annotation.subject)

    @grok.action('Set notification options')
    def set_options(self, **data):
        todo_annotation = ISetNotifications(self.context)
        todo_annotation.emails = data['emails'].split(',')
        todo_annotation.enabled = data['enabled']
        todo_annotation.subject = data['subject']
        todo_annotation.message = data['message']
        return self.redirect(self.url('set_notifications'))
```

We use the `grok.AutoFields` directive to construct a form automatically, by using the fields that we previously defined in the `ISetNotifications` interface. As with the `skin_chooser` form, we use the form template imported from the original application, in order to keep the look and feel of the site, the same.

In the `setUpWidgets` method, we get the `annotation` object with the `ISetNotifications(self.context)` call, which searches the registry for an adapter that implements `ISetNotification` and that is registered for the current context, which is the `todo` application. Once we have that, we use the `setRenderedValue` method of each widget to make the form show the currently stored value when the form is displayed. We also alter the size of the various text fields (although, at the moment, this is not important).

In the `set_options` form submit handler, we fetch the annotation object again, but this time we store the submitted values inside their corresponding properties. After that, we just redirect the user to the same form.

All that's left is to insert the form into a viewlet, and then add that viewlet to the `Main` viewlet manager in a view. The code for that is as follows:

```python
class SetNotifications(grok.View):
    grok.context(ITodo)
    grok.name('set_notifications')
    grok.require('todo.addprojects')

    def render(self):
        return master_template.render(self)

class SetNotificationsViewlet(grok.Viewlet):
    grok.viewletmanager(Main)
    grok.context(ITodo)
    grok.view(SetNotifications)

    def update(self):
        self.form = getMultiAdapter((self.context, self.request),
         name='set_notifications_form')
        self.form.update_form()

    def render(self):
        return self.form.render()
```

There is nothing new here. Just note that the permission to add projects will be required to edit the "e-mail notification" properties. The following screenshot shows the form in action:

Sending the e-mail

To send the e-mail, we need an e-mail delivery mechanism. Of course, the Zope Toolkit has a package called `zope.sendmail` that does this, so we just need to add this to our `setup.py`, file and then rerun the `buildout`, in order to use it. Edit the `setup.py` file, and add it to the `install_requires` line:

```
install_requires=[
    'todo',
    'zc.sourcefactory',
    'zope.sendmail',
]
```

Rerun the `buildout`. Now, we have to configure the mail delivery service. Unlike the Grok packages that we have used so far, this Zope Toolkit package requires configuration by using ZCML—the XML-based Zope configuration language. Open the `configure.zcml` file in the `todo_plus` package, and modify it to look like this:

```
<configure xmlns="http://namespaces.zope.org/zope"
        xmlns:mail=http://namespaces.zope.org/mail
        xmlns:grok="http://namespaces.zope.org/grok">

  <include package="grok" />
  <includeDependencies package="." />
  <grok:grok package="." />

  <mail:smtpMailer
    name="todoplus.smtp"
    hostname="mail.example.com"
    port="25"
    username="cguardia"
    password="password"
    />

  <mail:queuedDelivery
    name="mailer"
    permission="zope.Public"
    mailer="todoplus.smtp"
    queuePath="mailqueue"
    />

</configure>
```

Note the addition of the `mail` namespace at the top of the file. This allows us to use the mail directives that appear after the normal Grok configuration. The `smtpMailer` directive represents a named SMTP server. Its parameters are `host`, `port`, `username`, and `password`. If your mail host does not require a password, simply omit the `username` and `password` parameters.

The `queuedDelivery` directive sets up a queue to use to send the mail messages. This gets done in an independent thread to allow the application to keep working even when numerous e-mails are sent. The `permission` argument refers to the permission needed for sending e-mails. Be sure to use the same name for the `mailer` parameter that was used in the SMTP mailer definition, above.

Now we are ready to register the event for sending the e-mail. We'll use the `grok.subscribe` directive to register our handler with the `IObjectAddedEvent` of `Project` objects.

```python
import email.MIMEText
import email.Header
from zope.sendmail.interfaces import IMailDelivery

@grok.subscribe(IProject, grok.IObjectAddedEvent)
def send_email(obj, event):
    todo_annotation = ISetNotifications(obj.__parent__)
    if not todo_annotation.enabled:
        return
    sender = todo_annotation.sender
    recipient = todo_annotation.emails
    subject = todo_annotation.subject
    body = todo_annotation.message
    body = body.replace('${title}',obj.title)
    body = body.replace('${description}',obj.description)
    body = body.replace('${creator}',obj.creator)
    msg = email.MIMEText.MIMEText(body.encode('UTF-8'), 'plain',
      'UTF-8')
    msg["From"] = sender
    msg["To"] = ','.join(recipient)
    msg["Subject"] = email.Header.Header(subject, 'UTF-8')
    mailer = getUtility(IMailDelivery, 'todoplus')
    mailer.send(sender, recipient, msg.as_string())
```

The handler first finds the `annotation` object and checks the value of the `enabled` property. If it's `False`, the method just returns without doing anything else; if it's `True`, we get the property values and compose the message with the help of the Python e-mail module. One simple trick that we use here is to allow the message to insert the title, creator, and description of the newly created project by using simple string substitutions. Take a look at the screenshot under the *Creating a form* section of this chapter, to see how this works.

The `zope.sendmail` package registers the mailer utility by using an interface named `IMailDelivery`, so we import this and use the `getUtility` function from `zope.component` to find it and finally send the e-mail.

Displaying additional navigation links

So far, the to-do application has 'user management' and 'skin chooser' forms, but they don't show up in the site navigation. We have a viewlet manager set up for that in our original application, so we just need to register a viewlet with that manager and add a template, and we are done. This will demonstrate how easy it is to insert arbitrary page fragments in Grok, when the original views plan for it carefully.

Let's add two viewlets—one for regular user options, and one for manager-only options:

```python
class ManagerOptions(grok.Viewlet):
    grok.viewletmanager(ExtraNav)
    grok.context(Interface)
    grok.require('zope.ManageApplication')


class UserOptions(grok.Viewlet):
    grok.viewletmanager(ExtraNav)
    grok.context(Interface)
    grok.require('todo.changeitems')
```

Both of these viewlets are registered with the `ExtraNav` viewlet manager from the to-do application, but one requires only the `todo.changeitems` permission, while the other needs the `zope.ManageApplication` permission, which is usually assigned to the site manager. The page templates just include a couple of links. First, inside `manageroptions.pt`, we have:

```
| <a tal:attributes="href python:view.application_
url('userlist')">Manage users</a>
```

That's right, just a link to the `userlist` view, which will be inserted in the correct place by the viewlet manager.

The other template, `useroptions.pt`, is almost as simple:

```
| <a tal:attributes="href python:view.application_url('skin_
chooser')">Choose skin</a>
| <a tal:attributes="href python:view.application_url('set_
notifications')"> Set notifications</a>
```

That's all that is needed. You can see the result in the navigation section of the previous two screenshots of this chapter. The nice thing about this is that other third-party packages can add a navigation link as well, and this would be transparently integrated with the existing navigation options, without even having to know about the existence of these other packages.

Summary

This chapter discussed the main concepts behind the Zope Component Architecture, and showed how to use some of the ZCA's patterns to extend our application. Most importantly, we showed how to extend a package without touching its code. In the next chapter, we'll see how Grok uses a library called Martian to permit agile configuration, and learn how to benefit from it, for our own work.

12
Grokkers, Martian, and Agile Configuration

Agility is very important in Grok, and having to do less configuration to get an application running is the key to being **agile**. In Grok parlance, a **grokker** is a piece of code that allows developers to use framework functionality by making declarations in the code instead of using ZCML configuration files. In this chapter, we introduce **Martian**—the library that is used to create grokkers—and demonstrate how to create a simple one for our application. Among the subjects that we will cover are:

- What Martian is
- Why it is needed and how Grok uses it
- What a grokker is
- How to create a grokker

Agile configuration

As we explained at the very beginning of this book, when we use the Zope Toolkit without Grok, we must use ZCML to configure everything. This means that we have to add ZCML directives for every view, viewlet, adapter, subscriber, and annotation in our code. That's quite a lot of markup there, all of which has to be maintained along with the code. Agility is not the first thing that comes to mind when we think about this.

Grok's developers knew from experience that the Zope Toolkit and the **Zope Component Architecture (ZCA)** enable developers to create advanced object-oriented systems. This power comes at the cost of a raised barrier of entry for new developers.

Another thing that proved to be a problem for Zope Toolkit adoption, is its emphasis on explicit configuration. ZCML allows developers to be very explicit and flexible in their application configuration, but it requires separate files for configuration, and takes more time to create, maintain, and understand. You simply need more time to understand an application because you have to take a look at the different pieces of code and then consult the ZCML files to see how they are connected with each other.

Grok was designed in such a way that, if the developer follows certain conventions in his code, there is no need for configuration files. Instead, Grok analyzes the Python code for the use of these conventions, and then 'groks' them. Behind the scenes, everything is connected just as it would be if the configuration was written with ZCML, but the developer doesn't even need to think about that.

As a result of this process, known as 'grokking', the code for a Grok application is clean and uniform. The entire configuration is in the code, in the form of directives and components, so it's easier to follow, and more fun to develop.

Grok is definitely more agile than the Zope Toolkit alone, but it's not a subset or a 'stripped down' version of it. All of the power of the Zope Toolkit is available to the developer. Even explicit configuration can be used with ZCML when it's needed, as we saw when we configured the SMTP mailer, in the previous chapter.

The Martian library

The part of Grok that does the code 'grokking' has been extracted into a standalone library called Martian. This library provides a framework that allows configuration to be expressed in Python code, in the form of declarative statements. The idea is that, often, the structure of a piece of code can be examined and most of the configuration steps that it requires are deduced from this. Martian takes this a step further by using directives to annotate the code, making configuration requirements even more obvious.

Martian is published as a standalone library because even though, it's a key part of Grok, it can be very useful for adding declarative configuration to any kind of framework. For example, `repoze.bfg` (`http://bfg.repoze.org`), a minimalist web framework based on Zope concepts, uses Martian to optionally allow the view configuration without ZCML.

At program startup time, Martian reads the Python code in a module and analyzes all of the classes to see if they belong to a 'grokked' base class (or a subclass of one). If they do, Martian retrieves information from the class registration and any of the directives that it may contain. This information is then used to perform component registrations in the ZCA registry, much like the ZCML machinery does. This process is called 'grokking' and as you see, allows for quick registration of plugins within the framework. Grokkers allow us to write "agility" and "Zope Toolkit" in the same sentence again, without being ironic about it.

Understanding grokkers

A grokker is a package that includes a base class to be grokked, a series of directives for configuring that class, and the actual code that performs the registration process using Martian.

Let's take a look at a regular Grok view definition:

```
class AddUser(grok.View):
    grok.context(Interface)
    grok.template('master')
```

In this code, `grok.View` is a grokked class, which means that, when the "Grok time" comes at program startup, it will be found by Martian, 'grokked', and registered with the ZCA. The `grok.context` and `grok.template` declarations are the configuration directives available for this class. The actual 'grokking' is done by a piece of code associated with the grokked class, which registers a named adapter with the ZCA registry for the interface that is passed in the `grok.context` directive. The registration is done by using the class name to name the view, and whatever string value is passed as a parameter to the `grok.template` directive is used to name the associated template.

That's all that grokking means, so if we have the three required parts, we can easily make our own grokkers.

The grokked class

Any class can be grokked; there are no special requirements. This makes it easy for a developer to get started, and is a lot less confusing to work with. Imagine that we have some `Mailer` class that we want to grok. It can be as simple as this:

```
class Mailer(object):
    pass
```

Of course, it could be as complex as needed, but the point is that it doesn't need to be.

The directives

Once we have a class that we want to grok, we define the directives that we may need for configuring it. Again, there's nothing required of us here. We could perhaps perform our configuration without the need for directives, but most of the time we may need a couple of them.

```
class hostname(martian.Directive):
    scope = CLASS
    default = 'localhost'

class port(martian.Directive):
    scope = CLASS
    default = 25
```

Directives do need to inherit from the `martian.Directive` subclass. Also, they need to at least specify a scope, and probably a default value as well. Here, we defined two directives—`hostname` and `port`, which will be used to configure the mailer.

The class grokker

The final piece of our grokker is the one that does the actual registration, and it comes in the form of a class that inherits from `martian.ClassGrokker`:

```
class MailGrokker(martian.ClassGrokker):
    martian.component(Mailer)
    martian.directive(hostname)
    martian.directive(port)

    def execute(self, class_, hostname, port, **kw):
        register_mailer(class_, hostname, port)
```

The grokker class connects the grokked class with its directives, and does the grokking, or registration. It has to include an `execute` method that will take care of any configuration actions.

The `martian.component` directive connects the grokker with the class to be grokked, in this case, `Mailer`. The directive `martian.directive` is used to associate the various directives that we defined earlier with this grokker.

Finally, the `execute` method takes the base class and the directive values declared in the code that uses the grokker, and performs the final registration. Note that the `register_mailer` method (which would actually do the work here) is not present in the preceding code, because all we want to show here is the structure of a grokker.

The only ZCML you'll ever need

Once the grokker is available, it has to be configured to be initialized and used, by the Grok registration machinery at startup time. To do that, we have to use a bit of ZCML in a file named `meta.zcml`:

```
<configure xmlns:grok="http://namespaces.zope.org/grok">
   <grok:grok package=".meta" />
</configure>
```

If our `MailGrokker` class is inside the `meta.py` file, it will be initialized by the Grok machinery.

Creating our own grokker for zope.sendmail configuration

Now that we know how a grokker is structured, let's create one for the SMTP mailer from the `zope.sendmail` that we used in the section about adding e-mail notifications (in Chapter 11) to our application.

What we want is to have a simple `MailGrokker` class declaration with `hostname`, `port`, `username`, `password`, and `delivery type` directives. This will allow us to avoid using ZCML to configure the mailer, as we were required to do in the previous section.

We'll have to create a new package, so that our grokker is independent of the `todo_plus` code and can be used freely elsewhere.

Creating the package

We performed these steps in the *Creating the new package* section of Chapter 11. If you have any doubts, please refer to that section for details.

To create the package, go into the `src` directory of our main `todo` application, and type:

```
$ ../bin/paster create -t basic_package mailgrokker
```

This will create a `mailgrokker` directory. Now, navigate to this directory and add `grok`, `martian`, and the `zope.sendmail` package to the `install_requires` declaration:

```
install_requires=[
    'grok',
    'martian',
    'zope.sendmail',
],
```

In this way, we make sure that the required packages are present, once `mailgrokker` is installed. We also have to add our new `mailgrokker` package to the main `buildout.cfg` file at the top level of our project, immediately under `todo_plus`. Do this in both the eggs and the develop sections.

Writing our grokker

First, we'll add a `configure.zcml` file, which is just like the one in the `todo_plus` package. In fact, we can copy it from there:

```
<configure xmlns="http://namespaces.zope.org/zope"
           xmlns:mail="http://namespaces.zope.org/mail"
           xmlns:grok="http://namespaces.zope.org/grok">
  <include package="grok" />
  <includeDependencies package="." />
  <grok:grok package="." />
</configure>
```

Our grokked class will be inside the `component.py` file. Here, we are using only one base class, but a grokker project could include several base classes, and by convention they are defined here:

```
import grok


class Mailer(object):
    grok.baseclass()
```

This is just a simple base class with no methods. The `grok.baseclass` directive is used to mark it as a base class, although this is not mandatory.

The configuration directives are stored in a file named `directives.py`:

```python
import martian

class name(martian.Directive):
    scope = martian.CLASS
    store = martian.ONCE

class hostname(martian.Directive):
    scope = martian.CLASS
    store = martian.ONCE
    default = 'localhost'

class port(martian.Directive):
    scope = martian.CLASS
    store = martian.ONCE
    default = '25'

class username(martian.Directive):
    scope = martian.CLASS
    store = martian.ONCE
    default = None

class password(martian.Directive):
    scope = martian.CLASS
    store = martian.ONCE
    default = None

class delivery(martian.Directive):
    scope = martian.CLASS
    store = martian.ONCE
    default = 'queued'

class permission(martian.Directive):
    scope = martian.CLASS
    store = martian.ONCE
    default = 'zope.Public'
```

This is very straightforward. We just define all of the directives that we need, and then add a `martian.CLASS` scope. Each directive has its own default value, depending on its purpose. The intent of each directive should be obvious just by looking at the code, except perhaps for the `delivery` directive. This directive is needed because `zope.sendmail` includes two different delivery mechanisms—`direct` and `queued`.

Now comes the main grokker class, which we will add to the `meta.py` file. First, are the `import` statements. Note that here we import `martian` as well as `GrokError`, which is an exception that we can throw if the grokking fails. We also import everything that we are going to use from the `zope.sendmail` library.

```
import martian
from martian.error import GrokError

from zope.component import getGlobalSiteManager

from zope.sendmail.delivery import QueuedMailDelivery,
DirectMailDelivery
from zope.sendmail.delivery import QueueProcessorThread
from zope.sendmail.interfaces import IMailer, IMailDelivery
from zope.sendmail.mailer import SMTPMailer
from zope.sendmail.zcml import _assertPermission

from mailgrokker.components import Mailer
from mailgrokker.directives import name, hostname, port, username,
password, delivery, permission
```

The `register_mailer` function creates a `zope.sendmail` SMTP mailer object, and registers it as a named utility for `IMailer`, with the name taken from the `name` directive. Note the use of the `getGlobalSiteManager` function, which is really a fancy name for getting the component registry. We use the `registerUtility` function of the registry to add our newly created `SMTPMailer` instance.

```
def register_mailer(class_, name, hostname, port, username, password,
delivery, permission):
    sm = getGlobalSiteManager()
    mailer = SMTPMailer(hostname, port, username, password)
    sm.registerUtility(mailer, IMailer, name)
```

Continuing with the `register_mailer` code, we now use the selected delivery mechanism, which was passed as a parameter, to decide if we should initialize a `DirectMailDelivery` instance or a `QueuedMailDelivery` instance. Either way, we register the result as a utility.

In the case of a `queue` delivery mechanism, a thread that will take care of sending e-mail separately from the main application code is started.

```
    if delivery=='direct':
        mail_delivery = DirectMailDelivery(mailer)
        _assertPermission(permission, IMailDelivery, mail_delivery)
        sm.registerUtility(mail_delivery, IMailDelivery, name)
    elif delivery=='queued':
```

```
    mail_delivery = QueuedMailDelivery(name)
    _assertPermission(permission, IMailDelivery, mail_delivery)
    sm.registerUtility(mail_delivery, IMailDelivery, name)
    thread = QueueProcessorThread()
    thread.setMailer(mailer)
    thread.setQueuePath(name)
    thread.start()
else:
    raise GrokError("Available delivery methods are 'direct' and
'queued'. Delivery method %s is not defined.",class_)
```

The `MailGrokker` class declares all of the directives that we added to the
`directives` module, and associates itself with the `Mailer` class that it will grok. It
then defines the `execute` method that will call the `register_mailer` function to
perform the required `zope.sendmail` registrations.

```
class MailGrokker(martian.ClassGrokker):
    martian.component(Mailer)
    martian.directive(name)
    martian.directive(hostname)
    martian.directive(port)
    martian.directive(username)
    martian.directive(password)
    martian.directive(delivery)
    martian.directive(permission)

    def execute(self, class_, config, name, hostname, port, username,
                password, delivery, permission, **kwds):
        config.action(
                discriminator = ('utility', IMailer, name),
                callable = register_mailer,
                args = (class_, name, hostname, port, username,
                    password, delivery, permission),
                order = 5
                )
        return True
```

The only difference between the above code and the code that we showed earlier
is that instead of calling the `register_mailer` function directly, we wrap it inside
a `config.action` object. This is done so that Grok can perform the registrations in
an arbitrary order after the code is loaded, instead of doing that as it initializes each
package. This prevents any configuration conflicts, and allows us to be specific about
the registration conditions.

For example, the `discriminator` parameter, which could be empty, is, in this case, a tuple containing the string `utility`, the interface `IMailer`, and the value of the `name` directive. If any other grokker package uses this same discriminator, Grok will signal a conflict error condition.

The `order` parameter of the `action` is used to dictate the order in which the actions are called, although here it was added for demonstration purposes only. The `callable` parameter is the function that will perform the registration, and the `args` parameter contains the parameters that will be passed to it.

We now have our grokker in the `meta` module, and need to tell Grok to find it here, which we do by adding the small `meta.zcml` file discussed earlier:

```
<configure xmlns:grok="http://namespaces.zope.org/grok">
    <grok:grok package=".meta" />
</configure>
```

Finally, edit the existing `__init__.py` file, which is inside `src/mailgrokker/mailgrokker` directory, to look like the following code:

```
from mailgrokker.directives import name, hostname, port, username,
password, del ivery, permission
from mailgrokker.components import Mailer
```

This will allow us to use the directives simply by importing the main `mailgrokker` module, much in the way that `grok.*` directives work.

Using mailgrokker

Now that we are done with our grokker, the only thing that is missing is to show how it would be used inside an application. We will add it to the `todo_plus` package. Insert the following lines at the bottom of that file:

```
import mailgrokker

class TodoMailer(mailgrokker.Mailer):
    mailgrokker.name('todoplus')
    mailgrokker.hostname('smtp.example.com')
    mailgrokker.username('cguardia')
    mailgrokker.password('password')
```

Obviously, you should substitute the values shown here with the real values of your `smtp` server. You might also want to eliminate the mailer configuration that we placed in the `configure.zcml` file, earlier.

Done. We have now created a small grokker package that can be used in any of our applications in order to easily configure e-mail submissions.

Summary

In this chapter we learned about the Martian library and how it enables Grok to be an agile framework. We are now ready to discuss how to debug our applications.

13
Testing and Debugging

Throughout this book, we have been discussing how Grok offers an agile way of working with Zope. However, up to this point, we have neglected to perform one activity that is considered most important in agile projects: *testing*.

Grok offers some tools for testing, and in fact, a project created by `grokproject` (as the one that we have been extending) includes a functional test suite. In this chapter, we are going to discuss testing, and will then write some tests for the functionality that our application has so far.

Testing helps us to avoid bugs, but it does not eliminate them completely, of course. There will be times when we will have to dive into the code to find out what's going wrong in it. A good set of debugging aids becomes very valuable in this situation. We'll see that there are several ways of debugging a Grok application, and will try out a couple of them.

Some of the things that we will cover includes:

- The need for testing
- Testing in Grok
- Extending the functional test suite provided by `grokproject`
- Other kinds of testing
- Debugging tools

Testing

It's important to understand that testing should not be treated as an afterthought. It's just that in a book like this one, which focuses a lot on testing, it can be harder to follow explanations and code in the initial stages of your reading.

As mentioned earlier, agile methodologies place a lot of emphasis on testing. In fact, there's even a methodology called **Test Driven Development (TDD)**, which not only encourages writing tests for our code, but also encourages writing tests before writing a single line of code.

There are various kinds of testing, but here we'll briefly describe only two:

- Unit testing
- Integration or functional tests

Unit testing

The idea of unit testing is to break a program into its constituent parts and test each one of them in isolation. Every method or function call is tested separately to make sure that it returns the expected results and handles all of the possible inputs correctly.

An application that has unit tests that cover a majority of its lines of code allows its developers to constantly run the tests after a change, and makes sure that modifications to the code do not break the existing functionality.

Functional tests

Functional tests are concerned with how the application behaves as a whole. In a web application, this means, how it responds to a browser request and whether it returns the expected HTML for a given call.

Ideally, the customer himself has a hand in defining these tests, usually through explicit functionality requirements or acceptance criteria. The more formal that the requirements from the customer are, the easier it is to define appropriate functional tests.

Testing in Grok

Grok highly encourages the use of both kinds of tests, and in fact includes a powerful testing tool that is automatically configured with every project. In the Zope world — from where Grok originated — a lot of value is placed in a kind of test known as a "doctest", so Grok comes with a sample test suite of this kind.

Doctests

A **doctest** is a test that's written as a text file, with lines of code mixed with explanations of what the code is doing. The code is written in a way that simulates a Python interpreter session. As tests exercise large portions of the code (ideally 100%), they usually offer a good way of finding out of what an application does and how. So if an application has no written documentation, its tests would be the next obvious way of finding out what it does. Doctests take this idea further, by allowing the developer to explain in the text file exactly what each test is doing.

Doctests are especially useful for functional testing, because it makes more sense to document the high-level operations of a program. Unit tests, on the other hand, are expected to evaluate the program bit by bit, and it can be cumbersome to write a text explanation for every little piece of code.

A possible drawback of doctests is that they can make the developer think that he needs no other documentation for his project. In almost all cases, this is not true. Documenting an application or package makes it immediately more accessible and useful, so it is strongly recommended that doctests should not be used as a replacement for good documentation. We'll show an example of using doctests in the *Looking at the test code* section of this chapter.

Default test setup for Grok projects

As mentioned earlier, Grok projects that are started with the `grokproject` tool already include a simple functional test suite, by default. Let's examine this in detail.

Test configuration

The default test configuration looks for packages or modules that have the word 'tests' in their name and tries to run the tests inside. For functional tests, any files ending with `.txt` or `.rst` are considered.

For functional tests that need to simulate a browser, a special configuration is needed to tell Grok which packages to initialize in addition to the Grok infrastructure (these are usually the ones that are being worked on). The `ftesting.zcml` file in the `package` directory holds this configuration. This file also includes a couple of user definitions that are used by certain tests to examine functionality that is specific to a certain role, such as manager.

Test files

In addition to the already mentioned `ftesting.zcml` file, in the same directory there is a `tests.py` file added by `grokproject`, which basically loads the ZCML declarations and registers all of the tests in the package.

The actual tests that are included with the default project files are contained in the
`app.txt` file. These are doctests that perform a functional test run by loading the
entire Grok environment and imitating a browser. We'll take a look at the contents of
the file soon, but first let's run the tests.

Running the tests

As a part of the project's build process, a script named `test` is included in the
`bin` directory when you create a new project. This is the **test runner**, and calling
it without arguments finds and executes all of the tests in the packages that are
included in the configuration.

We haven't added a single test so far, so if we type `bin/test` in our project directory,
we'll see more or less the same thing that doing this on a new project would show:

```
$ bin/test
Running tests at level 1
Running todo.FunctionalLayer tests:
  Set up
 in 12.319 seconds.
  Running:
...2009-09-30 15:00:47,490 INFO sqlalchemy.engine.base.Engine.0x...782c
PRAGMA table_info("users")
2009-09-30 15:00:47,490 INFO sqlalchemy.engine.base.Engine.0x...782c ()

  Ran 3 tests with 0 failures and 0 errors in 0.465 seconds.
Tearing down left over layers:
  Tear down todo.FunctionalLayer ... not supported
```

The only difference between our output and that of a newly created Grok package
is in the `sqlalchemy` lines. Of course, the most important part of the output is the
penultimate line, which shows the number of tests that were run and whether there
were any failures or errors. A *failure* means that a test didn't pass, which means that
the code is not doing what it's supposed to do and needs to be checked. An *error*
signifies that the code crashed unexpectedly at some point, and the test couldn't even
be executed, so it's necessary to find the error and correct it before worrying about
the tests.

The test runner

The test runner program looks for modules that contain tests. The test can be of three
different types: Python tests, simple doctests, and full-functionality doctests. To let
the test runner know which test file includes which kind of tests, a comment similar
to the following is placed at the top of the file:

```
Do a Python test on the app.
```

```
:unittestt:
```

In this case, the Python unit test layer will be used to run the tests. The other value that we are going to use is doctest, when we learn how to write doctests.

The test runner then finds all of the test modules and runs them in the corresponding layer. Although unit tests are considered very important in regular development, we may find functional tests more necessary for a Grok web application, as we will usually be testing views and forms, which require the full Zope/Grok stack to be loaded, in order to work. That's the reason why we find only functional doctests in the default setup.

Test layers

A **test layer** is a specific test setup that is used to differentiate the tests that are executed. By default, there is a test layer for each of the three types of tests handled by the test runner. It's possible to run a test layer without running the others. It is also possible to create new test layers in order to cluster together tests that require a specific setup.

Invoking the test runner

As shown above, running `bin/test` will start the test runner with the default options. It's also possible to specify a number of options, and the most important ones of these are summarized below. In the following table, command-line options are shown to the left. Most options can be expressed using a short form (one dash) or a long form (two dashes). Arguments for each option are shown in uppercase.

Option	Description

`-s PACKAGE,`
`--package=PACKAGE,`
`--dir=PACKAGE`
	Search the given package's directories for tests. This can be specified more than once, to run tests in multiple parts of the source tree. For example, when refactoring interfaces, you don't want to see the way you have broken setups for tests in other packages. You just want to run the interface tests. Packages are supplied as dotted names. For compatibility with the old test runner, forward and backward slashes in package names are converted to dots. (In the special case of packages, which are spread over multiple directories, only directories within the test search path are searched.)

Option	Description
`-m MODULE, --module=MODULE`	Specify a test-module filter as a regular expression. This is a case-sensitive regular expression that is used in *search* (not match) mode to limit which test modules are searched for tests. The regular expressions are checked against dotted module names. In an extension of Python regexp notation, a leading "!" is stripped and causes the sense of the remaining regexp to be negated (so "!bc" matches any string that does not match "bc", and vice versa). This option can specify multiple test-module filters. Test modules matching any of the test filters are searched. If no test-module filter is specified, then all of the test modules are used.
`-t TEST, --test=TEST`	Specify a test filter as a regular expression. This is a case-sensitive regular expression that is used in *search* (not match) mode to limit which tests are run. In an extension of Python regexp notation, a leading "!" is stripped and causes the sense of the remaining regexp to be negated (so "!bc" matches any string that does not match "bc", and vice versa). This option can specify multiple test filters. Tests matching any of the test filters are included. If no test filter is specified, then all of the tests are executed.
`--layer=LAYER`	Specify a test layer to run. This option can be provided multiple times in order to specify more than one layer. If not specified, all of the layers are executed. It is common for the running script to provide default values for this option. Layers are specified regular expressions that are used in search mode, for dotted names of objects that define a layer. In an extension of Python regexp notation, a leading "!" is stripped and causes the sense of the remaining regexp to be negated (so "!bc" matches any string that does not match "bc", and vice versa). The layer named 'unit' is reserved for unit tests; however, take note of the *–unit* and *non-unit* options.
`-u, --unit`	Executes only unit tests, ignoring any layer options.
`-f, --non-unit`	Executes tests other than unit tests.
`-v, --verbose`	Makes the output more verbose.
`-q, --quiet`	Provides minimal output, by overriding any verbosity options.

Looking at the test code

Let's take a look at the three default test files of a Grok project, to see what each one does.

ftesting.zcml

As we explained earlier, `ftesting.zcml` is a configuration file for the test runner.
Its main objective is to help us set up the test instance with users, so that we can test
different roles according to our needs.

```
<configure
    xmlns="http://namespaces.zope.org/zope"
    i18n_domain="todo"
    package="todo"
    >

<include package="todo" />
<include package="todo_plus" />

<!-- Typical functional testing security setup -->
<securityPolicy
    component="zope.securitypolicy.zopepolicy.ZopeSecurityPolicy"
    />

<unauthenticatedPrincipal
    id="zope.anybody"
    title="Unauthenticated User"
    />
<grant
    permission="zope.View"
    principal="zope.anybody"
    />

<principal
    id="zope.mgr"
    title="Manager"
    login="mgr"
    password="mgrpw"
    />

<role id="zope.Manager" title="Site Manager" />
<grantAll role="zope.Manager" />
<grant role="zope.Manager" principal="zope.mgr" />
```

As shown in the preceding code, the configuration simply includes a security
policy, complete with users and roles, and the packages that should be loaded by
the instance, in addition to the regular Grok infrastructure. If we run any tests that
require an authenticated user to work, we'll use these special users.

The includes at the top of the file make sure that the entire Zope Component
Architecture setup needed by our application is performed prior to running the tests.

tests.py

The default test module is very simple. It defines the functional layer and registers the tests for our package:

```python
import os.path
import z3c.testsetup
import todo
from zope.app.testing.functional import ZCMLLayer

ftesting_zcml = os.path.join(
    os.path.dirname(todo.__file__), 'ftesting.zcml')
FunctionalLayer = ZCMLLayer(ftesting_zcml, __name__,
'FunctionalLayer', allow_teardown=True)

test_suite = z3c.testsetup.register_all_tests('todo')
```

After the imports, the first line gets the path for the `ftesting.zcml` file, which is then passed to the layer definition method `ZCMLLayer`. The final line in the module tells the test runner to find and register all of the tests in the package.

This will be enough for our testing needs in this chapter, but if we needed to create another non-Grok package for our application, we would need to add a line like the last one to it, so that all of its tests are found by the test runner. This is pretty much boilerplate code, as only the package name has to be changed.

app.txt

We finally come to the reason for this entire configuration—the actual tests that will be executed by the test runner. By default, the tests are included inside the `app.txt` file:

```
Do a functional doctest test on the app.
=========================================

:doctest:
:layer: todo.tests.FunctionalLayer

Let's first create an instance of Todo at the top level:

    >>> from todo.app import Todo
    >>> root = getRootFolder()
    >>> root['app'] = Todo()

Run tests in the testbrowser
----------------------------
```

```
The zope.testbrowser.browser module exposes a Browser class that
simulates a web browser similar to Mozilla Firefox or IE. We use that
to test how our application behaves in a browser. For more
information, see http://pypi.python.org/pypi/zope.testbrowser.
```

```
Create a browser and visit the instance you just created:

    >>> from zope.testbrowser.testing import Browser
    >>> browser = Browser()
    >>> browser.open('http://localhost/app')
```

```
Check some basic information about the page you visit:

    >>> browser.url
    'http://localhost/app/@@login?camefrom=%2Fapp%2F%40%40index'
    >>> browser.headers.get('Status').upper()
    '200 OK'
```

The text file has a title, and immediately after that a `:doctest:` declaration—a
declaration that tells the test runner that these tests need a functional layer to be
loaded for their execution. Then comes a `:layer:` declaration, which is a path that
points to the layer that we defined earlier in `tests.py`. After that comes the test
code. Lines starting with three brackets represent the Python code that is tested.
Anything else is commentary.

When using the Python interpreter, a line of code may return a value, in which
case the expected return value must be written immediately below that line. This
expected value will be compared with the real return value of the tested code, and
a failure will be reported if the values don't match. Similarly, a line that is followed
by an empty line will produce a failure when the code is executed and a result is
returned, because it is assumed that the expected return value in that case is None.

For example, in the last line of the Python doctest below the expression
`browser.headers.get('Status').upper()` is expected to return the value
`200 OK`. If anything else at all is returned, the test will fail.

Adding our own tests

Now, let's add a few functional tests that are specific to our application. We will need
to emulate a browser for that. The `zope.testbrowser` package includes a browser
emulator. We can pass any valid URL to this browser by using `browser.open`, and
it will send a request to our application exactly like a browser would. The response
from our application will be then available as `browser.contents`, so that we can
perform our testing comparisons on it.

The Browser class

Before writing our tests, it will be useful to see what exactly our `testbrowser` can do. Of course, anything that depends on JavaScript will not work here, but other than that, we can interact with links and even forms in a very straightforward manner. Here's a look at the main functionality offered by the `Browser` class:

Initialization	```>>> from zope.testbrowser.testing import Browser``` ```>>> browser = Browser()```
Page contents	```>>> print browser.contents```

```
>>> print browser.contents
<html>
  <head>
    <title>Simple Page</title>
  </head>
  <body>
    <h1>Simple Page</h1>
  </body>
</html>
>>> '<h1>Simple Page</h1>' in browser.contents
True
```

Headers
```
>>> print browser.headers
Status: 200 OK
Content-Length: 123
Content-Type: text/html;charset=utf-8
X-Powered-By: Zope (www.zope.org), Python (www.
python.org)
>>> browser.headers['content-type']
'text/html;charset=utf-8'
```

Cookies
```
>>> browser.cookies['foo']
'bar'
>>> browser.cookies.keys()
['foo']
>>> browser.cookies.values()
['bar']
>>> browser.cookies.items()
[('foo', 'bar')]
>>> 'foo' in browser.cookies
True
>>> browser.cookies['sha'] = 'zam'
```

| Links | ```
>>> link = browser.getLink('Link Text')
>>> link
<Link text='Link Text'
  url='http://localhost/@@/testbrowser/navigate.
html?message=By+Link+Text'>
>>> link.text
'Link Text'
>>> link.tag # links can also be image maps.
'a'
>>> link.url # it's normalized
'http://localhost/@@/testbrowser/navigate.
html?message=By+Link+Text'
>>> link.attrs
{'href': 'navigate.html?message=By+Link+Text'}
>>> link.click()
>>> browser.url
'http://localhost/@@/testbrowser/navigate.
html?message=By+Link+Text'
``` |
| Form controls | ```
>>> control = browser.getControl('Text Control')
>>> control
<Control name='text-value' type='text'>
>>> browser.getControl(label='Text Control') #
equivalent
<Control name='text-value' type='text'>
>>> browser.getControl('Text Control').value =
'Other Text'
>>> browser.getControl('Submit').click()
``` |

Now that we know what we can do, let's try our hand at writing some tests.

Our first to-do application tests

Ideally, we should have been adding a couple of doctests to the `app.txt` file every time we added a new functionality to our application. We have gone through the reasons why we didn't do so, but let's recover some lost ground. At the very least, we'll get a feeling of how doctests work.

We'll add our new tests to the existing `app.txt` file. The last test that we saw left us at the to-do instance URL. We are not logged in, so if we print the browser contents, we will get the login page. Let's add a test for this:

```
Since we haven't logged in, we can't see the application. The login
page appears:

    >>> 'Username' in browser.contents
    True
    >>> 'Password' in browser.contents
    True
```

As we mentioned earlier, when visiting a URL with the `testbrowser`, the entire HTML content of the page is stored in `browser.contents`. Now we know that our login page has a username field and a password field, so we simply use a couple of `in` expressions and check if these fields evaluate to `True`. If they do, it would mean that the browser is effectively looking at the login page.

Let's add a test for logging in. When we start the application in the tests, the user database is empty, therefore, the most economical way of logging in is to use basic authentication. This can be easily done by changing the request headers:

Let's log in with the manager user defined in `ftesting.zcml`. To keep things simple, let's use the basic authentication headers to get in:

```
>>> browser.addHeader('Authorization', 'Basic mgr:mgrpw')
>>> browser.open('http://localhost/app')
>>> 'Logged in as Manager' in browser.contents
True
```

That's it. We just add the header, "reload" the home page, and we should be logged in. We verify it by looking for the **Logged in as** message, which we know has to be there after a successful login.

Once we are logged in, we can finally test our application properly. Let's begin by adding a project:

We are now in. Let's create a project:

```
>>> browser.getLink('Create a new project').click()
>>> browser.getControl(name='form.title').value='a project'
>>> browser.getControl(name='form.description').value='The
description.'
>>> browser.getControl('Add project').click()
>>> browser.url
'http://localhost/app/0'
>>> 'Create new list' in browser.contents
True
```

First, we find the link on the home page that will take us to the 'add form' project. This is done easily with the help of the `getLink` method and the text of the link. We click on the link and then should have the form ready to fill in. We then use `getControl` to find each field by its name, and change its value. Finally, we submit the form by getting the submit button control and clicking on it. The result is that the project is created and we are redirected to its main view. We can confirm this by comparing the `browser url` with the URL that we would expect in this case.

Adding a list to the project is just as easy. We get the form controls, assign them some values, and click on the submit button. The list and the link for adding new items to it should appear in the browser contents:

We have added a project. Now, we'll add a list to it. If we are successful, we will see a link for adding a new item for the list:

```
>>> browser.getControl(name='title').value='a list'
>>> browser.getControl(name='description').value='The list
description.'
>>> browser.getControl(name='new_list').click()
>>> 'New item' in browser.contents
True
```

Good. Let's see how we are doing so far:

```
$ bin/testRunning tests at level 1
Running todo.FunctionalLayer tests:
  Set up
 in 3.087 seconds.
  Running:
.......2009-09-30 21:35:44,585 INFO sqlalchemy.engine.base.
Engine.0x...69ec PRAGMA table_info("users")
2009-09-30 21:35:44,585 INFO sqlalchemy.engine.base.Engine.0x...69ec ()

  Ran 7 tests with 0 failures and 0 errors in 0.428 seconds.
Tearing down left over layers:
  Tear down todo.FunctionalLayer ... not supported
```

Not bad. We now have four more working tests than when we started.

Note that the test browser handles HTTP errors gracefully, returning a string similar to what a real browser would return when running into an error. For example, take a look at the following test:

```
>>> browser.open('http://localhost/invalid')
Traceback (most recent call last):
...
HTTPError: HTTP Error 404: Not Found
```

That's the default behavior because this is how real browsers work, but sometimes, when we are debugging, it's better to take a look at the original exception caused by our application. In such a case, we can make the browser stop handling errors automatically and throw the original exceptions, so that we can handle them. This is done by setting the `browser.handleErrors` property to `False`:

```
>>> browser.handleErrors = False
>>> browser.open('http://localhost/invalid')
Traceback (most recent call last):
...
NotFound: Object: <zope.site.folder.Folder object at ...>,
          name: u'invalid'
```

Adding unit tests

Apart from functional tests, we can also create pure Python test cases that the test runner can find. Whereas functional tests cover application behavior, unit tests focus on program correctness. Ideally, every single Python method in the application should be tested.

The unit test layer does not load the Grok infrastructure, so tests should not take anything that comes with it for granted—just the basic Python behavior.

To add our unit tests, we'll create a module named `unit_tests.py`. Remember, in order for the test runner to find our test modules, their names have to end with 'tests'. Here's what we will put in this file:

```
"""
Do a Python test on the app.

:unittest:
"""

import unittest
from todo.app import Todo
```

```python
class InitializationTest(unittest.TestCase):
    todoapp = None

    def setUp(self):
        self.todoapp = Todo()

    def test_title_set(self):
        self.assertEqual(self.todoapp.title,u'To-do list manager')

    def test_next_id_set(self):
        self.assertEqual(self.todoapp.next_id,0)
```

The `:unittest:` comment at the top, is very important. Without it, the test runner will not know in which layer your tests should be executed, and will simply ignore them.

Unit tests are composed of test cases, and, in theory, each should contain several tests related to a specific area of the application's functionality. The test cases use the `TestCase` class from the Python `unittest` module. In these tests, we define a single test case that contains two very simple tests.

We are not getting into the details here. Just notice that the test case can include a `setUp` method and a `tearDown` method that can be used to perform any common initialization and destruction tasks that are required in order to get the tests working and finishing cleanly.

Every test inside a test case needs to have the prefix 'test' in its name, so we have exactly two tests that fulfill this condition. Both of the tests need an instance of the `Todo` class to be executed, so we assign it to the test case as a class variable, and create it inside the `setUp` method. The tests are very simple and they just verify that the default property values are set upon instance creation.

Both of the tests use the `assertEqual` method to tell the test runner that if the two values passed are different, the test should fail. To see them in action, we just run the `bin/test` command once more:

```
$ bin/test
Running tests at level 1
Running todo.FunctionalLayer tests:
  Set up
 in 2.691 seconds.
  Running:
.......2009-09-30 22:00:50,703 INFO sqlalchemy.engine.base.
Engine.0x...684c PRAGMA table_info("users")
2009-09-30 22:00:50,703 INFO sqlalchemy.engine.base.Engine.0x...684c ()
```

```
Ran 7 tests with 0 failures and 0 errors in 0.420 seconds.
Running zope.testing.testrunner.layer.UnitTests tests:
  Tear down todo.FunctionalLayer ... not supported
  Running in a subprocess.
  Set up zope.testing.testrunner.layer.UnitTests in 0.000 seconds.
  Ran 2 tests with 0 failures and 0 errors in 0.000 seconds.
  Tear down zope.testing.testrunner.layer.UnitTests in 0.000 seconds.
Total: 9 tests, 0 failures, 0 errors in 5.795 seconds
```

Now, both the functional and unit test layers contain some tests, and they are both run, one after the other. We can see the subtotal for each layer at the end of these tests for that layer, as well as the grand total of the nine passed tests, when the test runner finishes its work.

Extending the test suite

Of course, we have only scratched the surface of which tests should be added to our application. If we continue to add tests, we may have hundreds of tests, by the time we finish. However, this chapter is not the place to do this.

As mentioned earlier, it is much easier to have tests for each part of our application, if we add them as we code. There's no hiding from the fact that testing is a lot of work, but there is great value in having a complete test suite for our applications. This is even more so when third parties might use our product independently.

Debugging

We will now take a quick look at the debugging facilities offered by Grok. Even if we have a very thorough test suite, the chances are there that we will find a fair number of bugs in our application. When that happens, we need a quick and effective way to inspect the code as it runs and easily find the problem spots.

Often, developers will use `print` statements (placed at key lines) throughout the code, in the hopes of finding the problem spot. Although this is usually a good way to begin locating sore spots in the code, we often need some way to follow the code line by line in order to really find out what's wrong. In the next section, we'll see how to use the Python debugger to step through the code and find the problem spots. We'll also take a quick look at how to perform post-mortem debugging in Grok, which involves jumping into the debugger to analyze the program state immediately after an exception has occurred.

Debugging in Grok

For regular debugging, where we need to step through the code to see what's going on inside it, the Python debugger is an excellent tool. To use it, you just have to add the next line at the point where you wish to start debugging:

```
import pdb; pdb.set_trace()
```

Let's try it out. Open the `app.py` module and change the `add` method of the `AddProjectForm` class (line 108) to look like this:

```python
@grok.action('Add project')
def add(self,**data):
    import pdb; pdb.set_trace()
    project = Project()
    project.creator = self.request.principal.title
    project.creation_date = datetime.datetime.now()
    project.modification_date = datetime.datetime.now()
    self.applyData(project,**data)
    id = str(self.context.next_id)
    self.context.next_id = self.context.next_id+1
    self.context[id] = project
    return self.redirect(self.url(self.context[id]))
```

Notice that we invoke the debugger at the beginning of the method. Now, start the instance, go to the 'add project' form, fill it in, and submit it. Instead of seeing the new project view, the browser will stay at the 'add form' page, and display the **waiting for...** message. This is because control has been transferred to the console in order for the debugger to act. Your console will look like this:

```
> /home/cguardia/work/virtual/grok1/todo/src/todo/app.py(109)add()
-> project = Project()
(Pdb) |
```

The debugger is now active and waiting for input. Notice that the line number where debugging started appears right beside the path of the module in which we are located. After the line number, comes the name of the method, `add()`. Below that, the next line of code to be executed is shown.

The debugger commands are simple. To execute the current line, click on *n*:

```
(Pdb) n
> /home/cguardia/work/virtual/grok1/todo/src/todo/app.py(110)add()
-> project.creator = self.request.principal.title
(Pdb)
```

You can see the available commands if you type *h*:

```
(Pdb) h

Documented commands (type help <topic>):
========================================
EOF     break   condition   disable   help     list   q        step     w
a       bt      cont        down      ignore   n      quit     tbreak   whatis
alias   c       continue    enable    j        next   r        u        where
args    cl      d           exit      jump     p      return   unalias
b       clear   debug       h         l        pp     s        up

Miscellaneous help topics:
==========================
exec   pdb

Undocumented commands:
======================
retval   rv

(Pdb)
```

The list command `id` is used for getting a bird's eye view of where in the code we are:

```
(Pdb) list
105
106             @grok.action('Add project')
107         def add(self,**data):
108             import pdb; pdb.set_trace()
109             project = Project()
110  ->             project.creator = self.request.principal.title
111             project.creation_date = datetime.datetime.now()
112             project.modification_date = datetime.datetime.now()
113             self.applyData(project,**data)
114             id = str(self.context.next_id)
115             self.context.next_id = self.context.next_id+1
(Pdb)
```

As you can see, the current line is identified by an arrow.

It's possible to type in the names of objects within the current execution context and find out their values:

```
(Pdb) project
<todo.app.Project object at 0xa0ef72c>
(Pdb) data
{'kind': 'personal', 'description': u'Nothing', 'title': u'Project about
nothing'}
(Pdb)
```

We can, of course, continue stepping line-by-line through all of the code in the application, including Grok's own code, checking values as we proceed. When we are through reviewing, we can click on *c* to return control to the browser. At this point, we will see the project view.

The Python debugger is very easy to use, and it can be invaluable for finding obscure bugs in your code.

The default Ajax debugger

The other kind of debugging is known as *post-mortem debugging*. In the previous section, we stepped through the code at leisure while the application was in a stable and running condition. Many times, however, we can run into an error condition that stops the program and we need to analyze what the state of the program was at the time at which the error occurred. That's what post-mortem debugging is about.

We'll now intentionally introduce an error in our code. Remove the `import pdb` line from the `add` method, and change the first line after that to the following:

```
project = Project(**data)
```

The `Project` class' `__init__` method does not expect this argument, so a `TypeError` will be raised. Restart the instance and add a project. Instead of a view, a blank screen with the error message—**A system error occurred**—will be shown.

Recall that, so far, we have been using the `deploy.ini` file to start the instance, by using the following command:

```
$ bin/paster serve parts/etc/deploy.ini
```

To run a post-mortem debugger session, we have to start our instance with the debug profile instead:

```
$ bin/paster serve parts/etc/debug.ini
```

Try to add a project again. Now, instead of the simple error message, a full traceback of the error will be shown on screen, as shown in the following screenshot:

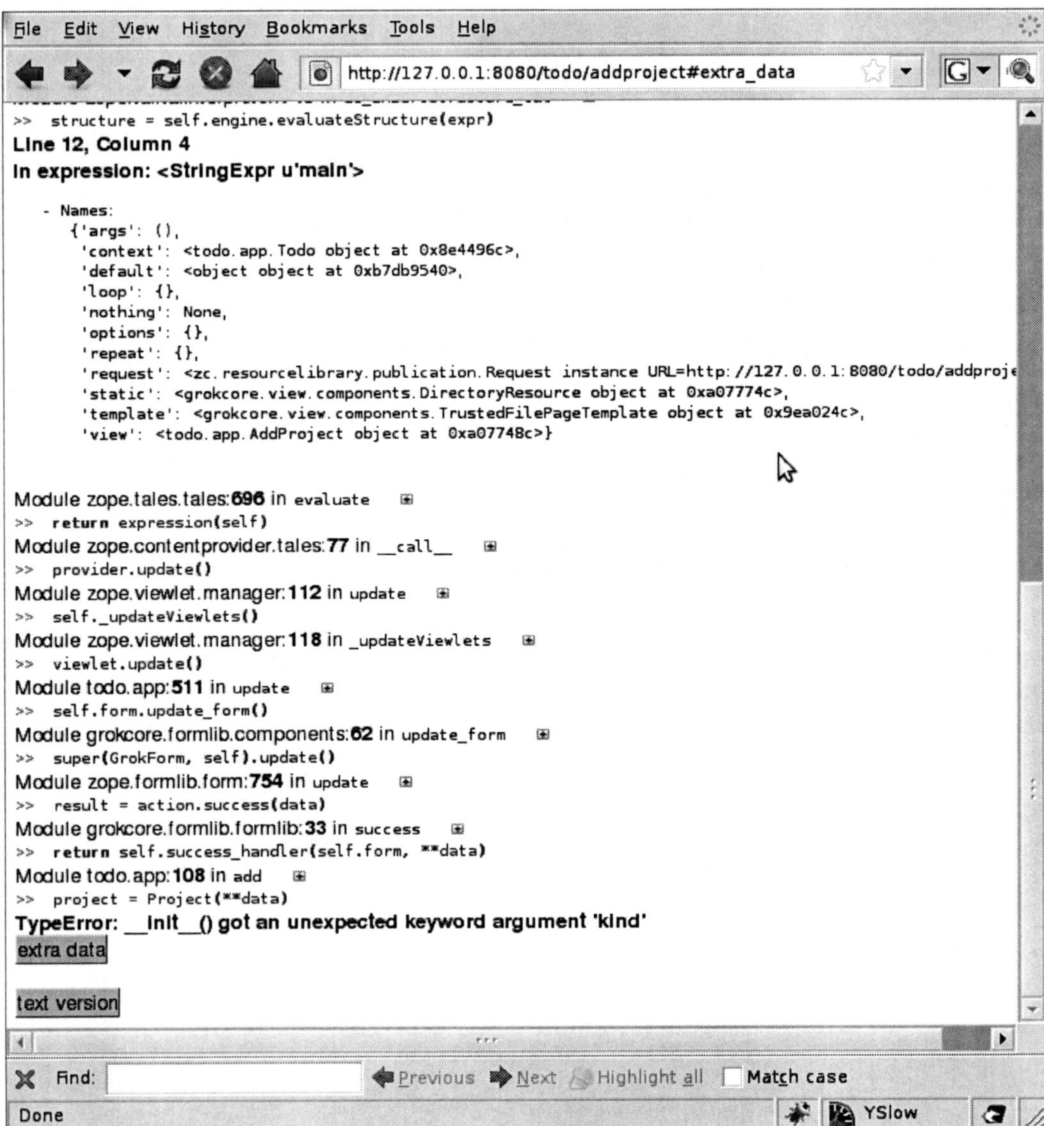

One nice thing about the traceback is that it is expandable. Clicking on the brackets to the left will show the lines of code around the line where the error occurred, while clicking on the plus sign to the right of a module and line message will show additional traceback information. Above this information you will also see a text box that can be used to evaluate expressions within the current context (refer to the next screenshot).

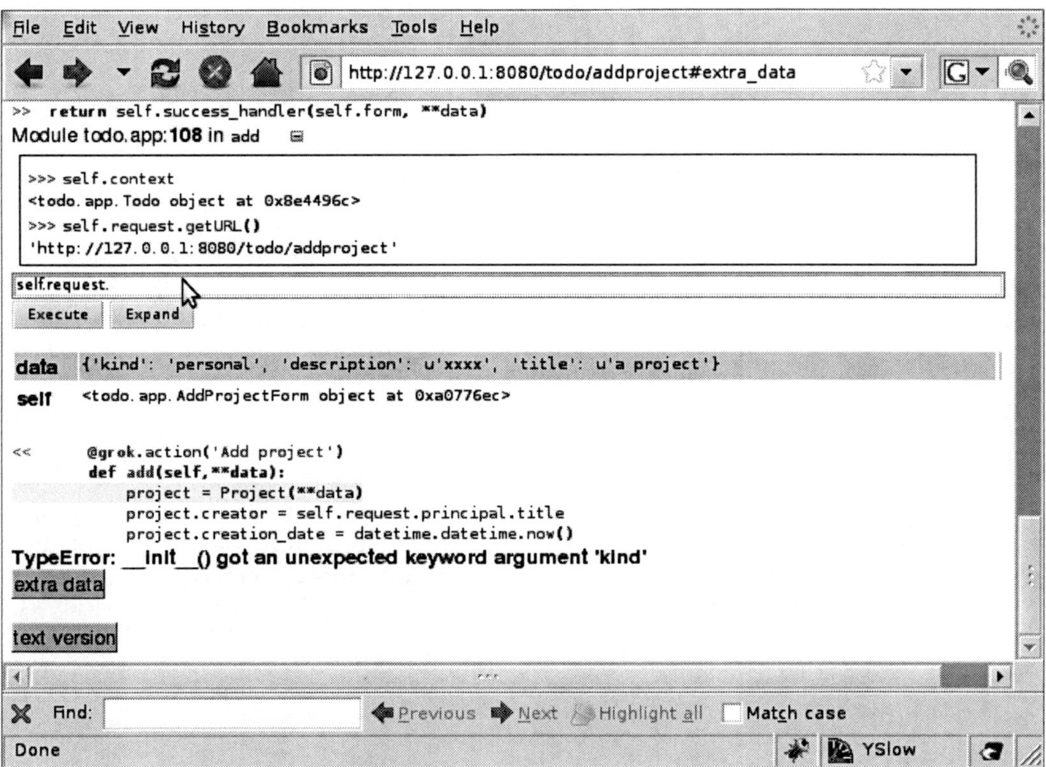

Post-mortem debugging with the Python debugger

The Ajax debugger is great, but if you are really used to the Python debugger, you might wish to use that instead for your post-mortem analysis. This is no problem; Grok comes prepared for this.

For a quick test, edit the `parts/etc/debug.ini` file in the project and change the word `ajax` to `pdb` in the `[filter-app:main]` section. It should look like this when you are done:

```
[filter-app:main]
# Change the last part from 'ajax' to 'pdb' for a post-mortem debugger
# on the console:
use = egg:z3c.evalexception#pdb  # <--- change here to pdb
next = zope
```

Now, restart the instance with the debug profile and try to add a project. Instead of seeing the Ajax screen, control will be transferred to the Python debugger on the console.

Keep in mind that we just modified a file that will be rewritten when we run the `buildout` again, so do this only for quick tests, as we just did, and never depend upon changes to the files in the `parts/etc` directory. In order to make this change permanent, remember to edit the `etc/debug.ini.in` file instead of the one in the `parts/etc` directory. You will then need to run the `buildout` again.

Summary

This chapter discussed how to test Grok applications and why it's important to do so. We also covered debugging, and looked at some useful debugging tools for the Grok developer. Now that we have added tests, in the following chapter, we'll see how to deploy our application.

14
Deployment

So far, we have been working in a development environment, and running our application on the console in 'foreground' mode, so that we can see the output for debugging and confirmation purposes.

Now that we have a more or less complete application, we may want to deploy it. Even for limited audience testing, we want the deployed application to run in the background. Later on, we probably want to use a full-fledged web server, such as Apache, for serving our application, and maybe others. Finally, for an application that expects lots of traffic and numerous visitors, we might want to balance the load over multiple instances of our application.

This chapter will discuss how to deploy our application by using the standard paster server. Then we'll find out how to run the application behind Apache, first by using a simple proxy configuration, and then under `mod_wsgi`. Finally, we'll explore how ZEO provides horizontal scalability for our application, and will briefly discuss how to make a site support high traffic loads by adding caching and load balancing into the mix.

Some specific topics that we will cover include:

- Simple deployment with paster
- Running behind Apache with proxy pass
- Running behind Apache with `mod_wsgi`
- Setting up a ZEO cluster
- Caching and load balancing

Moving an application to production mode

Before thinking about which web server we will use for our deployment, there is one step that we need to take for every production application. Grok offers a 'developer mode' for the application server, which enables some functionality intended to help developers debug and test their applications more easily.

The most noticeable effect of developer mode is that any changes made to templates are automatically taken into account by the server, without needing to restart. This imposes a penalty on application performance because the server has to poll files to find out if there were any changes made to a template.

It is recommended that you turn this functionality off when preparing an application for release. Further changes to templates will require a restart, but in web development, any performance gain must be welcomed.

To turn developer mode off, edit the `etc/zope.conf.in` file that was included in the package that was generated by `grokproject`. Find the line that says `devmode on`, and modify it to look like this:

```
# Comment this line to disable developer mode. This should be done in
# production
# devmode on
```

By commenting out the line shown in bold, the default will apply, which is for development mode to be off. However, note that this is not the actual configuration file, but a template used to generate it.

To make the change take effect, rerun the buildout, so that the actual configuration file at `parts/etc/zope.conf` is rewritten. When you next start the application, it will run in production mode.

Running the paster server in the background

By far the easiest way of deploying our application is to use the same paster server that we have been using for development throughout the book. The only thing that we need to do is to launch the server in 'daemon' mode, so that our application runs in the background:

```
$ bin/paster serve --daemon parts/etc/deploy.ini
```

The process will then start in the background. The PID for that process will be stored in the file `paster.pid`, which can be used to get status information for the running server. The `paster.if` filename is assumed by default, by other `paster serve` commands, so for example, to get the process status, you can type:

```
$ bin/paster serve --status parts/etc/deploy.ini
$ Server running in PID 11482
```

When we need to stop the server, we use the `stop-daemon` option, as follows:

```
$ bin/paster serve --stop-daemon parts/etc/deploy.ini
```

There are a couple of other options that can be useful. We might want the server to be restarted automatically in case, the server dies for whatever reason; that's what the `monitor-restart` option does:

```
$ bin/paster serve --daemon --monitor-restart parts/etc/deploy.ini
```

Finally, we may prefer to run the server continuously in the background and have it restart automatically when we change some files. This can be accomplished with the `reload` option:

```
$ bin/paster serve --daemon --reload parts/etc/deploy.ini
```

This setup could be considered as the minimum Grok deployment architecture, and its parts are shown in the following figure:

Running Grok behind the Apache web server

The problem with using the default paster configuration for production is that the URL for our site must include the application name. This might be acceptable in some cases, but almost always it's not good enough. The easiest way to overcome this problem is to put the application behind a web server, such as Apache, and use the powerful URL-rewriting tools available in most web servers to serve our application from any URL that we require.

Also, if our site will be running any other applications besides the one that we have developed, it is usually a good idea to let Apache or some other web server take care of centralizing the requests for multiple applications on the site.

Using mod_rewrite to serve our application from Apache

To set up this configuration, you will need to install the Apache web server, which is available for all platforms. Most Linux distributions will allow you to install it by using their package management tools.

For example, in Ubuntu or Debian, you can simply type:

```
$ sudo apt-get install apache2
```

Once you have Apache ready, the next step is to configure it to use the `mod_rewrite` module. Usually, the way to do this is to edit the `httpd.conf` file, which should be available somewhere inside the `/etc` directory of your server, under either the `apache2` or `httpd` subdirectory.

To load the required modules to make `mod_rewrite` work, the following general configuration is required:

```
LoadModule rewrite_module /usr/lib/apache2/modules/mod_rewrite.so
LoadModule proxy_module /usr/lib/apache2/modules/mod_proxy.so
LoadModule proxy_http_module /usr/lib/apache2/modules/mod_proxy_http.so


ProxyRequests off
```

The first three lines load the required modules, and the `ProxyRequests` line makes sure that the server can't be used as an involuntary proxy by third parties. Do not leave this line out.

Now that the "rewrite" functionality is enabled, we need to create a virtual host that will serve our application's requests. This virtual host will include the "rewrite" rule that will allow our application to be served by Apache. A sample virtual host definition looks like this:

```
<VirtualHost *:80>
  ServerName grok.example.com
  RewriteEngine On
  RewriteRule ^/(.*)
    http://localhost:8080/todo/++vh++http:grok.example.com:80/++/$1
    [P,L]
</VirtualHost>
```

In this simple example, we just set the server name, turn on the rewrite engine, and set up a rewrite rule. Before doing anything else, make sure that the server name is correct.

The rewrite rule is the important part of the configuration. Apache's `mod_rewrite` uses regular expression syntax for matching the part of a URL that will trigger the rule. In the configuration above, the first part of the rule tells the engine to match any URL that begins with a slash, which of course, will match any URL that will be served by this virtual host.

In regular expressions, when you enclose a subexpression in parentheses, it means that anything that matches the text inside them has to be saved in a variable. The first expression in parentheses that matches this text is stored in the variable `$1`, the second in `$2`, and so on. In this case, anything after the slash, which is the full path of the request, will be stored in `$1`.

The second part of the rule is dependent on Grok's virtual hosting tools. This will be the URL that will be looked up by the rule in order to get the actual content to be served at the matching location. For virtual hosting, Grok expects the full URL to the application that we are publishing (`http://localhost:8080/todo`), followed by the special virtual hosting syntax that will include the protocol, server name, and port, which will be used by Grok to translate all of the URLs present in the response, so that every link in it points to the correct host. Notice how, after the Grok `++vh++` rule, the full path for the request is appended to the end, by using the `$1` variable explained before.

The third and final part of the rule indicates to Apache that this is a proxy request (`P`) and that this rule should be the last rule applied, when it matches (`L`).

This is all that is needed to set up our application with `mod_rewrite`. To test this, first make sure that the paster process is running and that Apache is using the configuration that we added. Usually, the server is started automatically when it's installed, so you might need to tell it to reload the configuration. In Ubuntu or Debian, the way to do this is:

```
$ /etc/init.d/apache2 reload
```

Now you can go to the URL that you defined in the configuration (`http://grok.example.com`, in our example) and see your application work from behind Apache.

Installing and setting up Grok under mod_wsgi

Another great option for serving Grok applications behind Apache is `mod_wsgi`, which is an Apache module that serves applications under the WSGI protocol. In this section, we'll learn what WSGI is, and how to set up Apache to serve our application by using the `mod_wsgi` module.

WSGI: The Python Web Server Gateway Interface

WSGI is a Python standard for specifying how web applications can communicate with web servers and application servers. Its objective is to provide a simple interface that can support most interactions between a web server and a web framework (such as Grok).

WSGI also supports "middleware" components that can be used to preprocess or post-process a request. This means that it is used to create Python WSGI tools that "plug" into our applications and perform services such as profiling, error handling, and more.

Grok can run behind any WSGI server. We'll now look at how to install Grok behind the Apache web server and `mod_wsgi` on a brand new Linux virtual server.

Grok and WSGI

For Python web developers, WSGI holds the key to the Python web development future. As there are a number of important web development frameworks, and the power of Python makes it really easy to create new ones quickly, interacting with the best of breed applications developed in multiple frameworks could soon be the best way to create a new Python website.

Until relatively recently, Zope 3 and some of its derived applications, such as Grok, ran the risk of missing the WSGI party, but not anymore. Grok 1.0 is WSGI compatible and can therefore be integrated with the wide range of WSGI-based technologies available in the Python world today.

Why use Apache and mod_wsgi for Grok?

There are a number of WSGI servers available, but this chapter will focus on using `mod_wsgi`, which is a WSGI adapter module for Apache. There are a number of reasons for this.

First, Apache is the most popular web hosting platform, so there are many web developers and site administrators who are already familiar with it. Grok, for example, has been installed behind Apache for production servers by using `mod_rewrite`.

Second, there are also lots of Python applications that already run under Apache by using `mod_python`. There are a few WSGI adapters for this module as well, but `mod_wsgi` is written in C code, and has lower memory overhead and better performance than those adapters.

Also, one of the goals of `mod_wsgi` is to break into the low-cost commodity web hosting market, which would be good for Python, and ultimately for Grok and Zope.

Setting up a clean Linux server

In the discussion that follows, we'll use Linux as the operating system because, it's the most popular way to deploy web applications, by far. Ubuntu is the distribution that we'll cover, but these steps apply equally well to any Debian-based distribution. Other distributions use different package managers, and probably other system paths, but you should be able to easily figure out what you need in any case.

We can start with a clean install of a recent version of Ubuntu GNU/Linux. The first step is to install the necessary packages for both the correct Python version (Grok currently requires Python 2.5) and the Apache server.

Before that, it is necessary to install the required packages for being able to compile and build software using Ubuntu (other distributions usually don't need this). Be aware that both package installation and Apache module additions usually require root access. In the commands block, the prompt with $ is a user prompt, and the one with # is a root prompt that you can have with the command `sudo -s`. In this part, you'll use a root terminal so that you do not have to prefix each command with `sudo`. In the other parts, you'll use a user terminal where you add `sudo` before a command, if you need to execute something as root. You can have one terminal opened as root and another terminal as user.

```
$ sudo -s
```

```
# apt-get install build-essential
```

Next, install the packages for Python and Apache. As with most packaged Linux distributions, Ubuntu requires a separate install for the development libraries of each piece of software:

```
# apt-get install python2.5 python2.5-dev
```

```
# apt-get install apache2
```

The `apache2` package usually installs `apache2-mpm-worker`, but you may have the other version, `apache2-mpm-prefork`, installed. To check which one is installed, you can execute:

```
# dpkg -l|grep apache2
```

Next, install the corresponding development package, `apache2-threaded-dev` if `apache2-mpm-worker` is installed, or `apache2-prefork-dev` if `apache2-mpm-prefork` is installed:

```
# apt-get install apache2-threaded-dev
```

Grok uses Python's `setuptools`, so that package is needed as well:

```
# apt-get install python-setuptools
```

It's possible that the version provided by the Ubuntu package is not the latest. If you want to have more control of the installed version of `setuptools` and want to update it yourself when a new version is available, you can use the following method instead. Download `setuptools-0.6c9-py2.5.egg` manually (or latest version, choose py2.5) and execute the command:

```
# sh setuptools-0.6c9-py2.5.egg
```

You can later update it with:

```
sudo easy_install-2.5 -U setuptools
```

Installing and configuring mod_wsgi

Now, the server is ready to install `mod_wsgi`. There is a package `libapache2-mod-wsgi` in Ubuntu, but it's recommended that you build the latest version, in part because `mod_wsgi` has to be compiled with the same Python used by Grok. Please remove the `libapache2-mod-wsgi` package if you have installed it previously. We need to get the source directly from the download site, and then build it:

```
$ wget http://modwsgi.googlecode.com/files/mod_wsgi-2.6.tar.gz
```

```
$ tar xzf mod_wsgi-2.6.tar.gz
```

```
$ cd mod_wsgi-2.6
$ ./configure --with-python=/usr/bin/python2.5
$ make
$ sudo make install
```

Again, note that it is necessary to compile mod_wsgi using the same Python that you will use to run your website. As Grok requires 2.5, the --with-python option was used to point to the version of Python that we need.

Once mod_wsgi is installed, the Apache server needs to be told about it. On Apache 2, this is done by adding the load declaration and any configuration directives to the /etc/apache2/mods-available/ directory.

The load declaration for the module needs to go in a file named wsgi.load (in the /etc/apache2/mods-available/ directory), which contains only the following line of code:

```
LoadModule wsgi_module /usr/lib/apache2/modules/mod_wsgi.so
```

The configuration directives reside in the file named wsgi.conf next to wsgi.load file. We don't create it now, but it can be useful later to add directives to it, if you have more than one WSGI application to serve.

Then, you have to activate the wsgi module with:

```
# a2enmod wsgi
```

Note that a2enmod stands for "apache2 enable mod"—an executable that creates the symlink for you. Actually, a2enmod wsgi is equivalent to:

```
# cd /etc/apache2/mods-enabled
# ln -s ../mods-available/wsgi.load
# ln -s ../mods-available/wsgi.conf # if it exists
```

For Apache 1.3, or Apache 2 with an old directory layout, you may need to place the LoadModule line and the configuration directives (which you will see later) inside the httpd.conf file in your Apache's /etc directory. The soft links above will not be necessary in this case.

Configuring a Grok site under mod_wsgi

Grok can be installed with setuptools, and a Grok site can be easily created by using the included grokproject tool. As mentioned before, Grok can run behind any WSGI server, not just the paster server that is used by default. Now that we have a working mod_wsgi, we will look at how to run Grok behind it.

Getting the to-do application ready for mod_wsgi

WSGI applications use entry points to let the WSGI server know how to run the program. The **entry point** is usually a simple Python script that provides a function for calling the application and passing the appropriate initialization file to the server. Some servers, such as the paster server, need only the path to the `.ini` file, which is what we normally use to start up a Grok application. This doesn't mean that there's no entry point script for paster. In fact, the entry point is defined in the `setup.py` file, which is created by `grokproject` when a new project is initialized. Take a look at the last few lines of the file:

```
[paste.app_factory]
main = grokcore.startup:application_factory
debug = grokcore.startup:debug_application_factory
```

The heading `paste.app_factory` tells the server where to find the factory functions for each section of the `.ini` file. In Grok, a general application factory function is defined in the `grokcore.startup` package, which is what paster uses to start applications.

However, `mod_wsgi` requires a path to the factory, which would be cumbersome to include in our configuration, because this would mean that it would need to point to a file inside the `grokcore.startup` egg. As eggs include the version number, a simple update could crash our site if the old egg is removed. It would be better to have our own factory defined inside the application package.

Given that the factory code can be almost identical for different projects, it would be better to have it included automatically when we create the project, to avoid having to re-create the same script every time. Fortunately for us, Grok's use of buildout turns out to be very helpful in this case, as there is a buildout recipe available that creates the WSGI application factory for us.

The recipe is called `collective.recipe.modwsgi`. To use it, simply add a part to the buildout having a name such as `wsgi_app`. The recipe requires two parameters—the first being the eggs that have to be made available to the Python process that will run the app under WSGI, and the second being the path to the configuration file that will be used for the site. This last parameter `value` is the usual `parts/etc/deploy.ini` path that we have been using for running the application under paster. That's it. Edit the `buildout.cfg` file's `parts` list as follows:

```
parts =
    eggbasket
    app
    i18n
    test
    mkdirs
```

```
    zpasswd
    zope_conf
    site_zcml
    zdaemon_conf
    wsgi_app
    deploy_ini
    debug_ini
```

Next, add the following section anywhere in the file:

```
[wsgi_app]
recipe = collective.recipe.modwsgi
eggs = ${app:eggs}
config-file = ${buildout:directory}/parts/etc/deploy.ini
```

Note that the `eggs` parameter simply points back to the main egg section defined at the start of the buildout, to avoid repetition.

When the buildout is run again, we'll find a `parts/wsgi_app` directory (or whichever name we used for the buildout part). Inside that directory, there will be a `wsgi` file that can be used as is by `mod_wsgi` to run the application.

Configuring an Apache site to use mod_wsgi

The last step is to add a site to the Apache server that uses `mod_wsgi` to serve our application. This is standard `mod_wsgi` configuration; we'll just add the path to the application factory that we created in the previous section.

To set up the virtual host, create a file in the `/etc/apache2/sites-available` directory and call it, for example, "grok". Add the following code to it, assuming your to-do application is at `/home/cguardia/grok/todo`:

```
WSGIPythonHome /usr
WSGIDaemonProcess grok user=cguardia group=cguardia threads=4 maximum-requests=10000

<VirtualHost *:80>
  ServerName wsgi.example.com
  WSGIScriptAlias /todo /home/cguardia/grok/todo/parts/wsgi_app/wsgi
  WSGIProcessGroup grok
  WSGIPassAuthorization On
  WSGIReloadMechanism Process
  SetEnv HTTP_X_VHM_HOST http://wsgi.example.com/todo
</VirtualHost>
```

This will run `mod_wsgi` in 'daemon' mode, which means that it will launch a number of processes in order to run the configured WSGI application instead of using the Apache process. If you are using virtualenv, the `site-packages` directory of the virtual Python, which is used to run it, needs to be passed in the `WSGIPythonHome` variable. To tell `mod_wsgi` which WSGI application to run, we use the `WSGIScriptAlias` directive, and pass to it the path to the application factory that we created earlier.

Note that we assign a user and group to run the process. It is required that this user has access to the application directory.

The PYTHON_EGG_CACHE directory

Note that when the application is started, all of the eggs will be automatically extracted in the `PYTHON_EGG_CACHE` directory, normally `~/.python-eggs`. This directory depends on the `HOME` environment variable. The `HOME` apache user `www-data` is `/var/www`. You may get the error, **[Errno 13] Permission denied: '/var/www/.python-eggs'** in your `error.log` apache file if you don't configure the user or the `python-eggs` variable in the `WSGIDaemonProcess` directive. You can also add a `python-eggs` parameter to tell `mod_wsgi` to use an alternative directory for the egg cache:

```
WSGIDaemonProcess grok threads=4 maximum-requests=10000
    python-eggs=/tmp/python-eggs
```

In this example, the process belongs to `www-data`. The `www-data` and `python-eggs` cache directory will be `/tmp/python-eggs`.

Running the application

Once the configuration is ready, we need to enable the site in Apache, because we just created it. This is necessary only for the first time we run it:

```
$ sudo a2ensite grok
```

This command will create a link from the Apache `sites-enabled` directory to the "grok" site that we just configured, which is enough to make it active. Then, we can start serving our application from Apache by simply reloading the configuration for the server:

```
$ sudo /etc/init.d/apache2 reload
```

When you visit the site in a browser (`http://wsgi.example.com/todo`), you should see the Grok admin UI. You should be able to log in by using the admin login name and password.

Adding a ZEO server

By default, `mod_wsgi` will use a single process to run the application. As this configuration is intended for production use, it may be desirable to have a higher number of processes available to serve the application. The ZODB that Grok uses comes with a server named **Zope Enterprise Object (ZEO)**, which allows us to add as many processes to our configuration as our system permits, providing unlimited horizontal scalability. Typically, the recommended number of processes is one for each core in the system's processors. Let's set up a ZEO server and configure the Grok process to connect to it.

Buildout recipe for the ZEO configuration

Once again, the easiest way to get ZEO running is to use an existing buildout recipe. This time we'll use the one named `zc:zodbrecipes`. Add a `zeo_server` part to your `buildout.cfg` file, as shown below:

```
parts =
    eggbasket
    app
    i18n
    test
    mkdirs
    zpasswd
    zope_conf
    site_zcml
    zdaemon_conf
    zeo_server
    wsgi_app
    deploy_ini
    debug_ini
```

Next, add a `zeo_server` section as follows:

```
[zeo_server]
recipe = zc.zodbrecipes:server
zeo.conf =
  <zeo>
    address 8100
  </zeo>
  <blobstorage 1>
      blob-dir ${buildout:directory}/var/blobstorage
    <filestorage 1>
      path ${buildout:directory}/var/filestorage/Data.fs
    </filestorage>
```

```
    </blobstorage>
    <eventlog>
      level info
      <logfile>
        path ${buildout:directory}/parts/log/zeo.log
      </logfile>
    </eventlog>
```

This will add the ZEO server, and configure it to listen on port 8100. The rest of the configuration is pretty much boilerplate, so just copy it to new projects when you need ZEO there. The `blobstorage` section sets up a file storage with blob handling enabled; the `logfile` sections tells the server where to store the log file.

Next, we need the buildout to add scripts for starting and stopping ZEO. This is easily accomplished by adding the ZODB3 egg to our app section:

```
[app]
recipe = zc.recipe.egg
eggs = gwsgi
    z3c.evalexception>=2.0
    Paste
    PasteScript
    PasteDeploy
    ZODB3
```

Configuring the ZEO client

Currently, the Grok application that we are using is working with the regular Zope server. To use ZEO, we need to change the configuration to connect to the server at port 8100. Fortunately, the required changes already come inside the regular `zope.conf` file that is created inside the Grok project, so we only need to uncomment those lines. Uncomment the following lines inside the `zope.conf.in` file in the `etc` directory of your Grok project:

```
# Uncomment this if you want to connect to a ZEO server instead:
<zeoclient>
    server localhost:8100
    storage 1
    # ZEO client cache, in bytes
    cache-size 20MB
    # Uncomment to have a persistent disk cache
    #client zeo1
</zeoclient>
```

The important line here is the one with the ZEO server address. In this case, we are using the same host as the Grok application, and the port that we defined in our ZEO configuration in the previous section.

Launching the ZEO server

After running the buildout again, we'll be ready to start the ZEO server in the background. To do this, we have to run only the server script that was automatically created for us. The name of the script is the same as the name of the part in the buildout where we configured the server:

```
$ bin/zeo_server start
```

Our Grok application is now running! To stop it, you can use the following command:

```
$ bin/zeo_server stop
```

Augmenting the number of processes

Recall that we mentioned earlier that mod_wsgi runs the application in a single process by default. To really take advantage of ZEO, we want to have more processes available. We need to make a small addition to our mod_wsgi Apache virtual host configuration for that. Change the WSGIDaemonProcess line, near the top, to look like the following code:

```
WSGIDaemonProcess grok user=cguardia group=cguardia processes=2
threads=4 maximum-requests=10000
```

Remember to reload the Apache configuration to be able to see the new setup in action. In this example, we'll have two processes running, with four threads each. By using ZEO and mod_wsgi, we now have a scalable site.

More scalability: Adding caching and load balancing

The configurations that we just discussed will be enough for most kinds of sites. However, there are times when a site is required to handle high traffic loads, and measures need to be taken to ensure that it will not go down under pressure.

Caching proxies

One very effective thing that can be done is to add a caching proxy in front of the Apache server. A **caching proxy** reduces bandwidth and improves response times by saving a copy of the most frequently used pages of a site and serving that copy directly on further requests, rather than connecting to the server again.

Two very popular caching proxies are Squid (`http://www.squid-cache.org`) and Varnish (`http://www.varnish-cache.org`). A detailed discussion of how to set these up is beyond the objectives of this chapter, but, interestingly, there are buildout recipes available for setting them up automatically. Take a look at the Python Package Index and see how these recipes help to build and configure a caching proxy. For Squid, there's `plone.recipe.squid` (`http://pypi.python.org/pypi/plone.recipe.squid/`), and for Varnish, the corresponding `plone.recipe.varnish` (`http://pypi.python.org/pypi/plone.recipe.varnish`).

Load balancers

A **load balancer** sits in front of two or more instances of an application and distributes the incoming requests evenly between them. This is a very powerful solution when you can have several machines serving the application.

There are several load balancers available as open source; for example, Apache itself has a load-balancing module. However, one of the most popular load balancers to use with Zope Toolkit-based applications is "Pound" (`http://www.apsis.ch/pound/`).

Pound does a lot more than just distributing the load. It can keep session information and send a request from the same origin browser to the same destination server used on the first request. Pound can also distribute requests among servers according to its URL. Finally, it can act as a failover server, because it's smart enough to notice when a backend server fails and will stop sending requests to it until the server recovers.

There is, of course, a buildout recipe available for setting up Pound, appropriately named `plone.recipe.pound` (`http://pypi.python.org/pypi/plone.recipe.pound`).

A high-traffic architecture for Grok

Now that we know about some mechanisms for improving our application's performance, it can be helpful to visualize how the different parts relate to each other. In our case, a good way of organizing a system to support high traffic loads would be to put a caching proxy such as Varnish at the front and configure it to pass requests to the Pound load balancer.

Pound would be configured to distribute the load among a number of separate servers, each one of them running Apache configured with `mod_wsgi`, and running several processes that would talk to a number of ZEO clients running our Grok application. Using this architecture, depicted in the following figure, we could scale our application to deal with very high traffic.

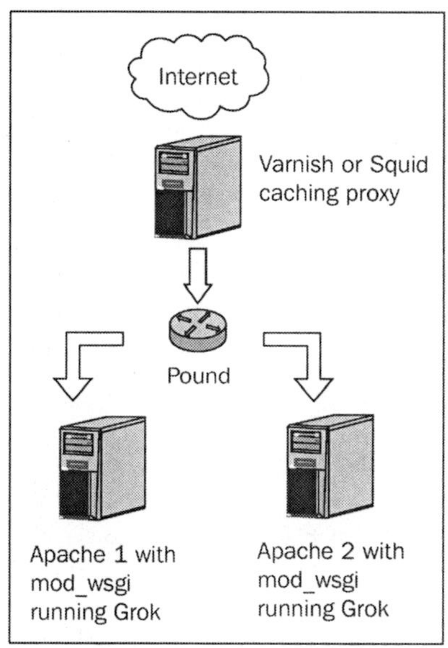

Summary

This chapter discussed how to approach application deployment, and explored various possibilities for deploying our sample application, from a simple setup to a scalable configuration with ZEO.

We have reached the end of our journey with Grok. Hopefully, you'll find that Grok is a good addition to your web arsenal, and will think about how its strengths could help you reach your goals whenever you need to develop a web application. In this Internet age, it's very easy to reach out and communicate with people who can help us with many kinds of technologies. Grok developers and users are no exception, so please do not hesitate to ask for advice, by using Grok's mailing lists or IRC channel. We'll be glad to help you, and will be happy that you took Grok out for a spin.

Index

request 142
response 142
static 142
update(**kw) 143
url(obj=None, name=None, data=None)
    142
views
about 31, 32, 141
modifying, to use master templates 149,
    150
names, setting 71
redirecting 72
reorganizing 70
views, redirecting
deleteList method 73
deletelist view 72
redirect method 72
setTitle view 73
Todo model 73
Virtualenv
about 21, 22
default application, running 23-25
first project, creating 23
Grok installing, grokproject used 22

W

web application 31
Web Server Gateway Interface. *See* **WSGI**
widgets
and form fields 86
WSGI
about 264
and Grok 264, 26

X

XML-based Zope configuration
        language 221
XML configuration file 27
XMLHTTP Request object 57
XML namespace 33

Z

ZCA
about 8, 196
adapters 198, 199

components 9, 196, 225, 226
events 205
interface 197
interfaces 196
marker interfaces 198
utilities 203
ZEO
about 162
client, configuring 272, 273
configuration, buildout recipe 271, 272
number of processes, augmenting 273
server, adding 271
server, launching 273
zeopack 175
ZODB
about 10, 62, 159
ACID properties 160
committed 160
features 161
maintenance 173
transaction 160
transparency 160
using 162
using, without Grok 176
versus relational database 193
working 159
ZEO 162
ZODB, features
Blobs (Binary large objects) 162
history 161
in memory caching 161
packing 162
pluggable storages 162
save points 161
undo 161
ZODB, maintenance
automatic packing 174, 175
backing up 175
file storage 173
ZODB, using
by Grok 163, 164
persistence, rules 163
traversal 163
zope.app.undo package 172
Zope Component Architecture. *See* **ZCA**
Zope Enterprise Object. *See* **ZEO**
Zope Enterprise Objects. *See* **ZEO**

Expert Python Programming

ISBN: 978-1-847194-94-7   Paperback: 372 pages

Best practices for designing, coding, and distributing your Python software

1. Learn Python development best practices from an expert, with detailed coverage of naming and coding conventions

2. Apply object-oriented principles, design patterns, and advanced syntax tricks

3. Manage your code with distributed version control

Python Testing: Beginner's Guide

ISBN: 978-1-847198-84-6   Paperback: 256 pages

An easy and convenient approach to testing your powerful Python projects

1. Covers everything you need to test your code in Python

2. Easiest and enjoyable approach to learn Python testing

3. Write, execute, and understand the result of tests in the unit test framework

4. Packed with step-by-step examples and clear explanations

Please check **www.PacktPub.com** for information on our titles

Matplotlib for Python Developers

ISBN: 978-1-847197-90-0   Paperback: 308 pages

Build remarkable publication-quality plots the easy way

1. Create high quality 2D plots by using Matplotlib productively

2. Incremental introduction to Matplotlib, from the ground up to advanced levels

3. Embed Matplotlib in GTK+, Qt, and wxWidgets applications as well as web sites to utilize them in Python applications

4. Deploy Matplotlib in web applications and expose it on the Web using popular web frameworks such as Pylons and Django

Solr 1.4 Enterprise Search Server

ISBN: 978-1-847195-88-3   Paperback: 336 pages

Enhance your search with faceted navigation, result highlighting, fuzzy queries, ranked scoring, and more

1. Deploy, embed, and integrate Solr with a host of programming languages

2. Implement faceting in e-commerce and other sites to summarize and navigate the results of a text search

3. Enhance your search by highlighting search results, offering spell-corrections, auto-suggest, finding "similar" records, boosting records and fields for scoring, phonetic matching

Please check **www.PacktPub.com** for information on our titles